READ FOR
YOUR LIFE

"It hung upon a thorn, and there he blew three deadly notes"—painting by N. C. Wyeth as an illustration for *The Boy's King Arthur* (1917) by Sidney Lanier; reprinted with permission of Charles Scribner's Sons.

READ FOR YOUR LIFE

Turning Teens Into Readers

GLADYS HUNT
AND BARBARA HAMPTON

ZondervanPublishingHouse
Grand Rapids, Michigan

A Division of HarperCollins*Publishers*

Read for Your Life
Copyright © 1992 by Gladys Hunt and Barbara Hampton

Requests for information should be addressed to:
Zondervan Publishing House
Grand Rapids, Michigan 49530

Library of Congress Cataloging-in-Publication Data

Hunt, Gladys M.
  Read for your life : turning teens into readers / Gladys Hunt and
Barbara Hampton.
     p. cm.
   ISBN 0-310-54871-3 (paper)
   1. Bibliography—Best books—Young adult literature. 2. Young
adult literature—Book reviews. 3. Young adult literature—
Bibliography. 4. Reading—Parent participation. 5. Teenagers—
Books and reading. I. Hampton, Barbara. II. Title.
   Z1037.AIH87   1992
   [PN1009.A1]
   016.809'89282—dc20   92–6834
                                                                          CIP

Edited by Shelley Townsend-Hudson
Designed by Rachel Hostetter
Cover design by Terry Dugan Design

Printed in the United States of America

92 93 94 95 96 97 / CH / 10 9 8 7 6 5 4 3 2 1

CONTENTS

Dedicated to our book lovers
Jedediah
Austin
Jenny
Ellen
Karen
who are always eager for
the adventure of a good story!

A WARNING TO PARENTS

WARNING: This book may hook you into becoming a reader.

Read for Your Life is an all-purpose generic book. It's for anyone who can read, even though it is pitched toward young adults. While the "you" in this book is aimed primarily at teenagers, it could be anybody who wants to take seriously the ideas presented.

Parents, teachers—any adult—could profit from reading the book because everyone needs encouragement to read, as well as help in learning *how* to read. In fact, the best way to influence the teenagers in your life is to become a reader yourself. They might be quite impressed if they know that you are learning from this book, too. Besides, you probably missed reading some really good books as you were growing up. Now is a good time to read them. The reading list at the back of this book is an education in itself.

We have high respect for the abilities of young adults. We haven't simplified either the language or the ideas in this book. Instead, we have "put the cookies on the top shelf." You will have to reach for some of the ideas in this book. And you will want to use the Glossary at the end of the book to check on the meaning of words that may not be in your daily vocabulary. "Look it up" is the watchword of good readers.

One of the most helpful parts of the book deals with learning to evaluate what you read and to ask questions about the worldview of the author. That exercise is training for life and a skill that we can learn together, as young or older adults. Talking about books makes for the best kind of companionship.

Sharing ideas and feelings about books is foundational to the purpose of *Read for Your Life*. The classroom, the living room of your home, around your dining table, riding in your car, eating lunch in the cafeteria, lying on the beach and talking to your best friend— what great places to grow close to each other by sharing what touches our hearts, what causes our minds to grow big with wonder, what injustices anger us, what questions the plot of the story insists upon asking.

Though this book is meant to be the private possession of a teenager, it will fit in any library and prove useful in the study of literature in the classrooms.

INTRODUCTION

Honey for a Child's Heart has been one of the most satisfying books I have written. It is an annotated guide to selecting books for children, and through it thousands of parents have introduced their families to good books. That reality is awesome. I feel privileged to have entered the lives of so many people, and I am especially glad to receive letters like this one:

> When your book *Honey for a Child's Heart* was featured on the magazine cover, I knew that it is what I wanted for our kids: honey for their hearts. Imagine my delight when my husband brought your book home for our family to use. I began marking the books that I wanted for the children and hunted for them in the library. Can you believe that I was the valedictorian of both my high school and college class and had never been in a public library?
>
> We have been reading ever since. We read *The Secret Garden* during a family vacation in the hill country of Texas. We read *Heidi* during a camp in the Colorado mountains. We've recently read *Where the Red Fern Grows* and included another family in the reading. We've read the favorites: the "Laura" books (the kids were indignant that the TV Pa didn't have a beard—and Jack wasn't the right kind of dog), the Pooh books, the Narnia books, and because of you I am finishing C. S. Lewis's science-fiction trilogy, and Craig has read Tolkien. We loved *The Good Master* and Lamb's *Shakespeare* for children. And the real version of *Mary Poppins*.

For me it's more than receiving a positive letter; it's imagining all those parents, children, teens—having fun with books! I feel bonded with them and with their parents, all of whom are finding out what good books can do.

Honey for a Child's Heart has been revised three times so that new books could be included in the recommended reading list. As many of the children who were influenced by the first edition grew older, they began asking me about books for teenagers and recommending some of their favorites to me. Others were confused by the enormous number of books labeled *Young Adult Fiction* that poured from the publishing houses—a category of books that hardly existed when I first wrote *Honey for a Child's Heart*. And still others, who were avid readers in elementary school, stopped reading altogether as they got older.

So I knew then that I wanted to write a book for all these teenagers. And I began reading. I thought I might never get around to putting my ideas on paper until, in the wonderful way old friends meet again after a long absence, I met Barbara Hampton at a summer camp. I knew that she loves books. She had written journal articles about books for children and teens. I knew that her values were like mine. So Barbara and I began to talk book-talk. Here, I thought, is someone I can trust to read and review books for teenagers with me. She had already read more of that kind of book than anyone else I had ever met. So I proposed that we work together on a book for teenagers—and their parents—a book that would inspire them to read.

Barbara Hampton is the mother of three book-reading, teenage daughters. She has degrees in journalism and English from the University of Michigan and the University of Wisconsin. She is presently a freelance writer and a consultant at the Reading and Writer Center of the College of Wooster, Ohio, where her husband, Charles, is a mathematics professor. Since agreeing to help me with this book, she has read, evaluated, and annotated hundreds of books.

The project has been exhilarating. When I think about the richness that books can bring to your life, I want to shout about the importance of being a lifelong reader. A German philosopher named Oswald Spengler once said that music is the only art that can convey the idea of God and that fiction may be the only art to convey the idea of man and what it means to make wise choices. Good books can show you your heart and your values. Books can illuminate life's choices.

The wonderful thing about books is that while building strong values in us, they are pure pleasure to read. We laugh, we cry, we sit on the edges of our chairs in suspense, we create kings and kingdoms and whole new worlds in our heads. We underline important ideas and share a good story line with our friends. Memorable characters are forever etched in our minds. Language from the story becomes part of our daily idiom.

Our hope—Barbara's and mine—is that reading this book and using its bibliography will spur you on to even greater treasures of literature.

Gladys Hunt
Ann Arbor, Michigan

Solid food is for the mature,
who by constant use have trained
themselves to distinguish good from evil.
Hebrews 5:14

1

Three Cheers for a Good Book!

*We can strip the knight of his armor,
to reveal that he looks exactly like us,
or we can try on the armor ourselves
to experience how it feels. Fiction
provides an ideal opportunity to try on
the armor.*

C. S. Lewis

Dinner was over at 6:30. We switched the telephone ringer to the off position and went into the living room to read the next chapter of J. R. R. Tolkien's *The Fellowship of the Ring.* Just as we sat down, the doorbell rang. It was Mark's friend from down the street who wanted to hear the chapter with us. The two of them sprawled their lanky teen-age bodies across the floor, and Father began reading. It took twenty minutes to read the chapter aloud, and the length of the next chapter was too long to allow us to sneak in a second one. We all made some kind of noise at the end of the reading: a sigh, comments on the adventure and the plot line, or pleasure at "words fitly spoken." Then we got up and left the world of the shire and hobbits and went about our business— homework, a meeting, the dishes.

After we had begun reading the book aloud in the car on the

way home from skiing one weekend, we knew that we had to finish the experience together. When we completed this first book of the trilogy, we were hooked on the adventure of these hobbits and easily wooed into the second volume. By the time we got to the third volume, *The Return of the King,* summer had come and we were all together, canoe-camping on the edge of a lake in Canada. Each night we read around the fire in the fading light, with the night sounds of loons echoing across the lake. Even on the day it rained and the wind blew its arctic coldness into our campsite, we all huddled into one tent, snuggled into sleeping bags, and took turns reading chapter after chapter, going on an adventure far beyond the one we had canceled because of the rain. Sometimes the reader would have to pause because a lump in the throat was stopping the words. We would look around to find tears trickling from everyone's eyes. Feelings of closeness and understanding are woven into our memories of the marvelous adventure of the Tolkien trilogy—because we shared the books together.

Books are meant to be shared. Sometimes they are read aloud together. Often they are simply shared in answer to the question, "Have you read any good books lately?" It's a question we ought to ask regularly because we don't want to miss any good ones. I will always be grateful for teachers who handed books to me, saying, "I think you'll like this." In the same way, I will always be grateful for all the times teenagers have given me books—and still give me books, saying, "This is a good book. You'll like it." We respect each other's opinions. Sharing a book makes for a delightful companionship. It is sharing yourself.

Probably everyone has had the experience of reading a book so good that they could hardly wait to find someone who has read it too. When ninth-grader Tim read *A Day No Pigs Would Die* by Robert Newton Peck, the story evoked deep and even confusing emotions inside him, and he wanted to talk with someone about it. Since the story is about a young man and his father, he asked his dad to read it. His dad had a similar reaction to the story, and one evening they went for a walk together—just to talk about it.

Barbara Hampton's family reads aloud as they travel. She says they have a good time because everyone is together, and reading makes the miles pass quickly. One day, reading Arthur Ransome's *We Didn't Mean to Go to Sea* as they traveled, they became so engrossed in the story that they missed their exit and ended up in another city. They hadn't meant to go to Canton, Ohio!

When our son was a freshman in college, he came home for spring break one time, bearing Charles Williams's *Descent Into Hell*, and he suggested that we read it together on our trip to Florida. As we drove down Highway 19, we neared the end of the story just as we were nearing our destination. Since we wanted to finish the story before arriving, we found ourselves driving more slowly so as not to break the spell of the story. It is one of our favorite memories.

Just last summer fifteen-year-old Lindsay excused herself from a conversation with me and rushed off to catch up with a friend who was passing by. She called back over her shoulder to me as she left, "I want her to read this new book by Janette Oke. It's great; they don't come any better than this!"

Jim Trelease, author of *The Read-Aloud Handbook*, says that next to being hugged, reading aloud is probably the longest-lasting experience of childhood. Reading aloud together is important for all the reasons that talking together is important—inspiration, guidance, education, bonding, communication, understanding, and sharing. When people read together, they give each other a piece of their mind and a piece of their time, and that says a good deal about human worth. If your family doesn't read together already, why not start reading to them? Find something wonderfully funny, interesting, or beautiful and read it aloud to them. You'll come to know them in a new way.

When our son, Mark, found the girl he wanted to marry, they spent evenings together reading aloud. They read *Alice in Wonderland*, *The Wind in the Willows*, *Robin Hood*, and all the other books that she had never read that were an important part of Mark's past. Then they read from her list. I thought, "Not a bad idea." It gives them a common cultural heritage as well as a bond of sharing.

Sharing books makes for good companionship. It is the special fellowship of "readers." It opens up a whole new world for those who enter it. If you have never experienced it, begin soon. Share a good book with someone you care about.

Why Read?

When asked why they read, some teenagers answer bluntly, "Because my teachers and parents make me." My suspicion is they have only experienced books as "have-to" projects. They've never found out what stories are for. They think of reading only for assigned book reports in which they must follow a dull formula to analyze its meaning, identify the main character, write two paragraphs to summarize the plot, tell whether they'd recommend it to a friend, and so on. In many cases it's done the night before, with a quick flip through the pages to find the main character and an attempt to rewrite the blurb on the book cover.

But that's not what reading is all about. A good story is meant to be a *treat*, not a treatment. Stories are for magic, for grand adventure, for making you feel and see things, to take you places you've never been. A book is the greatest learning device ever invented. You can take it with you, loan it to a friend, put it on a shelf, and pass it on to your children years later. Books offer sheer enjoyment. They give the reader remarkable new insights, even if it is only learning to laugh a bit harder at what is ridiculous in life. They nourish the inside of you, speak to your fears and dreams without your knowing it, and give you a wider look at the world. Books become friends. You get so you can't wait to meet up with a new one, hoping it will be the best you have ever read!

A woman, humorously exaggerating her addiction to books, tells how she used to walk a hefty distance to get to the library every week and how the librarian would save special books for her to try. She writes, "I married young and continued to read. My children used to take the book from my hand in order to capture my attention and stick notes under the bathroom door when I retreated there with my book for the requisite solitude. Finally I became a librarian . . . and I am deliriously happy to be paid for indulging my personal inclinations."[1]

In my own experience, my mother would take the book from my hands, too, to bring me back to the real world to clean my room. In a task-oriented day and time, reading in the middle of the day was a time-waster. But I've resisted this all my life and consider any day spent reading is "a most delicious day."

What Do Books Do for You?

More than you think. More than the enjoyment of being transported into another world and meeting the people there. Good books evoke feelings and teach us to understand these feelings. I see what selfishness does to a life; I see how necessary compassion is in human relationships; I understand what it means to be honest and have integrity. The story shows me the hard choices that make up life, and because the story is about someone else, and not me, I am more open to understanding exactly where the choices may lead. Good books are always about the fight between good and evil. That is the basic story line of the universe.

Books widen our world and take us on adventures we may never have. I won't ever wander across Europe finding my way home after having been interned by the Communists following World War II. But reading Ann Holm's *North to Freedom* can open up new appreciations of beauty and goodness, besides giving me a vicarious experience of what it was really like. Robert Louis Stevenson's *Treasure Island* can be read from youth through adulthood—read repeatedly because of the skill the author used in portraying his characters and the detail of life in past times. I feel richer having seen Jim's courage in action and facing his choices with him. And besides that, it is a great adventure. *My Antonia* by Willa Cather puts me inside the life of early pioneers on the prairie, and their love for the land becomes my own. The struggle, the hardships, the raw courage and Cather's descriptions and word choices make me glad that I can read.

Good stories put flesh on abstract ideas. It's difficult to fathom what it means to be noble, valiant, courageous, or even unselfish, unless we meet people in stories whose actions show us what these things mean. What would you understand about "beauty" if you had never seen or heard anything beautiful? A young woman once wrote to Tolkien, "You have made truth and honor more meaningful to me." If you have read *The Lord of the Rings* and followed the courageous Sam Jamgee and Frodo on their adventure, you already know why she wrote to Tolkien in this way. All of us face choices that involve honor and truth.

Once, while reading one of George MacDonald's stories, I came across this description of a certain person, "Never suspecting what a noble creature he was meant to be, he never saw what a poor creature he was." This seemed to me to be an apt description of a person, maybe a nonreader, who has never looked beyond his own small life to see the possibilities that human beings have. Good books show us our potential.

We learn how to use the English language when we read good writing. It's a by-product. We come to admire the right word in the right place—and we are amazed at what it can convey. Reading from Tolkien's trilogy, our family found what has become a favorite description of joy. After one of the hobbits had just experienced an incredible victory, someone asked him how he felt. He said, "I feel like spring after winter, and sun on leaves and like trumpets and harps and all the songs I ever heard."

Slowly and imperceptibly we develop our language skills and learn to choose the right words when expressing ourselves. We learn spelling and punctuation too. Words help us shape what is happening to us. The use of language enables us to drop verbal crutches (like "you know") that plague our conversation, demanding that the listener fill in the blank spaces. All of which makes your personal life more interesting and contributes clarity and precise thinking to the world—which is not a bad contribution, when you think of it.

We are, after all, word partners with God. He has given us these shining symbols known as "words" and lets us communicate with each other and with him, which is nothing short of amazing when you consider all the possibilities for not understanding each other. In one of her lectures Katherine Paterson said,

> Words are humanity's greatest natural resource, but most of us have trouble figuring out how to put them together. Words aren't cheap. They are very precious. They are like water, which gives life and growth and refreshment, but because it has always been abundant, we treat it cheaply. We waste it, we pollute it, and doctor it. Later we blame the quality of the water because we have misused it.[2]

I can use words to tell you truth, to help you find the way when you are lost, to make you understand who I am inside, to make you feel loved and understood, and to tell you the assignment you missed in history when you were out with the flu. It's good if I know how to use them well. They aren't cheap, if I try to say or write the right things. Sitting before a piece of blank paper with an assignment to write an essay convinces me of this. Books show all of us the awesomeness of words.

What Are Reading Skills?

Reading is like other skills. The more you do it, the better you can do it. The less reading you do, the more difficult it is.

You need to be honest with yourself. If you say, "I hate to read," are you really saying, "I can't read very well" or "I read so poorly that I don't feel good about myself when I do it, so I don't read"?

Reading is one of the most complex tasks a person can undertake. And one of the most important. Reading is a way of defining a civilization. When we give statistics about a nation, we talk about its "literacy rate"—the percentage of its people who can read. That is the way an individual's cultural level is judged as well.

Do You Read?

The willingness to read and the skill to read are tied together. Every child by third grade (and usually earlier) knows how special it is to be able to read and begins to feel like a second-class citizen if he can't read well. Then begins the big cover-up. The student reads less and less instead of more and more. I am amazed at the strategies that people have developed to hide the fact that they have trouble reading. I know a man who buys an evening paper every day and carries it home under his arm on the commuter train as a way of saying to the world he is a reader, when, in fact, he cannot read.

As a substitute teacher, I once taught an eighth-grade English class. I called on a student to read aloud the next paragraph from the story we were reading in class. He did not refuse, but he was so intimidated by the words on the page that he made no attempt to read them. He had been listening, so he simply made up some words. I could feel the eyes of the entire class on me, waiting to see what I would do. When he finished, I went on with the class as if nothing unusual had happened. Later, I saw him after class and apologized for putting him on the spot. We talked about his reading. He wanted to read, and so we went to work on some ways for him improve. One of these was to be tutored.

Young men make up most of the students in remedial reading classes—as many as 75 percent. That says something to teachers and to parents. Boys don't make up 75 percent of the poor readers in Japan or Germany or Nigeria. What has happened in our culture? And where are the dads to model reading habits? If Dad sits in front of the television every night, claiming that he is too tired to do anything else, he not only stunts his own growth but his children's as well. Fathers need to let their sons know that athletics and reading are not mutually exclusive interests.

My own dad spent hours reading the newspaper. I have often thought how much broader his world would have been if he had read more books. In today's world we are living with a cultural liability because too many mothers and fathers simply do not read at all.

You may never have admitted to yourself honestly that you have a reading problem. It's not a moral problem; it doesn't mean you are not a capable and good person. You just got skipped over at a critical stage in your reading. Now is the time to do something about it. You should ask for a reading test. Then take advantage of the many kinds of help available—such as private tutoring—to get your reading level up to where it should be.

If you have trouble getting into a book because the words seem scary, try watching a video production of a well-known book. If the story is appealing, get a copy of the book and read it. Knowing the story line may make it easier to read. The characters are already familiar from the video, and they entice you into the story.

You can do some other things. Ask the librarian to help you find a good book on your reading level—one that will capture your interest. Then make an agreement to read every day for ten or fifteen minutes. Ten minutes a day times seven days results in over an hour of reading each week. That may not seem like much, but it's a beginning. You are now reading for enjoyment, not to give a report. You don't have to impress anybody; you can just enjoy the book. If you read fifteen minutes every day, then you can read at least fifteen books a year. But I often tell teenagers: No one can help your reading skills except *you*.

The Right Environment Helps

Parents need to have books and good magazines around the house that invite browsing. Both mothers and fathers should be readers if they expect their children to be; and talking about books makes for good conversation. But people don't read unless there is something on hand to read. I'm amazed at how many people turn on the television as soon as they walk into the house, because that kind of distraction does not encourage reading. Everyone needs to read, because reading opens up our world. Teenagers have no corner on that.

Good lamps are necessary for reading. Maybe no one reads in the home because the one lamp in the living room has only a fifty-watt bulb and does not provide enough light. Experts say that a one-hundred watt bulb is the minimum for easy reading, and some even recommend a total of two hundred watts. Abraham Lincoln read by firelight, but I wouldn't recommend that kind of light today. Better to have more than one place with a good light in the living room and a lamp by your bedside so that you can get your fifteen minutes in before falling asleep.

Learn to use the library. Go often enough so that you recognize it as a friendly place. Libraries have all kinds of people who will help you. I have never yet met one who acted as if my questions were dumb. Librarians don't guard the books to keep them away from you; instead, they are shouting "Look at what you can borrow for free! Let me help you find something good." If you don't like the book someone recommends, you don't have to read it. You can say it didn't interest you or that you found it too hard. The secret is not to give up. Look for one that does interest you. You would be strange indeed if in a library with thousands of books you didn't find one you couldn't put down once you've started reading it.

The more a person reads, the easier it will get, and an attitude change will take care of the rest of the problem. No one should miss out on the excitement. The world out there is bigger than you know.

Here is a prayer for teenagers to help them on their way:

A TEENAGER'S PRAYER

O Supreme Being, and I don't mean me;
Give me the vision to see my parents as human beings
   because if they aren't, what does that make me?
Give me vocabulary, because the more I say "*you know,*"
   the less anyone does.
Give me freedom from television, because I'm beginning
   to suspect its trivial plots.
Give me homework to keep me from flunking Free Time.
Give me a map of the world so I may see that this town
   and I are not the center of it.
Give me a love for books so that I can understand
   the choices facing me.
Give me understanding that nobody ever grows up in

a group so I may find my own way.
Give me limits so I will know I am loved.
And give me nothing I haven't earned so that my
   adolescence
will not last forever. Amen.[3]

Notes

1. Anna A. Flowers, *A Passion for Books*, published in *The Horn Book Magazine* (March/April 1985), 237.

2. Katherine Paterson in the Velma Varner Lecture, December 8, 1979.

3. Adapted from Richard Peck's prayer in *Young Adult Books*, published in *Horn Book Magazine* (September/October 1986), 621.

2

Is Imagination Going Down the Tube?

Television has become our imagination, and in a sense, almost eliminates the necessity of thought. Television has many of the properties of an addiction.

Dorothy A. Singer and
Jerome L. Singer
Psychologists, Yale University

"Television is like a drug," someone said. "A little always leads to more and it dulls the mind, the body, and the soul. It's the "Plug-in" drug.

Television doesn't need to be addictive; you are the one who decides if it will be. Neither is it totally negative. In fact, it's an incredible invention. I like watching certain programs: sporting events and some public television programs, in particular. Television has unlimited potential for educating, for broadcasting significant cultural events, and for entertaining. But it has not lived up to its potential—and neither have its viewers. A television in a room ought to be simply that: a television. It has no life of its own.

People are in charge, not the television. To willingly become a slave of something with an "off" switch is failure to control your own life.

In its short life, television has led to more empty-mindedness than any other gadget invented. Research estimates that most young men and women have watched over 15,000 hours of television by the time they reach age seventeen. That cuts out a lot of living. TV requires little of its viewers and tends to make them lonely and lethargic. Like skywriting, it gets a lot of attention but doesn't last long.

Television may not require much from the viewer but it does, however, affect you. It is not a totally passive activity. Think of your mind as a pad of paper with blank sheets. What are you writing on the pages that will be stored away in your inner computer forever? For one thing, what you look at affects your values. It uses up time; it takes space in your life. We need to decide how we want to fill up the pages of our minds.

Television is the direct opposite of reading. Reading lets us use our imaginations; television does it all for us. The action in most television programming consists of rapid transitions. Instead of holding our attention, allowing us to think, it constantly interrupts our thought processes. We can't ask questions of a television program; it allows for no interaction. Education leaders believe that this is why children are restless and have short attention spans. Television simply doesn't teach you to think, nor will it enhance your verbal skills. But *books* do.

Perhaps one of television's worse offenses is its display of antisocial behavior. Even cartoon characters are constantly bopping each other over the head. After so much exposure to violence, the average person is desensitized and can even accept violence as "normal behavior." Human life is devalued. Oddly, if animals die, the story line is often full of pathos, whereas humans are gunned down with hardly a second thought. Even the so-called humorous barbs in sitcoms are like arrows shooting down another human being. They don't model much that is good for human relationships. The constant flow of crises and devious behavior in the afternoon soaps gives a skewed view of life and is not good training for a happy home life. One young woman told me "the soaps" were her main source of information about sex "and stuff." I hardly knew where to begin to unravel all that misinformation.

I make no claim that books are free from violence or antisocial behavior. But you would have to read a stack of carefully chosen books to get as much violence as you get in two or three evenings of prime time television (unless you are reading Stephen King!). Obviously, you have to be as careful about what you read as what you watch. Many contemporary books have unsavory behavior as their main point. These scenes fill the blank pages in your mind, too, and can cause you more than a little trouble.

Videos have made all kinds of movies available for inexpensive and relaxing evenings at home. The great movies of the past—the classics—are available for those who missed them the first time around or who want to see them a second time. A good drama is worth seeing more than once. But some videos are on a different level entirely. I don't have to elaborate the behavior they incite or the feelings they evoke. The kind of stuff that exploits its viewers, that controls thought-life and behavior in a negative way, well, who needs that? I want to be my own person and make my own decisions about values and behavior, based on something more than a movie that manipulates my senses. I do that by taking care with what I watch and what I read.

If it is true that television makes people think less, feel less, speak less, and imagine less, why are people so hooked on it? You don't have to throw out the television, you just have to *control* it. A good rule is this: However much television you watch, watch less. What kind of person do you want to be? You decide. To arrive at the end of life and realize that you didn't use even a fraction of your potential seems incredibly sad to me. It makes being created a human being seem pointless.

In the story of the remarkable Ben Carson called *Gifted Hands*, Dr. Carson tells of growing up black, with his older brother, Curtis, and a determined, inspiring mother who worked two jobs to keep her family together.[1] She was constantly challenging her boys to do better in school than their grades showed. When Ben brought home a D in math, she drilled him on his multiplication tables night after night until he could answer without hesitation. School became more enjoyable, but still his mother was not satisfied, and encouraged improvement.

"I've decided you boys are watching too much television," she said one evening, snapping off the set in the middle of a program. She was not swayed by the protests of her sons and stood by her firm decision that they would watch only three programs a week.

Then she added another demand. "You boys are going to the library and check out books. You're going to read at least two books every week. At the end of each week, you'll give me a report on what you've read." Ben thought that the rule was impossible; he had never read a book on his own in his whole life. But he and Curtis did what their mother asked, reluctantly at first. As time went on, he and Curtis discovered the treasures of the library. Ben checked out books on nature and became a fifth-grade expert on things of a scientific nature. The librarians noticed the boys and began to recommend books to them. As they read, their vocabulary improved. Their schoolwork improved; their self-images improved; their attitudes toward school changed.

There is much more to the story. Curtis Carson graduated from the University of Michigan as an engineer. Ben Carson went to Yale, then went on to medical school at the University of Michigan, and now has a worldwide reputation as a pediatric neurosurgeon at Johns Hopkins University. He was raised in inner-city Detroit by a mother with a third-grade education. His future did not look bright. His mother, Sonya Carson, had twenty-three siblings and had married at age thirteen, but she had a vision for her sons. Again and again she said, "Bennie, if you read, honey, you can learn just about anything you want to know. The doors of the world are open to people who can read. And my boys are going to be successful in life, because they're going to be the best readers in the school."

Gifted Hands is a fine, inspiring biography, worthy of a "good read" for more than the paragraphs I have quoted. But as I read the story of Ben Carson's life, it occurred to me that the story might have been very different if Ben's mother had not insisted that the television be controlled and that her boys learn to read.

Why this sermon about television? Because I am talking about books and reading and enriching your life, and I know that probably the biggest enemy to personal growth is sitting in a prominent corner in a room of your house. All chairs are facing it—as if this electrical box were the source of a message from on high.

The human imagination is one of our greatest gifts. Don't let it go down the tube.

Note

1. Ben Carson (with Cecil Murphey), *Gifted Hands* (Grand Rapids: Zondervan, 1990), 34–37.

3

How to Read a Book

Stories are a way of teaching. Our own lives are mirrored and intensified by stories. We learn the connection between things by reading stories.

Robert Coles

We had been watching together a dramatized version of a poem by Robert Browning, called *The Pied Piper of Hamelin,* one story in a series for public television called "Long Ago and Far Away." The Pied Piper, hearing that rats have taken over the city of Hamelin, offers to "pipe" them out of town with his flute—for a price. As he plays his pipe, the rats rush out from every nook and cranny in the city to follow the piper to their destruction. Afterward, the town fathers refuse to pay him the agreed-upon price. The Pied Piper warns that he might use his pipe another way if they delay. And when they do, the Pied Piper sounds his pipe and all the children of the village run out to follow him. Singing, laughing, and dancing, they follow him up the mountain path, when suddenly the mountain pass closes like a door behind them and they disappear forever. Only one small boy on crutches, who couldn't keep up with the crowd, is left in the village, where people are mourning the loss of all their children.

It was an absorbing, effective production of a story that raised many questions. When it was over, James Earl Jones, the program's host, asked, "Was the Pied Piper good or was he bad, or was he both?" We discussed it among ourselves. Ten-year-old Jedediah made a quick judgment based on getting rid of the rats and then changed his mind. One of us mentioned the injustice of the town fathers; they hadn't kept their word. Austin, who was six, felt sorry for the moms and dads who were missing their children.

Jedediah came to me later and asked if we could read the poem from which the story was taken, hoping that he could get some more clues. After we read it, we talked more about the story. Finally, he said, "The children followed him without asking him where he was going. It was like someone fooling you with promises of adventure and excitement, like taking drugs. The children didn't know they could never come back to their parents. I think the Pied Piper fooled the children." He has since watched the tape of this story many times and is still asking himself questions about the story.

I wonder if he would have questioned the story if the host hadn't asked that one single question. Stories often touch us deeply, leaving us wondering, sometimes feeling pain inside, or confusion. (That's when it is good to know someone else who has read the same story or seen the same film.) We need to be aware that stories do affect us profoundly. They can change the way we think or feel and even the way we behave. When we ask questions about the story and our feelings, we begin to understand more clearly.

I don't mean that you should weigh stories down with the baggage of moral lessons so that the fun of the story sinks and disappears. Stories should be read for the enjoyment they bring. Reading should not be a chore, a drag, or just another lesson. A good story is sufficient in itself. It is complete as it stands. But when you were younger, whatever point the story was making was right out front. No one recommends analyzing *Peter Rabbit*. To my knowledge, none of the other stories on "Long Ago and Far Away" had such a weighty question about the main character—is he good or is he bad? After all, the point of *Saint George and the Dragon* is pretty obvious. He is called Saint George because he killed the dragon and saved the people. However, Saint George, and others like him, did not "pack the emotional wallop" that the Pied Piper did.

The *Pied Piper of Hamelin* is adult poetry made into a fairy tale. The story demands a question. As you read more complex novels and stories, you will find that what you read demands a question so that it can make sense. It is not an "unwanted lesson"; instead, it is the exhilaration of getting the point. That is the "double fun" of reading. You have the enjoyment of a good story, plus the inner delight of understanding what it is about. It is somewhat like getting the point of a joke.

Questioning the story is one way of describing what is done in literary criticism. No one will really be a good reader before learning how to ask questions about what he reads. He may read the words flawlessly, but *reading* is getting the meaning behind the words. It is not so much learning to read as it is *learning to think*.

Learning to Think

Everyone is a philosopher. All people have some life-view, even if they don't know how to express it. By life-view I mean the things that people believe give life meaning and help it make sense. A person's life-view, or worldview, gives that person the values he or she lives by. It is a belief system. It determines not only what people value but how they think and act.

Suppose a certain man's speech and behavior are so full of anger that few people want to be around him. You might think that person doesn't have any life-view or belief system. Yet he does have his own limited view of the world, albeit a pretty confusing one.

Whenever anyone opens his mouth to speak, some elements of his belief system are evident. All the films you see, the books you read, the way your friends talk, the news stories on television—all of them tell you something of that writer's view of the world. All of them are "philosophical statements" to some degree.

While having a worldview is a good and necessary thing, most adolescents are in the process of forming a worldview or a belief system. Young adults are inevitably influenced by the worldview of their parents. As they grow on the inside, they may begin to affirm certain values of their parents and sometimes choose others of their own. Often they are easily swayed because they haven't thought their values through to logical conclusions. This is not unique to young adults; many people in their thirties and forties are still being tossed about by every new idea that comes along because they don't have a framework for evaluation. People of all ages need a measuring rod by which to measure their values, to see if they are on track.

Adults who cherish their own worldview sometimes want to press it on to young people, getting them to give assent to values that they haven't thought through. It is good to believe something definite, but too many people have a collection of half-baked ideas. (I like that phrase "half-baked" because it indicates that the person does not stay with it long enough to see if it is worth eating!) If you accept someone else's worldview without thinking it through, it won't really be yours. Many ideologies produce "group-think" but not necessarily informed thinking or consistent people. You can recite back a string of truths to someone, but unless they are your own, because you are convinced about them, you will be like a robot instead of a thinking person.

It can work two ways. On the one hand, a teenager can be overprotected from ideas that parents or teachers think are unacceptable or perhaps even dangerous. At its worst, this is what censorship is all about, although it can also be a safety factor insofar as it helps keep the teenager from trouble. But too often it keeps the teenager from thinking. Being overprotected from ideas can make a person suspicious of everyone who has a slightly different idea; it doesn't usually lead to the ability to ask questions to discover what is true.

On the other hand, it is not only naïve but downright

nonsensical to think that we can consume any idea, without question, and that it won't hurt us. Some people have thought that about pornography and have been surprised at what a strong hold a vulgar, indecent mental image can have on them.

Because everyone has some sort of worldview, we don't have to look too far to find that some of these worldviews are hostile to Christian truth. Look at what happened to the children who followed the Pied Piper. They didn't ask where they were going and have never been heard from since.

What Is the Author Saying?

You might think that the sheer enjoyment of a good story is enough, and many stories do delight us. But novels are always saying more than what is on the surface. We will find the story more valuable if we learn to ask questions—like the following—about what we are reading:

(1) *Let the story answer questions*
Why did this book tug at me?
What themes are found in this story? (A theme is the dominant idea or topic in the story.)
What tests (physical, moral, mental, or spiritual) do the characters in the story face?
What are the important traits of the characters in the story? (For example, is the character unstable or does he "hang in" even when the going is tough?)
How do the characters change or develop?
How did the characters know (and choose to do) what is wrong or right?
How do the characters treat each other? What does this reveal about their values?
Is this story like life as I know it? Do I find myself saying, "That's the way it is". . . or "Wait a minute?"
Who is responsible for the way things turned out?

In an excellent essay on literary criticism, the poet T. S. Eliot says that you cannot judge literature apart from theology, that the "greatness" of literature cannot be determined solely by good writing but must include an evaluation of what is Truth. We are not reading stories well if we keep our religious beliefs in a separate compartment. Especially today, when there is no common agreement on what is true or right, it is more necessary than ever for readers to "scrutinize their reading," especially the reading of novels. Eliot writes, "It is commonplace that what shocks one generation is accepted quite calmly by the next. This adaptability to change of moral standards . . . is only evidence of what unsubstantial foundations people's moral judgments are."[1]

An author whose belief system is very different from ours may tell the truth by portraying the world and people in it so accurately that he is saying more than he knows. Sometimes an evil person well portrayed, for example, can be *truth*. A story tells the truth when we understand that this is the way things may happen. It tells a greater truth when it gives us new insights into *why* things happen that way and shows us what we may have believed to be vaguely true but had never put into words. Then the story qualifies as great literature and helps us clarify and interpret life.

   (2) *Question the story with your theology or belief system*
      Does this story tell the truth about the human heart?
      Does the story unmask evil (show it for what it really is) or
         does it encourage it?
      Does this story awaken good in me?
      Does it enlarge my worldview?
      Is it a helpful presentation of human experience?
      Is this story (which may not mention God) compatible with
         biblical values?

People who are trying to develop their literary tastes need to read widely. I think that everyone goes on reading "binges" at some time or another. Remember reading all the Hardy Boys books or Nancy Drew? Some teenagers read everything Janette Oke writes. Some years back I went on a wonderful adventure reading everything Anne Morrow Lindbergh had written. One author can almost take possession of us for a time, and we end up feeling an affection for certain writers because we have read so much of their writing. But as our critical powers grow, we are protected from being dominated by one writer. As we read, we are affected by one writer after another and are no longer overly influenced by any one of them. This allows us to better arrange and define our own life-view. But there are other questions we need to ask of the books we read.

(3) *Question the writing style of the book*
Is the writing good prose—strong, clear word choices?
What metaphors or imagery have left a lasting picture in your mind?
How does the book help you to see, feel, hear—and use another of your senses—to make the story more real to you?
In what ways did this book inspire you?

Language well used is a delight. It has a beauty and a rhythm that makes us say to ourselves, "This is what words were meant to do." Chaim Potok's books are examples of excellent writing for adults and teenagers alike. I read his *Gift of Asher Lev* while on vacation, thoroughly enjoying every page. I could hardly wait until my husband—and then the two friends who were with us—finished it. We talked about it endlessly over every meal we ate together later that week. I went on to read Frank Peretti's *This Present Darkness*, and, while I became absorbed in the book and the adventure and insights it offered me, I had trouble getting into it at first because of the great contrast in the quality of the writing. Both were good stories, worth reading. Potok's writing, however, is great *literature*. It will be around a long time.

We might want to include another question to ask of any book: Is it easy to read? First let me define *easy reading*. Some people like large print and a limited vocabulary, so that defines easy reading for them. But by my definition, easy reading means that without a struggle you get the gist of what the author is saying. Some contemporary authors deliberately fill their stories with dissonance, making it hard to figure out motives and even what is happening. That represents their view of the world and makes for anxious reading. At the same time, some of the things that are the easiest to read can have the most negative influence on us or, at best, do not add anything to our lives. For example, too many formula-written romance novels can skew the reader's understanding of real life.

Should We Censor Books?

Whenever you or I decide not to read "trashy" books, we are censoring. We have to recognize that some writing is good and some is not. At the back of this book you will find over three hundred book annotations in the bibliography—books that we consider good writing. A few are questionable, and you can tell that easily from the annotation. These are popular contemporary books that many teenagers are asked to read for school. We do not think that reading any of them will corrupt readers or their beliefs. In fact, we hope that you will see them for what they are: an expression of the worldview of an author who thinks this is the way the world is. That is why we need to ask hard questions about books.

Most public and school libraries do not carry trash. They try to carry the really worthy books. Sometimes librarians get taken in by liberal reviewers who use descriptions like "tender" and "poignant" for questionable books. The standards of what makes a worthy book will vary according to contemporary worldviews. The old favorites will be there, along with some excellent new books. Not every book the library chooses is appropriate for every reader. But that is precisely why it is so important to learn how to critique what we read. If we ask the right questions, there may even be some books that we may not want to finish. Good readers often say, "This book isn't for me. I don't like it."

Sometimes we read books even when we do not value them. I

call these the "shrug your shoulders" kind of books. No book will hurt you if you know how to evaluate it and have developed a principled and moral life-view. If you lack the principles to protect yourself, then no rules can keep you safe, because there is too much "out there" with destructive potential. Rules like "Don't read that; don't go there; don't do that"—are never as effective in guarding your life as an inner decision to choose what is good.

In the end, the only discipline that really works is self-discipline. You must choose; you must decide between good, better, and best—and often between good and evil. As someone has said, "It's important to have an open mind—but not so open that your brains fall out."

C. S. Lewis, author of the wonderful Narnia Chronicles, said that the best antidote to evil and falsity in fiction, as in life, is saturation in the good and genuine. The bibliography at the end of this book will help you learn to have discriminating taste in reading and saturate your reading with the good and genuine. The reader bears the responsibility for judging any work of art—novel, play, or poetry. We need to expand our reading experience to know how to judge.

Reading on Two Levels

There are two ways to read even the best of writing and to hear what it is saying. If you have read C. S. Lewis's *The Lion, the Witch and the Wardrobe* from the Narnia Chronicles, you already know it's a ripping good adventure. It is enjoyable on that level alone. But Lewis gives us more than adventure. The book is even better when it is read on a second level—as an allegory of life. As you read, you learn something about the clever enticements of evil and what evil does to the world—and about the necessity of redemption from evil. It is true that the book can be read only as an adventure, but think what the reader misses when it is read that way.

The Narnia Chronicles are relatively simple illustrations of reading on two levels. The more complicated the novel, the more readers need to judge what they are reading. *The Tale of Two Cities* by Charles Dickens is often read as preparation for studying the French Revolution. The social structure of French society: the poverty, the injustice, the abuses of power are the obvious message of the book. But it is also a story about good and evil. It too is a story about redemption. The thoughtful reader finds significant themes running throughout the book.

Nancy M. Tischler, a professor of English at Penn State University, comments that "Graham Greene's *The Power and the Glory* makes a powerful statement about God and his priests in a most effective form. But many readers enjoy the novel for its degrading portrayal of the whiskey priest who fathered an illegitmate child, missing the central point altogether."[2]

That is why it is important to learn to ask questions about what you read. If you'll carefully identify the themes in the book, you'll be surprised at what you'll find. Often you will be profoundly gripped by spiritual truths that heighten your understanding of God's character and the nature of evil. But this takes looking for more than what is on the surface, and it takes experience.

When novelist Aleksandr Solzhenitsyn writes in *One Day in the Life of Ivan Denisovich*, you know that the author understands the nature of evil even if he doesn't refer to the "Fall." When you see moments of generosity, heroism, integrity in Solzhenitzyn's characters in the prison camp, people living above their demeaning surroundings, then you understand new things about what it means to be made in the image of God.

Many well-intentioned people, who may not know how to ask questions of literature, want to protect others by giving them only books in which the message is flatly and firmly evident. Many of these books have thinly veiled plots whose primary purpose is propaganda. They may serve a moral and spiritual function, but for the most part, they do not qualify as literature. This kind of writing lacks beauty or substance. In good writing, the morality of a story is not laid on top of the narrative; it is woven into the fabric of the story so that whatever is true comes out of the characters' beings and the plot of the story. People are mixtures of good and evil, not one or the other, and the plot of any story should reveal this complexity.

Readers need to exercise their freedom carefully so that they do not abuse their liberty in reading. If we are free to read, then we must show a willingness to think, to evaluate, to examine. Above all, we must be honest in our reading.

What About Bad Language?

Authors of inferior literature often use explicit sex scenes or profanity in such a way that they become the point of the story; there is no second level of meaning except to show the degradation that comes when one lives without rules. Some writing (and some movies) exploit the reader in this way. These qualify as X-rated and bring the reader's or viewer's thought life down to the level of that of the writer. I simply refuse to let an author do this to me.

We live in a fallen world. Good literature does not avoid that fact. But it does not revel in it, either. In good writing, the author portrays evil behavior as a way of exposing it for what it is. *Les Miserables* by Victor Hugo is a prime example. It is true that sometimes evil properly portrayed exposes the real character of evil. In the same way, King Ahab and Queen Jezebel in the Old Testament show the lengths to which some people will go.

Good literature may sometimes include rough language. It is entirely believable for some characters to use profanity. A writer may use profanity as a tool or technique to make characters come alive, to be more authentic. How does the reader handle this? By focusing on the author's intent. The point of a story should always transcend the writer's techniques.

You, as a reader, are the judge of right and wrong, and you cannot blame a book for your own behavior or language. It is always a challenge to keep your integrity. You can read something and become "earthy" or "carnal" yourself. That's what happens when people don't ask questions like, *What is the point of this story? What is it really saying?*

Read at Your Own Level

Teenagers and adults alike should take care not to read beyond their level of understanding, otherwise they'll miss the point of the story. While reading books that are too advanced, they will be readers who are missing all the good books that have been written for their present emotional and intellectual level. No one gains adulthood by reading books beyond his or her ability to understand. We grow by understanding and coping with what is meant for us today.

In some schools a kind of intellectual snobbery exists. I remember talking some years ago with a twelve-year-old who told me he had read *Dr. Zhivago* and loved it. He spoke of the writing style and the plot structure, but I had an uneasy feeling that he was faking it, that the evaluation had come from someone else. He felt so smug about his maturity in reading an adult book. But the years have proven him to be very immature. He is always pretending to have the necessary insights, but rarely does anyone see the fruit of good insights in his now forty-year-old life.

John Milton, the fifteenth-century English poet, believed that in our long-term reading we are collecting "bits of perfection." By that, he meant insights that reveal reality. Our job is to collect, to judge, and to select those bits that truly belong to God and make use of them in our lives. They will enrich both our life and our faith. "A phrase, an idea, or a situation will suddenly catch our attention and magically illumine our lives." These bits of truth point to *the* Truth that holds our lives together.

We as readers already know what is good and right. Part of maturity is shown in self-censorship. Quality life always comes from making the right choices, of choosing what we consider valuable. What do you want to put on "the pages of your mind"?

Parents should read the books their children are reading. In fact, teenagers should encourage their parents and teachers to read the same books they themselves are reading, so they can talk together about them. This not only gives them a sounding board for evaluating but enlarges understanding on both sides. Sharing is enriching, and neither teenagers nor adults have enough of it. Teens *can* make value judgments, recognize truth, and make good decisions.

All of us need to learn to ask questions of life, of the books we read, of the sermons we hear, of the television programs we watch, of the commercials and the newscasts. Don't be a sponge. Instead, ask yourself, "Is this true?" Remember the Pied Piper.

Notes

1. T. S. Eliot, "Religion and Literature," from *The Christian Imagination: Essays on Literature and the Arts* by Leland Ryken (Grand Rapids: Baker, 1981), 142–44.

2. Nancy M. Tischler, *The Christian Reader,* first published in *Christianity Today* (June 8, 1973).

4

What Makes a Good Book?

> *A book is good if it permits, invites or even impels a good reading, one in which the reader has submitted himself to the text, entering the "made" experiences, and been taken beyond himself. While good books can be read badly, bad books cannot be read well. The question is not whether it is a good book, but whether the book compelled a good reading.*
>
> C. S. Lewis

"This novel won't let go of me."

"I don't know how to say what happens when you read a good story: it's not TV and it's not reading the papers. It's not the movies, because you get into them faster, but you're out real fast; you forget what you've seen because the next flick has come and you're looking at it. With a novel . . . you take things slowly and get your head connected to what you're reading. Then the story becomes yours."[1]

We read for many reasons; mostly for the pleasure and entertainment it offers. Good books help us shape and express our own feelings; they stimulate us intellectually. We don't read for long unless the story is interesting. Books give us insights and sometimes answers. Stories show how complex life is and the possibilities of being a human being. Francis Bacon once remarked that "Some books are to be tasted, others to be swallowed, and some few to be chewed and digested."

How does one identify a "chewable" book? Do we know how to identify a good book, a book that compels good reading? Without insisting that we all like the same books, we do have some standards.

A good book has life; it releases something creative in the mind of the reader. The author has captured reality, the permanent stuff of life, and something enduring is planted in the heart. It may be fantasy, mystery, historical fiction, or whatever, but a profound morality comes out of the story.

The idea behind the book will determine something of the value of the story. What is the author trying to say about life, about the people in the story? That is the theme of the book. A weak or superficial theme means a weak story. Many books written today exploit the natural curiosity of adolescents about the facts of life; therefore, such books have shallow plots and superficial characters.[2] The theme behind the story is not compelling enough nor sufficiently significant to give the books a long life either on the shelf or in the heart. A large and enduring theme handles the large and enduring truths or choices that make up the human experience.

A good writer has something worth saying and says it in the best possible way and respects the reader's ability to understand. Language is used well. The word choices make us see, feel, hear, taste, smell, decide. The action of the story and the descriptions have a crisp leanness because strong verbs and simple descriptions are used. The Bible is a model for this kind of writing. With an economy of words, lasting pictures are painted. Consider, for example, what pictures are painted in your mind from a short story that the prophet Nathan told David, after David had stolen the affections of Uriah's wife.

> There were two men in a certain city, the one rich and the
> other poor. The rich man had very many flocks and herds;
> but the poor man had nothing but one little ewe lamb,
> which he had bought. And he brought it up, and it grew up
> with him and with his children; it used to eat of his morsel,
> and drink from his cup and lie in his bosom, and it was like
> a daughter to him. Now there came a traveler to the rich
> man, and he was unwilling to take one of his own flock or
> herd to prepare for the wayfarer who had come to him, but
> he took the poor man's lamb, and prepared it for the man
> who had come to him. (2 Samuel 12:1–4 [RSV])

Notice that the story doesn't say, "The poor man really loved
his lamb and had made a pet of it." Instead, you are led to that
conclusion from the description of actions taken by the poor man. It
is not only that he was poor that made the rich man's action unjust.
A whole layer of emotion and feeling, of hope and encouragement,
are latent in the description. What would the fact that it was a "ewe
lamb" have meant to the poor man? The story doesn't need to use
many adjectives to describe the rich man. His action shows what
he was like. That's the mark of good writing.

*A good story has characters of depth, not superficial
stereotypes; they inspire the inner life of the reader.* The
characters—whether animals, people, or creatures created by the
author—must be believable, not one-dimensional actors who
deliver a thinly disguised message or react with some unreal
heroism. Heroes we like, but let them resemble someone we know,
at least a little human—like Toad in *The Wind in the Willows* or
Jody in *The Yearling* or Dicey in *Dicey's Song* or even Winnie-the-
Pooh in Milne's stories.

Literature presents human experience. Fiction is not untrue
just because it is called fiction. Good fiction contains truth. It is not
the Truth, but it serves as a signpost to the Truth, to the reality of
God, and of our need for redemption. Like John the Baptist crying
out, "Prepare the way for the Lord," literature focuses on our
deepest needs, and that is why it moves us so profoundly. We see
reality in what we read. The story may take us on adventures or
introduce us to people not remotely related to our lives. Because

people are the same on the inside and have to make the same kind of choices, the story is true and can teach us. Good fiction does not always have a happy ending, but it always shows possibilities of how to act or resolve the conflict. It ends with *hope*, with some possible good in sight, some redeeming vision.

What About Tragedy, Despair, and Hope?

Some contemporary writers depict their own meaningless world and foist it on the reader instead of wrestling with life to give it order and meaning. They delight in depravity, snigger at morality, throw into the plot bits of pornography that appeal to our baser values. The end product reveals their life-view: meaninglessness. It leaves the reader empty. Despair is a hard commodity to build on. It may be a true description of some people in the world and, in that sense, it presents human experience. We need to know that there are some people who look at life this way. But a constant diet of books gives us neither insight nor understanding. When we read the literature of despair, our best response is compassion and pity for those caught in this trap.

A story of despair is different from a tragedy. Some facet of human values, some meaning is always present in the great tragedies of literature. Shakespeare, who wrote many tragedies, always showed the moral result linked with the deed itself. In *Hamlet*, eight tragic deaths take place because of one murder. *Romeo and Juliet* is another example of great drama, though an incredibly tragic one. Whenever I read it or see it portrayed on the screen, I want to stop the action and tell them how they could put this whole situation right. Threads of human values and choices run through the tragedy. It is cause and effect at work. The fact that it has a sad ending does not indicate lack of meaning. Many situations in life do not have happy endings, but we learn from tragedy. And, in contrast to the literature of despair, people are "choosers," not hapless victims.

Readers have written to Katherine Paterson, expressing disappointment about the ending of her story *The Great Gilly*

Hopkins. When streetwise Gilly has been moved to another foster home and made the responsibility of frumpy Maime Trotter, she is drawn into a circle of love. However, she lives with dreams of what could be and plans her own rescue by getting in touch with her real mother. Her mother doesn't turn out to be wonderful and responsible and all that Gilly had dreamed about.

> She'd come because Nonnie had paid her to. And she wasn't going to stay, And she wasn't going to take Gilly back with her. "I will always love you." It was a lie. Gilly had thrown away her whole life for a stinking lie.

When she called Trotter to tell her she was coming home, Trotter hears her pain and tells her,

> "Sometimes in this world things come easy, and you tend to lean back and say, 'Well, finally, a happy ending. This is the way it is supposed to be.' Like life owed you good things. And there is lots of good things, baby. Like you coming to be with us here this fall. That was a mighty good thing for me and William Ernest. But you just fool yourself if you expect good things all the time. They ain't what's regular—don't nobody owe 'em to you."[3]

Paterson, in an article called "Hope is More Than Happiness" writes,

> This world looked at squarely does not allow optimism to flourish. Hope for us cannot simply be wishful thinking, nor can it be only the desire to grow up and take control over our own lives. Hope is a yearning, rooted in reality, that pulls us toward the radical biblical vision of a world where truth and justice and peace do prevail, a time in which the knowledge of God will cover the earth as the waters cover the sea, a scene which finds humanity . . . walking together by the light of God's glory. Now there's a happy ending for you. The only purely happy ending I know of.[4]

All of us need hope; people can't live without it. Good stories have it, but it may not look like the happy endings of fairy stories. At the end of Gilly's story we aren't sure whether she will stay on with her grandmother or return to Trotter, but somehow we know that Gilly will be all right. Her pain is not trivialized or erased, but you feel deep in your heart that she will grow up to become a wise and compassionate woman even though she will forever miss the mother she wanted.

More About What Makes a Good Book

The plot of the story is part of its genius. Plot doesn't only answer "what happened next?" It tells you why it happened. Plot is the design of the idea behind the story. Good plots grow out of strong themes, the quality of the idea. The plot holds the story together in such a way that the story takes on meaning. Add to that, memorable characters and good use of language, and you have a winner. These are the ingredients of a good book.

No one has produced a magic formula or set of rules that produce a good story. The quality of the writing comes from the quality of the writer. Add to that the quality of the reader, and you have the right combination. *Good stories have an excellent spirit about them.* They are an experience—imaginative, intellectual, social, spiritual—and a sense of permanent worth surrounds them.

All of these characteristics are also found in books that make us laugh. Everyone profits from a well-written story that brings laughter. Consider James Thurber. We used to read aloud his *The Thirteen Clocks* every Halloween night for fun. Farley Mowat's *The Dog Who Wouldn't Be,* along with his other books, relate such believable, ridiculous incidents that you will find yourself chuckling all the way through the book. Edmund Love's *The Situation in Flushing* is a delightfully humorous tale of life in the town of Flushing. *Absolute Zero* by Helen Cresswell, a British writer, is full of wonderful characters and hilarity. Books like *I Remember Papa, Cheaper By the Dozen,* and others of that genre should be part of everyone's reading. Life can become too serious. A good laugh can often do more for us than anything else.

But some readers still may wish for something more concrete in defining what makes a good book. Something more tangible. It's hard to describe a good book. Once a book leaves the author's hands, it becomes the property of the reader. Each person who reads it will see different things in it—often, things that the author didn't necessarily intend. What is a good book in one person's eyes may not be so in another's. That's fair enough. It's important not to weigh books down with, "You must like this." At the same time, you do need to learn to discriminate between the awful, the good, the better, and the best—not just in reading but in *all* of life.

Writer Leon Garfield tried to tackle the problem of what is good. He wrote,

> Certainly not those bland, lifeless romances, those empty tales of wish fulfillment that are more like shampoo advertisements than honest pieces of fiction. Like sugar candy that rots the teeth, they rot the mind. Nor do I have much affection for those dreadful efforts, purporting to be helpful to troubled teenagers, that, in effect, are little better than sly pornography.[5]

But he doesn't tell us what is good, except to say that a book should have the spark of vitality and a glint of indignation.

It's easier to describe what isn't good writing. Garfield, and others like him, have plenty to say about how standards for contemporary books have "fallen into the mud." He worries that responsible editors are a vanishing breed and have been replaced by the hirelings of the accountants who consider the quick salability of a book more important than quality.

The best hope of promoting quality lies in the better education of the reader. If you have a taste for what is really good reading, I don't think you will acquire an appetite for what is not. I remember noting with surprise a book that our teenage son had brought home from the library. I had read one of that author's books and suspected its racy content. He left it on the coffee table one day, and I asked him how he liked that author. He said, "Next to other books I have read, this one ranks at the bottom of the list. There's really not much to the story. Have you ever read any of her books?" Yes, I had, and we had a good conversation about what we suspected were the author's goals for the story.

So much for that kind of reading. Excellence has a way of

eliminating inferior products. That is true in reading, at least for thoughtful people, and we need more thoughtful teens to help save our world from "the mud."

When all is said and done, a good book is a good book. You have to find the ones you like, by trial and error. But the point of this book is to spare them from some of that. The entries in the bibliography will give you some ideas. The annotations show how we evaluated the books.

For you to like all the books in our bibliography would be expecting too much. But there are good ones for nearly everyone to try out. Some of you will love books that are not on our list and ask, "Why did you leave this one out?" I hope that you do. The list could go on and on. You should share that book with someone else and thus supplement our listing.

Notes

1. From an interview with a teenager named Linda done by Robert Coles and recorded in his book *The Call of Stories* (Boston: Houghton Mifflin, 1989), p.64

2. Judy Blume's Margaret in *Are You There, God? It's Me, Margaret* has a serious concern over the fact that her friends have begun menstruating and she hasn't. This hardly makes an enduring or enlightening theme for a book. Yet stories are about human experience, and because preadolescents are curious about the subjects she writes about, her books, which I would not classify as "good literature," are extremely popular with certain readers. Blume's books reflect her own secular values, and her plots are thin.

3. Katherine Paterson, *The Great Gilly Hopkins* (New York: Harper & Row, 1978), 148.

4. Katherine Paterson, *New York Times Book Review* (December 25, 1988).

5. Leon Garfield, "The Outlaw," written for *Horn Book Magazine* (March/April 1990), 170.

5

What Is Happening to Books?

It is tragic that many writers who look down on stories of the supernatural are writing things for young people which are nothing but sheer chaos.
Isaac Bashevis Singer

No formula; no uplifting moral; no climactic heroics; just the turbulence of adolescent life.
Jack Forman

"These days," an editor said, "the decision to publish a book lies 80 percent with the sales and marketing department and 20 percent with the editor." Why the emphasis on the sales potential of a book? Books have to sell to keep publishers in business, and since there is more competition for a young person's time, the trend has been to print books that speak to our present culture. These so-called "issue" or "problem novels" that deal with "realism" have essentially redefined reality. It means, among other things, handling issues like adult betrayal, violence, sexual encounters, alcoholism, and the Big Ds: death, divorce, disease, and drugs.

My premise throughout this book has been that stories should represent what is true and real. "Real" means that a story should reveal values that the reader can build on. We do not live in a vacuum as if no one before us had ever discovered what is true and worthy. "Real" stories build on these values and give hope while exposing the result of choices. Although such stories do not hide what is wrong, the focus is on greater truths. The characters live and grow. And like Rat and Mole in *The Wind in the Willows*, one hears "the thin, clear, happy call of distant piping," an insight into deeper truths.

Many contemporary authors, however, define "real" as taking on societal problems. Much of what is being written might be described as "slice of life" or "coming-of-age" stories in which teenagers struggle through the process of *becoming* adults, while dealing with chemical dependency, sexuality, illness, family quarrels, abandonment, and more. Some of the stories give more negative ideas than positive ones. Their characters live impulsively as if there were no foundations to build on. They simply invent life as they find it. Growth is beside the point. Such books are problem-oriented and can become "those gray, heavy stories" that one teenager complained about.

In 1968 Paul Zindel paved the way for this new kind of book with what some librarians call the first "young-adult novel." The book was *Pigman*. From the first, I thought *Pigman* questionable. I still don't understand why anyone thinks it is an exemplary young-adult novel.

Two teenagers, John and Laurie, skip school to con a lonely old man named Mr. Pignati into giving them money for charity. They really intend to buy beer with his contribution. He is so delighted to have company that he invites them in and serves them some wine, thus beginning their involvement in his life. Mr. Pignati doesn't have a good grasp on reality, which inability John and Laurie tend to exploit. While he is in the hospital, they hold a party in his house, which gets out of control. Mr. Pignati returns home by taxi midway through the party, and what he sees does him in. The redeeming words of the story come as John and Laurie realize that their selfishness has caused Mr. Pignati's death. "There was no one else to blame anymore . . . And there was no place to hide . . . Our life would be what we made of it—nothing more, nothing less."

This novel was a first of its kind and took the publishing world by storm. It is well-written and engaging. And while the moral lesson of responsibility has some merit and could promote a lively classroom discussion, the circumstances of the story are bizarre and do not represent American teenage life.

Such novels have led Isaac Bashevis Singer to write, "A lot of the evil taking place today, I often feel, is the result of the rotten stuff this modern generation is reading in its school days." The same may certainly be said of television, whose scripts authors often mimic. Readers need to ask questions about the values and ideas that come from stories and TV. Are they seducing us into cynicism, or are they helping us to develop our values?

Pigman was written more than twenty years ago, and in the meantime a flood of books on contemporary problems have hit the teenage market. Their basic theme is mirrored in the words of a character in *I Am the Cheese* by Robert Cormier: "It's a terrible world out there. Murders and assassinations. Nobody's safe on the streets. And you don't even know who to trust anymore." All of us can relate to this to some degree, but how really typical and how representative is such a hostile world? Have publishers and authors who reside mostly in either in New York City or California become so removed from the average teenage life that they must convey such utter hopelessness?

Classroom discussions on S. E. Hinton's *Outsiders* convinced teachers that these books, pitched according to the violence of the eleven o'clock news, excited students to greater discussion than the more "real" books—books that reveal values that the reader can build on. Jim, the seventeen-year-old protagonist in Richard Peck's *Father Figure*, cries out, "Why do you have to know all this just because it happens to be true?" Peck's story has a mugging, the suicide of the boy's mother, a forced reunion with the father who had abandoned him, and the boy falls in love with his father's girlfriend. Robert Cormier, M. E. Peck, Norma Klein, Judy Blume, Brock Cole, Margaret Mahy, Harry Mazer, Cynthia Rylant, and others have all followed suit in the themes they have written about. The subjects have become more daring and now include homosexuality, incest, and abortion.

Sheila Egoff, a Canadian professor and librarian, gives some of the characteristics of these problem novels. Typically the new social realism has (1) a grievance-laden yet egocentric teenager, usually alienated from his or her parents; (2) a confessional, first-person style, using colloquial language, often with expletives (swearing); (3) a setting in upper middle-class suburbs in the East and in California; (4) parents who are physically or emotionally absent, often as selfish as their children; (5) "the problem" as its theme, not so much with the intent to apply standards of good and evil, but for its own sake.

Barbara Hampton, who has read hundreds of teenage books, adds two other typical characteristics: (6) the books are depressing and cynical; (7) teenage sex is taken for granted.

Don't Paint with Too Broad a Brush.

Not all contemporary authors write what is labeled "realism" even when writing about real life in this present decade. Madeleine L'Engle, Paula Fox, Sue Ellen Bridgers, Ursula LeGuin, and Mildred Taylor are not usually put in that category. Katherine Paterson, for example, writes from a different worldview than most of the other "contemporary realism" writers. She says she has never created a character "that some corner of her soul does not personally claim." She wants you to know her characters and understand them, but she stops short of telling sordid details. As an author she wants to guide teenagers around the "bogs and sloughs" that could suck them in and instead show them the great open spaces where their imagination can soar.

Madeleine L'Engle has taken it on the chin for her stories about the Austin and O'Keefe families because they are too wholesome.

Meanwhile her books have been eagerly snapped up by teens, who can't get enough of them. Everyone longs for the kind of family life she writes about, and it is not unreal. But other writers of teenage fiction claim L'Engle does not write realistic fiction, and I suspect that even her editors have suggested that she still writes for teens living in the fifties rather than in the eighties and nineties. Perhaps as a result, L'Engle wrote *A House Like a Lotus*, another book about Polly O'Keefe, but a book with a very different tone from the other O'Keefe stories. She has been forced to defend this story to her loyal readers, some of whom were outraged. I, for one, do not think the book is either good or realistic. Polly's parents, who have been models of wisdom, suddenly show poor judgment, and Polly herself is an intellectual bore. I wonder if this book didn't emerge out of "publishing pressure."

For the last twenty years and more we have been pushing books carrying heavy, adult problems onto younger and younger people. What used to be read in college is now read in high school, and what used to be read in high school is now read in later elementary school and middle school. Most of these stories have heavy ambiguities that confuse even adult readers.

I have always thought it an unmerciful act to give teenagers (who are trying to figure out their mood swings, their identity, and their self-worth) a book about someone as mixed-up as Holden Caufield. *Catcher in the Rye* is written with J. D. Salinger's sensitive ear, acutely sympathetic for Caufield, but it is not a picture of adolescent life so much as a picture of the human condition. Should Holden Caufield himself read *Catcher in the Rye* at age thirteen? Golding's *Lord of the Flies* is written for adults, not young adolescents. It is a story about evil in human nature as the cause of evil in society, not about children. Why are adults pushing cosmic problems onto their kids? That's why I have urged readers not to read books beyond their understanding. Such is not the path to maturity so much as the path to confusion. If the action of any story bothers you, don't read it. If you think you may not be getting the point of the story, put it away until another day. Younger children don't try to be more grown-up by pretending to like books too far beyond them. They are smarter sometimes than the rest of us.

What Is the Author's Worldview?

Most serious novels follow a pattern: spiritual quest that leads to new insights, that moves from problem to solution or meaning within the imagined world. Sometimes it is the hero leaving home, undertaking ordeals that test his powers; he overcomes the obstacles and returns in triumph. The details of the motif differ. How the story works out in detail depends on the author's worldview.

The writers of contemporary fiction are good writers, particularly the ones we have highlighted in the bibliography. Some of these are writing "social realism" (Cormier, Coles, Mazer, M. E. Kerr, Brooks, Bridgers, Mahy, Peck, Rylant). Others are not. The "social realism" authors are productive and popular. You need to know about them. They write stories that invite questioning. Is this true? What philosophy of life comes through the author's writing? Ask the questions in chapter 3 of every book you read.

In preparing the elaborate bibliography in this book, Barbara Hampton has included special annotations about most of these authors. They will give parents and teenagers clues about the authors' writing style and worldview. Be sure to read them.

As teenagers put together their own worldviews, they need to be able to verbalize what they believe so that they can share it with others—and so you can examine it and see if it lives up to Truth. This is a significant step toward maturity. You also need to be sufficiently aware of the worldviews of others to identify them when you read. First, let's look at the questions we ask in determining a worldview. (I have adapted the following information about worldviews from an excellent book, *The Universe Next Door* by James W. Sire.[1])

What do we believe? How do we find out what our worldview is? Our basic worldview should answer the following questions.

(1) *What is the really real?* Is it God or the gods, or the material universe?

(2) *What is the world around us like?* Is it created? Is the universe chaos or ordered? How do we relate to it?

(3) *What is a human being?* A machine? A sleeping god? A person made in the image of God? A naked ape?

(4) *What happens at death?* Extinction? Transformation to a higher state? Resurrection? Is there life after death?

(5) *Why is it possible to know anything at all?* Made in the image of an all-knowing God? Rationality developed in process of evolution?

(6) *How do we know what is right and wrong?* Tradition? Made in the image of God whose character is good? Human choice? Result of means of survival?

(7) *What is the point of human history?* Where is it going? Is history taking us somewhere? Does it move in a line with an ending, or does it go around in cycles?

Some people may look at those questions and think, "Wow, how do you know the answers to questions like these?" The Westminster Catechism isn't a bad place to begin. It's a condensation of the biblical doctrines on which the civilization of the Western world is built. It summarizes what most would call the Christian worldview.

Let's look briefly at what this and some other popular worldviews believe:

A. *Christian theism.* God is beyond measurement (infinite) and yet personal. He is not a substance or a force, he is HE. God is also beyond us (transcendent) and yet everywhere present. He is the Creator, all-knowing, good, and human beings are made in his image. This God has communicated with us so that we can know him. Human beings were created good, but since the Fall the image of God has been marred (sinful) and is restored through the work of Christ, who redeems those who trust in him. Death is the gate to life with God or to eternal separation from God. Right and wrong is based on the character of God. History is linear; it is going someplace, to the fulfillment of God's purposes. Because of the Bible, this is the most clearly spelled out worldview.

B. *Deism.* God, like someone winding a clock, created the universe and then left it to run on its own. God is distant, foreign, and alien. Thus human beings are on their own. The universe is a closed system; everything can be explained. It operates according to the law of cause and effect. There are no miracles. Human beings are part of the clockwork—personal and yet unrelated to God. The Fall does not exist, so that what is wrong or right is God's responsibility. How things are is his fault. The course of the world was determined at Creation. K. M. Peyton's books reflect this worldview.

C. *Naturalism.* God does not exist. Matter is all there is. Carl Sagan says, "The Cosmos is all that is or ever was or ever will be." Human beings are complex machines—with mind and personality as a function of the machine. There is but one substance with various modifications. Death is extinction. History is cause and effect but has no purpose. Values are man-made. Secular humanism (as opposed to Christian humanism) and Marxism both are forms of naturalism. Probably Leon Garfield, K. M. Peyton, and Isaac Asimov reflect this worldview.

D. *Nihilism* (pronounced NEE-hill-ism). Nihilism is more a feeling than a philosophy. It is really not a philosophy at all, because it denies the possibility of knowing anything or that anything is valuable. Nihilism is negative about everything. Modern art galleries are full of its products. Samuel Beckett's play *Waiting for Godot* is a prime example of nihilism. Beckett's *Breath* is a thirty-five-second play that has no human actors. The props are a pile of rubbish on stage. There are no words, only a recorded cry at the opening of the play, an inhaled breath, an exhaled breath, and a closing cry. That is Beckett's worldview. Nihilism is really unliveable. Robert Cormier has a nihilistic point of view in some of his stories.

E. *Existentialism* (pronounced ex-i-STEN-shal-ism). Reality is subjective and objective. The world merely is. There is no God. Human beings define themselves and are totally free and determine their own destiny. The world does not have meaning unless people revolt and create meaning. Both Margaret Mahy and Cynthia Voigt's books give evidence of this worldview. "Theistic existentialism" believes in an infinite God and is closer to theism except that people are center stage and responsible.

F. *Pantheism.* Eastern religions are pantheistic. Pantheism takes various forms. God is in everything. There are many gods. Each person is God. God is in all. Some things are more One than others, but many roads lead to the One. The goal is to become one with the cosmos and thus pass beyond good and evil. Death ends the individual, but his essence goes on into something else (reincarnation). Nothing of value perishes. History is cyclical; it goes round and round. Some of Gary Paulsen's books reflect this worldview.

G. *New Age.* New Age thinking borrows heavily from Eastern religion, from theism, and from naturalism. There is no Lord of the universe. Self is the kingpin. People use their senses to get in touch with the invisible universe through "doors of perception" like drugs, meditation, trance, biofeedback, acupuncture, ritualized dance, certain kinds of music, and so forth. Self can get in touch with Mind at Large, which does not obey the laws of the universe. The conscious self can travel across the earth and into time and space. Some New-agers are heavily into the occult. They believe that extraordinary power and energy can surge through a person and be transmitted to others. Shirley MacLaine is a proponent of this worldview. People have adopted it without even knowing what it is about, believing in a person's power to heal self, consulting channelers and the stars for guidance. It's a hodge-podge worldview in which humans are god.

Now perhaps I've told you more than you ever want to know, but there it is, and it is something you need to know about if you are to face the world squarely. You don't need either to memorize these worldviews or feel overwhelmed by them. It helps you simply to know that they exist. You can always refer to these pages as you read and ask questions of the novels you read. The most important observation to make in determining a worldview is to notice who acts as god in the story.

"I just sort of accept the world the way it is, and don't think much about it," is a common remark. Too many people go through life with a careless belief system—a little of this and a little of that—making themselves the final judge of whether it is a good system or not. And when you read books, you will find that the authors reveal their worldview, if you notice what values they are encouraging. Questions, questions. Always ask questions.

What About Books and God?

In a paper read at a literature conference at Syracuse University School of Education, Charlotte Huck from Ohio State noted nine changes in books for children and young adults. There are fewer strong male characters in comparison with female characters. There is less humor and joy, and when we do laugh it is so that we won't cry. Another was that religion seemed to be the only taboo left in literature for children or young adults. Authors may write on child abuse, sex, and death but don't mention belief in God.

The Children's Literature Association Quarterly (Summer 1986) carried an editorial by Perry Nodelman in which he commented on the omission of the Bible on a list of touchstone books that are a vital part of our literary heritage. He wrote, "The list ignores the one book that most clearly underlies contemporary culture and that has had the most direct influence on the history and characteristics of our literature: the Bible." He writes that those who teach literature have become fearful of the Bible and have given it a sinister reputation that it doesn't deserve. Why? He tells us,

> Many of those obnoxious people who want to keep good books out of the hands of children because they think children are weakminded enough to adopt every dangerous idea and attitude they read about often use the Bible as the authority for their narrow-minded bigotry.

However, there is a vast conspiracy of silence about children's literature with a spiritual emphasis. The books available don't get reviewed or recommended for public libraries or even discussed in journals like this one. We simply act as if this massive body of literature did not exist at all. Now I am not myself a Christian, I have no special axe to grind. But this reveals a common form of intolerance by theoretically tolerant people, an intolerance that amounts to censorship. It seems to be based on the peculiar assumption that, in order to have true religious freedom, we must never express a religious idea. . . . This is an act of intense bigotry.

Alice Bach, who reviews children's novels for *The Horn Book Magazine* and other journals, tells of her own search for God as a secular New Yorker and her subsequent coming to faith.

I needed to write about faith, to examine the consequences of having faith or not having it, for adolescents who are the protagonists in my novels. At first my proposal to write novels centered around faith was not met with great editorial enthusiasm. But fortunately a Dell book editor agreed to a proposal that became *He Will Not Walk With Me*. In talking with adolescents, I have found that all of them think about God. They are eager to explore not only how to find God in their own lives but how to deal with the moral issues around them.

It is my hope that adults who direct what children read will allow young readers to wonder about God, to come to know God, through books that deal with present issues in a tough, straightforward manner. Let me be clear. I am not suggesting pretty posies that present God as a magical godfather who removes all pain and suffering from the lives of the righteous—because every child knows that all life has pain and suffering. And to lie about the function of God is to keep a child from knowing God. What we as writers and publishers can do is permit the reader to intuit the magnificence of God, who suffers with each of us over hardship and grieves with us and watches over us, and who is always present in our lives.[2]

Nobel-Prize-winning writer Isaac Bashevis Singer writes,

> No matter how young they are, children are deeply
> concerned with so-called eternal questions: Who created the
> world? Who made the earth, the sky, people, animals? If I
> had my way, I would publish a history of philosophy for
> children. Children, who are highly serious people, would read
> this book with great interest. In our time, when the literature
> for adults is deteriorating, good books for children (and
> young adults) are the only hope, the only refuge.

There you have it. Book editors and writers have admittedly felt uncomfortable about books that mention God. While it is true to say that a book that does not mention God may have a profoundly positive spiritual impact, it is still prejudice and fear on the part of the editors that prevent books from addressing the spiritual issues young people wonder about.

Now you see why I think it is important that you have a worldview and that you can answer questions about reality, God, truth—and all the things that make up a worldview. Some people are writing as if none of this matters, but we are all constructing a belief system of some kind.

What the book publishing industry needs is more skillful writers who can write the kind of books that expose children, young adults, and adults to a biblical worldview. T. S. Eliot pleads for writers who can make a relationship between religion and literature, a literature that should be *un*consciously, rather than deliberately and defiantly, Christian. I would further add that what is needed is something like the writings of Chaim Potok, which, in the course of his stories, exposes the reader to the Jewish worldview. Failure of the book industry to publish stories like this will be a mark of bigotry, as Mr. Nodelman noted in his editorial.

A Look to the Future

We can expect that some authors will turn to increasingly bizarre themes, with an eye more on dollars than on good literature. Movies and television talk shows have already led the way. The latest fad is the "horror" genre of books, which has taken some readers captive. Stephen King, the best-known of these writers, states his purpose without apology: "I write to terrorize the reader. But if . . . I cannot terrify . . . I will try to horrify, and if I cannot horrify, I'll go for the gross-out. I'm not proud." His high sales have not gone unnoticed by other writers and publishers. The book market now has a whole new cadre of horror writers who are exploiting teens. Remember that a book is as good as its theme. When "horror" is the theme, do you expect reality or corruption? Whatever "cosmetic dressing" publishers put on their reasons for producing these, be suspicious and ask hard questions. These books will eventually "run out of gas"—victims of the desensitizing that they encourage. "Horror" will eventually bore its own readers.

Already the appetite for young-adult stories is changing. The super-realism in some contemporary novels seems to be fading. Readers are asking for something more positive, more hopeful. After a long period of decline, innocence is reclaiming its lost ground in American youth literature. It will not happen overnight, but a renewed craving for community, for the positive side of life is coming back to novels. We have a basic need for something that assures us that life is essentially good and can be wonderful—that we may not know all that is rich and marvelous in the world. This return to balance and optimism is welcome. Stories that leave anxiety on our doorstep—like an abandoned baby that we wonder what to do with—may have run their course.

Fiction can't help having an ethical dimension. Everything we do *means* something. Fiction should teach us to be good, or at least what good is.

Notes

1. James W. Sire, *The Universe Next Door*, (Downers Grove: InterVarsity Press, 1988).

2. Alice Bach, essay on *He Will Not Walk With Me*, in the *Dell Carousel*, a publication of Dell/Doubleday.

6

Fantasy in a Real World

Creative imagination is more than mere invention. It is that power which creates, out of abstractions, life. It goes to the heart of the unseen, and puts that which is so mysteriously hidden from ordinary mortals into the clear light of their understanding. . . . Writers of fantasy, more than any other writers except poets . . . are able to evoke ideas and clothe them in symbols, allegory, and dream.

Lillian H. Smith

It does not do to leave a dragon out of your calculations if you live near him.

J. R. R. Tolkien

Once upon a time there was a dragon, or *In a hole in the ground there lived a hobbit.* It is by such beautiful non-facts as these, wrote Ursula LeGuin, that we fantastic human beings may arrive at the truth.

Fantasy is reality in unreality. The question about fantasy is not whether the story has happened in our history but is there truth in what happened? In fact, the power of fantasy is that it knows nothing of the limitations of the modern world. In the real world that has "exiled gods and heroes" we need the help of fantasy to express all the Truth of transcendent themes like deity, glory, heroism, courage, goodness, or beauty. Fantasy is always bigger than life and yet it must reveal life. It takes place in a world remote from ours, yet at the same time it is rooted in our world. Just because we live in time doesn't mean that we have to stay in time.

In a fine essay on myth, Thomas Howard writes that we don't want myths crowded or spoiled by the immediate world, but we do want them to ring bells that our ears can hear.

> A Christian, especially, living as he does in a huge universe all ringing with the footfalls of hurrying seraphim, cherubim, archangels, angels, men, and devils, will never be too quick to judge what creatures aren't in on the traffic. He can only demur and say, "Elves? I don't know much about them. I've never come across one (worse luck)."[1]

Howard is essentially saying that Christians know they can't explain everything, that what is real is not necessarily seen. The question about fantasy is *How true does it ring?* Is there consistency in the world that has been created by the writer? Does it live by its own laws so that it hangs together? Does it show me reality in a way that I can understand?

The fantasies of writers like C. S. Lewis and J. R. R. Tolkien are not only first-class adventures but their visions of a golden-maned lion named Aslan and the courage of valiant hobbits have nourished the understanding of countless readers. Some have wondered if it is possible to describe the Christian experience effectively outside of fantasy. Katherine Paterson writes about Tolkien's trilogy:

> Those of us who have followed Frodo on his quest have had a vision of the true darkness. We know that we, like him, would have never gotten up the steep slope of Mount Doom had the faithful Sam not flung us on his back and

carried us up, crawling at the last. We know, too, that we would never have parted with the baneful ring or power had not the piteous Gollum torn it from our bleeding finger and, in the effort, fallen screeching into the abyss, clutching his damned treasure and ours.[2]

Our response to such a story is surely, "That's me." We recognize the awfulness of the way we clutch at the control over our own lives, our rebellion, our cowardice, our sin. Fantasy stands off from our experience but is about our experience. Howard insists that "excursions into that world are never a flight away from reality; they are, rather, a flight to reality."

Fantasy demands something extra of its readers; it asks them to pay close attention to the rich details of the story. Fantasy invites you to read and reread it, like exploring a gold mine for nuggets. Our imaginations can soar. I, for one, did not want to watch a cartoon-like production of Tolkien's *The Lord of the Rings* because I didn't want anyone to spoil my mental image of what a hobbit looks like. I felt the same way about the Narnia Chronicles in cartoon fashion although the most recent productions using real children have been well done and better than I expected.

Fantasy can also put our personal problems into perspective. When you get carried away with a really large story, your own dark moments disappear. It's rather like Alice in Wonderland falling mile after mile down the rabbit's hole until she thinks she might be near the center of the earth. "Well," thought Alice to herself, "after a fall such as this, I shall think nothing of tumbling down the stairs."

A twenty-year-old student wrote to author Susan Cooper about her fantasy books, "You give all of us the chance to leave the mundane struggles we face and enter a slightly grander struggle for a while." Another wrote to her, "Your books are my escape from the world I live in. I often wish I were one of the Old Ones, fighting the Dark and protecting Mankind from harm."

All of us need adventure, and it is easier to handle through the pages of a good book than when it actually arrives. Afterward, if an adventure does happen to overtake you, somewhere in your subconscious mind you will be equipped to endure and handle it.

Michele Landsberg in her book *Reading for the Love of It* tells a wonderful story about her son, Avi, who was a very bright, gifted child, reading at an early age. One day when she went into his room she found this six-year-old weeping over a book. She took him on her lap as he sobbed out, "I can't go on. Drem has failed his wolf slaying." She assured him that things would get better and read aloud from his story, Sutcliff's *Warrior Scarlett*, until Avi had composed himself. Three years later, Avi agreed to work on his lateral lisp with a speech therapist. In fewer than three weeks the childhood lisp had disappeared. His mother was amazed. How had he managed to deal so swiftly with this trial in his life? "I remembered Drem," Avi said. "He was handicapped like me." Drem had slain his wolf, and Avi had determined to slay his as well.

Susan Cooper, who writes fantasy, complains that Americans have increasingly taken all ritual out of their lives. That is why people join fraternities, sororities, the Elks, and even country clubs—which all thrive on rituals of membership. American football is the ritualization of rugby, in her mind. She fears that the newest and fastest growing new ritual imposed on our lives is that of the computer, whose complexities amount to a new language and a new way of thinking. She writes, "There are no longer any sacred festivals in the American calendar, religious or otherwise; there are only celebrations of commerce. We don't have heroes; we have celebrities."[3] Cooper believes that young people long for rituals and that these are given them in the mysterious world of fantasy. She urges families to establish rituals, to find special ways of celebrating. And above all, she urges young people to read fantasies.

Is Fantasy for Everyone?

You will notice that the bibliography has a sizable listing of fantasy books. All of them are winners. Many readers have read Madeleine L'Engle's *A Wrinkle in Time* and its sequels. John Bibee (and his Magic Bicycle series) is a fairly recent author in this category. Ursula LeGuin writes wonderfully and needs a thoughtful, mature reader to get all the nuances of her stories. John White (*Tower of Geburah*) began writing a series of four fantasies in response to his children's lament that they wished there were more Narnia Chronicles. His Gaal is a different Christ-figure from Aslan. Pat O'Shea takes the reader into the richness of Irish myths. Patricia Wrightson has written a series of wonderful fantasies set in Australia. And there are still more to discover. Teenage readers especially ought to try more than one of these.

Not everyone takes to fantasy. Some readers want only real-life, contemporary stories they can relate to without having to translate too many allegories or symbols. Often these readers are more drawn to nonfiction than to fiction in any form. Some people have difficulty believing anything they can't see.

Over the years, I have received letters from parents who have told me in one way or another that they only give their children books that contain true things. Animals don't talk, so they think it is misleading to give children books in which animals do. They believe that many of the books on my children's list, because they are not true, are not good for children.

I maintain that when a child reads *Stuart Little*, the fact that Stuart is a mouse is no problem to boys and girls. They do not wish he were a boy. They love him for his integrity and fortitude. When someone says that Stuart is "just the best kind of mouse," we know they are not talking about how he looks but of what he is inside. And think of Winnie-the-Pooh and missing out on his wisdom, merely because he is stuffed!

Jane Stephens, an English professor, tells how she used to talk with horses as a small girl. Driving along, her parents had to stop for any horse who came to the fence, so that she could talk to it. But when *Mr. Ed* came on television, she was horrified. She knew that horses could talk, but they did not talk as loudly as Mr. Ed and never to a whole room full of people. And they did not say the kind of things that Mr. Ed said.

All parents have to do what they think is best in selecting books for younger children, but I always respond with the challenge not to make their world too small. Life is largely understood through metaphors. We use metaphors when we say, "This is like that"; "Jack is a mad dog when he gets angry"; "The room was a beehive with people going in all directions"; "War is hell." None of these statements are literally true, but they convey a picture.

Think of the imaginative ways the Bible describes the joy of Creation: the trees clapping their hands and the morning stars singing together. Twenty-five percent of the Bible is poetry; and Job contains thirty-four verses about the glory of the crocodile and ten verses on the hippopotamus. Why does God get so carried away with his own creation?

Imagination is one of the chief glories of being created human, in the image of God. No other created being can imagine things that can't be seen and then make connections between what is visible and what is invisible. For Christians, whose most important investment *is* in the invisible, the imagination is of greatest importance. Czeslaw Milosz, the Nobel-prize-winning poet, said that the minds of Americans have been dangerously diluted by explanations. He is convinced that our educational process has left us with an inadequate view of the world. The universe has space and time—and nothing else—no values, no God—and human beings end up being no different from bacteria. Our educational system is imagination-deficient.[4]

Imagination is important. C. S. Lewis calls it the organ of meaning. It is the way we sub-create, as those who are related to the Creator. We take the stuff of this world, including words, and put them together into new forms to say what is true. That is the basis of all art. Creativity is a way of noticing. Praise is also a way of noticing. Could it be that the two are connected? Grown-ups sometimes feel uncomfortable with questions. They want to give answers. They like to act as if all the answers are already in. That kills creativity.

Why Are People Sometimes Afraid of the Imagination?

It may be because,

Explanation pins things down so we can handle and use them—obey and teach, help and guide. Imagination opens things up so that we can grow into maturity—worship and adore, exclaim and honor, follow and trust. Explanation restricts and defines and holds down; imagination expands and lets loose. Explanation keeps our feet on the ground; imagination lifts our heads into the clouds. Explanation puts us in harness; imagination catapults us into mystery. Explanation reduces life to what can be used; imagination enlarges life into what can be adored.[5]

Surely imagination without explanation is a disaster. Imagination is only useful if it relates to reality. But maybe we need to think more about how flat explanations are without imagination. Both are needed.

When a teacher once read to her class from one of C. S. Lewis's Narnia books, some parents went to the principal, complaining that they did not want their children reading about witches. I've known people to question *The Witch of Blackbird Pond* by Elizabeth George Speare, a novel about the witch-hunts in the 1600s, that won the Newbery Medal back in 1959. It would be better if parents had read *The Lion, the Witch and the Wardrobe* or *The Witch of Blackbird Pond* before making their complaints. The witch is the right symbol in the first novel, and the second novel is historically based. Certainly with the increase of satanism and interest in the occult, parents are rightly concerned about forces that might entice their children into occultic beliefs. But fear can be eased by knowing the reputation of the authors or by actually reading the works themselves.

Good writers define reality; bad ones merely restate it. A good writer turns fact into truth; a bad writer will, more often than not, accomplish the opposite. A good writer writes what he believes to be true; a bad writer puts down what he believes that his readers should believe to be true. Good writers write about the eternal questions; inferior writers deny the eternal.

A few years ago a priest wrote an article in his diocesan newspaper in response to a question about developing a young person's spirituality. His short answer was "flip" but true. "Give them A. A. Milne, the brothers Grimm, Kenneth Grahame, J. M. Barrie, C. S. Lewis, J. R. R. Tolkien, Shel Silverstein, and Ursula LeGuin . . . and get out of their way." All of these authors write imaginative fantasy. How did he dare say that? Because a good story always has a spiritual dimension and speaks about what is real and true.

The practice of questioning the story applies to fantasy as well as to other stories. If we ask questions about meaning, about truth, about intent of the fantasies we read, if we ask, "What is this story really saying?" we will know if the book has enough substance to qualify as good literature.

Notes

1. Thomas Howard, "Myth: A Flight To Reality," an essay in *The Christian Imagination*, 202

2. Katherine Paterson, "Yes, But Is It True?" in *Gates of Excellence* (New York: Elsevier/Nelson Books, 1981), 59.

3. Susan Cooper, "Fantasy in the Real World," *Horn Book Magazine* (May/June 1990), 310.

4. Czeslaw Milosz, interview in *New York Times Book Review* (February 27, 1986).

5. Eugene H. Peterson, "Masters of Imagination," in *Eternity Magazine* (January 1989), 20–21.

7

Read for Your Life

*One of the gifts of knowing how to
read is knowing what is best to read.*
—anonymous

One of my professors during my freshman year in college asked each student to prepare a paper giving his or her personal worldview. What did we perceive to be true and what was the basis for that perception? I spelled mine out in detail and gave the Bible as the basis for my belief system. Later, as he listened to my fervent assertions, he asked, "About basing your beliefs on this book, have you read all of the Bible?" He pointed out that it was pretty dumb to claim to believe what a book says if you hadn't even read it.

The Bible is the most relevant and challenging book I have ever read. I urge others to read it, not just because it is good for them but because it is a good book. Everyone should know what it says. It may be the best book they've ever read! And its claim to be the very Word of God is awesome!

Think of how long the Bible has been around, still a bestseller to this very day. Think of its influence on our civilization. You can hardly read a book that doesn't have a biblical allusion, and you never write a letter or a check without indicating the date, which is simply the number of years since the time of Christ. Often we write dates with an A.D. attached; that means *Anno Domini*—the year of our Lord. You cannot understand our culture without knowing the roots from which it has come.

In 1350 a college student at Oxford, named John Wycliffe, risked his life to translate the Bible from the Latin into English so that the common people could read it. Subsequently, many people died for the right to read and preserve the book. In 1990, students in eastern Europe and the USSR who had been denied access to this book snatched up copies as quickly as they were produced. Why? Well, read it for yourself. Why let someone else tell you what this book says?

Only 10 percent of the Bible is written as the logical presentation of abstract ideas. Those are the epistles, or letters, included in the New Testament. These powerful letters explain not only what Christians believe but the lifestyle of those who are believers. These letters need to be read the way you read any letter—from beginning to end in one sitting. Taking a phrase or a sentence or two from a letter is hardly a way to understand its message.

Four books of the Bible—Matthew, Mark, Luke, John—are given to the story of Jesus' life and what he taught. Dorothy Sayers once dedicated a book: "In the name of the One who assuredly never bored anyone in the thirty-three years He passed through the world like a flame." What did she know about Jesus that caused her to do that? How can you know anything about who Jesus is if you don't read his story and try to comprehend what he said? Too many teenagers are in the third grade when it comes to understanding about God, even though they may be seniors in high school.

The rest of the Bible contains love stories, drama, history, poetry, and parables, with humanity and truth presented as realistically as in any of the world's greatest literature.

> A farmer went out to sow his seed . . .
> There was a man who had two sons . . .
> The Lord is my shepherd . . .
> When Sanballat heard they were rebuilding the wall, he became angry . . .
> So she let them down by a rope through the window . . .

An enormous red dragon with seven heads and ten
horns . . .

Excerpts like these are enough to show you that the Bible is
not a "theological outline with proof texts attached." It is filled with
stories, poems, visions, and letters. It contains more than most
people realize.

To say that the Bible is literature, or that it is imaginative, is not
to say that it is fictional rather than historical and factual. To say
that it is literature is to say that *it needs to be read.* Too many
people take bits and pieces from the Bible and never think of
reading the books within it. We don't read anything else that way.

While it is *more than* literature, the Bible is certainly a model of
the finest literature. In terms of the use of language, it is a
masterpiece.

Who has measured the waters in the hollow of his hand,
  or who with the breadth of his hand marked off
    the heavens?
Who has held the dust of the earth in a basket,
  or weighed the mountains on the scale
  and the hills in a balance?
Who has understood the Spirit of the Lord,
  or instructed him as his counselor?[1]

Is it possible that the artistic craftsmanship of the Bible tells us
something important about God? Is it not significant that a book we
regard as sacred is not a dull book but an interesting one?

Literature presents human experience. The Bible does this in
profound ways. It tells stories. In terms of reality, it tells the truth. A
Jeremiah can end up in a pit; a saint named John can end up in a
lonely exile on Patmos. How things worked out for Hosea are quite
unclear: Why the Holy God told this man to marry a harlot, raises all
kinds of questions. The fact that Job had many good things at the
end of his life hardly erases the excruciating loss of loved ones
along the way.[2]

And as for adventure, mystery, rescue, suspense, pageantry,
celebration, heroes, and villains, the Bible has plenty of them. The
story of Paul's journey to Rome aboard a ship in the storm (Acts
27–28) grips the imagination. In the Old Testament, one man's
large family was given hospitality in Egypt and multiplied into a great

nation. The story of their exodus into a promised land is one of the most significant stories of history. One night, after we had finished reading about Joseph's being kidnapped by his brothers, sold into Egypt, and later saving his family from famine, our little boy sighed and said, "I like God. He likes adventure." Indeed, God is the greatest adventurer of all.

Some people do not like thinking of the Bible as literature, almost as if that would take away its sacredness. "Sacredness" sometimes makes a thing untouchable. People use its sacredness as an excuse not to read it. The Bible is meant to be read and understood. It covers subjects that are basic and enduring in our human experience—God, nature, love, relationships, death, evil, guilt, salvation, family life, judgment, and forgiveness.[3] If you read it carefully, you will understand yourself and the world better.

How to Read the Bible

One day I encountered a middle-aged man who had just taken an old Bible off the shelf. He riffled through its pages and said to me, "Where does a person begin to read in a book like this?" It was a good question.

The Bible is a collection of books. It is a library of books, in a sense. While everyone needs to put together the big picture of this "library" eventually, you can still read individual books according to your interests.

Genesis and Exodus cover creation and the beginnings of the history of the Jewish people. The third book, Leviticus, is largely a book of rules for the children of Israel and, though it is not an unimportant book especially in terms of Jewish history, it is better understood after the reader has picked up the themes of some of the other books in the Bible. If one likes ancient history, he or she should read the books of Joshua through Esther.

The Gospels in the New Testament may be the most relevant place to begin. They tell the reader who Jesus is and what he said about himself, about us, about religious people, about faith. Why did he die? Was that the end of the story? Then the story of how the Christian church began is told in Acts.

How should you read the Bible? By asking it questions, as you do any other piece of literature. You can ask questions about the literary style: Is this narrative, poetry, history, or teaching? That helps you understand how to read and what you are reading.

Three Questions to Ask the Bible

(1) *What does it say*? Make observations about what you are reading. What are the facts? Ask, Who? When? What? How?

(2) *What does it mean*? Interpret the meaning of what you have read, based on your observations of what the chapter of the book has said.

(3) *What does it mean to me*? What can I learn from this? How does what I have read affect the way I think, act, or believe?

If you get in the habit of asking these questions of the Bible, you will learn from your reading. These three questions are essentially the same questions you should ask as you read history or geography or whatever. A notebook and a pencil are good tools to help consolidate the answers.

Even from a totally secular point of view, people ought to know what is in the Bible, because it is the touchstone of our whole value system. It has always seemed strange to me that those who claim to believe it, often know so little of its contents.

Don't be someone who gets on the *Jeopardy* show and avoids the biblical category until all the other categories are finished. Know who Abraham is and why we refer to Solomon's wisdom, or why Israel and Judah separated from each other, or why Daniel was in Babylon. And for goodness' sake, don't be ignorant of the marvelous *evangel* the angels heralded to shepherds one night on a Judean hillside. It could change your life.

Notes

1. Quote from Isaiah 40:12–13.
2. Philip Yancey, *Open Windows* (Westchester, Ill.: Crossway Books, 1982), 170.
3. Addison H. Leitch, "Reality in Modern Literature," an essay in *The Christian Imagination* by Leland Ryken (Grand Rapids: Baker, 1981), 194.

8

Feed Your Heart

I was always told that I should read The Odyssey. *It popped up in small doses in English and Latin textbooks as I was growing up. But somehow I never got around to the whole thing until I was forty-six years old. I gave myself the assignment to read* The Odyssey *(Rouse's translation) all the way through from the beginning to end. Do you know why* The Odyssey *has lasted for nearly three thousand years? Because it is a simply marvelous story. Why did people keep telling me that I ought to read it so that I could be an educated person? I can't imagine anyone who had ever really read it, telling someone else to read it because it was good for him. Read it because it's one of the best stories you'll ever read. Read it because it's one of the best stories I ever read.*[1]

Katherine Paterson

Reading the Tried and True

We ought to go after the tried-and-true books (listed in the bibliography) for the same reason that Paterson encourages people to read *The Odyssey.* If a book lasts beyond a generation, it is one that everyone should read. There is nothing "mere" about the characters in the tried-and-true books. You won't have to sigh or groan or read against your will. A really good book hypnotizes the reader so that he or she *wants to* read it. The writer gives us words and ideas that are like food that we want to keep on eating.

For over a hundred-fifty years the exciting plot of *The Last of the Mohicans* has kept readers on the edges of their chairs. Suspense, pursuit, captivity, rescue, Indian lore—all masterfully woven into this tale by James Fenimore Cooper. *A Tale of Two Cities* is one of Charles Dickens's finest novels. The film version cannot match the reading of the book. What memorable characters are Charles Darnay and Sydney Carton! Some characters we read about evaporate quickly from our memory. Others will haunt us all our lives. That's how DuMaurier's *Rebecca* affected me.

Sixteen-year-old Ellen Hampton informed me that Lloyd Douglas's *The Robe* is the best book she had ever read. Her recommendation is sound, but I have to admit she says this about every book she reads! That's the way it is with good books; each seems better than the one before.

There are many great writers: Rumer Godden, Elizabeth Goudge, Alan Paton, Harper Lee, and hundreds of others. Our list isn't complete—just enough to give a taste of lasting literature. Don't even think of them as classics (although they are that!), for that might intimidate some readers. If you found a chest full of buried gold, you wouldn't avoid it because it's old. Reading tried-and-true books gives us immediate rapport with a great host of other readers, who, on seeing you reading a certain book, might say, "Oh, you, too? I thought I was the only one!"

Most of the tried-and-true books listed in the bibliography are for late-teen readers, because they are essentially adult books. Reading them too soon can cheat readers from appreciating them. Young adults themselves should decide when they can handle them. Though written for adults originally, these books were quickly purloined by young adults.

Why Not Go On an Adventure?

Where did I learn to love Alaska and dream of adventure whenever I picture it in my mind? Surely it began with meeting the marvelous dog Buck in *The Call of the Wild* in Jack London's story set in the gold rush days. Using a contemporary setting, Gary Paulsen also writes about Alaska in *Dogsong*, a Newbery Honor book. Ivan Southall writes stories set in contemporary Australia, another frontier country. His characters confront the challenges of an untamed land; his stories are wonderful tales of human endurance and enterprising action.

When a librarian friend sent me a copy of *The Outlaws of Sherwood* by Robin McKinley, I could hardly put it down—I think it is the best retelling of the popular Robin Hood legend I have ever read. And no teenager should become an adult before first enjoying Robert Louis Stevenson's *Kidnapped* and *Treasure Island*. They are two of the most gripping tales ever written.

Animal stories are closely linked to adventure books. *The Yearling* by Marjorie Rawlings and *Where the Red Fern Grows* by Wilson Rawls are worth reading more than once. Both these books make you weep.

Others make you laugh. Our family read James Herriot's *All Creatures Great and Small* aloud together on a trip through Yorkshire country in England and sometimes feared we might be thrown out of our lodgings because we had laughed so loudly into the night. Look for others in this category. Robert Siegel's *Whalesong* seems to contain all the wonderful mystery of the sea.

Mystery stories. Many younger teenagers get into reading mysteries through The Hardy Boys series or Nancy Drew's adventures. (For those who haven't met her yet, Nancy Drew has been brought up to date. She now has a luxuriant swing of blond hair, wears designer jeans, and has even discovered kissing. A cadre of writers have been churning out updated versions during the late 1980s. She is no longer Nancy Drew.) The predictability of the characters in these stories soon led mystery lovers to look for others. Today many fine suspense and mystery stories are published for all ages.

The appeal of mysteries will last well into adulthood when a reader discovers such writers as Agatha Christie, Dorothy Sayers, Josephine Tey, and Ellis Peters (whom I just recently discovered and like very much!). We have even put Frank Peretti's popular *This Present Darkness* in the mystery category because the suspense of his story will capture you. (This book could also have been placed in the fantasy category.)

We have included a number of writers of contemporary realism in this category, including Stephen King. Read the annotation about King's book carefully. What do you think about King's intention in writing his books? We put this book on the list, not to recommend it so much as to make you think about the purpose of his writings, since we know they are very popular with certain readers.

The best mystery stories have strong themes of good and evil, which explore human nature. Alexander Pope's couplet: "Oh, what a tangled web we weave / When first we practice to deceive," underlies most mystery stories. I am always amused to find theologians, philosophers, and scientists with shelves full of mystery novels.

Science fiction falls in this same genre. Escape to hair-raising tales and other worlds with Ray Bradbury, John Christopher, Ursula LeGuin, C. S. Lewis, Jules Verne, and H. G. Wells. When you have read the ones on our list, the shelves still contain others for your pleasure. Be sure to evaluate the "universes" created by these authors. For example, compare what C. S. Lewis creates in *Perelandra* with H. G. Wells's *The War of the Worlds*. Mysteries and science fiction keep you reading carefully, examining the clues, and asking questions. It's a good exercise, as well as enjoyment.

Historical Fiction: The Real Stuff of Life

Historical fiction is often more real than "contemporary realism." That is, it isn't based on faddish interests or a tendency to make reality bizarre. It must be true on two levels: It must be true to its setting and time, and have true characters.

Historical fiction is anchored in the past but peopled with characters the reader can relate to even though continents and circumstances are vastly different. People are the same in every age, at least on the inside, with the same dreams and fears and hopes. The plots in historical fiction may sweep across time and events that are new to the reader, but the people and the circumstances will be familiar. The people are like us or like someone we know. This allows the writer to plot the story in the past and people it with characters that we can identify with. Those of you who have read Joan Blos's *A Gathering of Days* or Elizabeth George Speare's *The Bronze Bow* will know exactly what I mean.

Good historical fiction gives a fascinating "read." Esther Forbes's *Johnny Tremain* may be the book that could best introduce readers to this category. Leon Garfield's books give a realistic picture of life in eighteenth-century London, and his characters are fascinating. I love Esther Hautzig's *The Endless Steppe*, about a Polish girl exiled to Siberia. More mature readers will enjoy John Hersey's *The Wall*. Irene Hunt's *Across Five Aprils* makes the struggles of the Civil War seem more personal and tragic. What a terrible thing to have members of the same family divided by loyalty to different sides of a war. It is interesting to compare this book with Bruce Catton's nonfiction about the Civil War, books very popular with teenage men.

Kenneth Roberts' novels, set during the Revolutionary War, have been family read-alouds for us. Roberts' careful historical research and strong writing make you care about his characters. Most of his books are about the bravery and daring of the early colonists. But I had never thought about what it would be like to be a loyalist during the Revolutionary War until we read his *Oliver Wiswell*. It's a wonderfully compelling look at the rag-tag army of the colonists and the problems facing the nonrevolutionaries.

Some historical fiction picks up more recent events. Readers are sure to enjoy Sonia Levitin's *The Return*, a story of an Ethiopian

Jewish girl airlifted during the 1984 Operation Moses rescue mission.

Historical fiction must be one of the most satisfying kinds of writing to do because there is so much of it. It certainly is satisfying to read. What we have listed for you in the bibliography will whet your appetite for more.

Biography and Nonfiction

The lives of other people are not only intriguing but give us concrete examples of courage, heroism, sorrow, and success. Such books show us a broad sweep of human lives, and their appeal is ageless.

Virginia Hamilton's *Anthony Burns: the Defeat and Triumph of a Fugitive Slave* is one such story; Phillip Hallie's *Lest Innocent Blood Be Shed* is another true story, set in a far different world from anything Anthony Burns knew, yet their themes are similar.

Biographies are always enriching reading experiences; they do something special for their readers—encourage, motivate, inspire. We have chosen stories of people our typical reader would not normally meet. For one thing, reading these books will widen a reader's understanding of people and ways of behaving. Their stories give us new friends, people whom we think we surely must know by the end of the book. Many leaders point to the reading of biographies as their most influential exposure to books—reading that gives inspiration, encouragement, and motivation.

Several of the biographies in our bibliography center on events surrounding World War II, the Holocaust, and the Nazi prison camps. Corrie ten Boom's *The Hiding Place* has been one of the most inspiring of these. Other biographies center on the African-American experience. *Black Like Me* by John Howard Griffin tells a real story about prejudice; Haley's *The Autobiography of Malcom X* is a "shocker," but it articulates the rage prejudice produces.

You'll not want to miss in some other nonfiction works the fun of *The Thurber Carnival,* and the beauty of "noticing" nature in *Pilgrim at Tinker Creek.* You'll love meeting Gerald Durrell's zany family in *Birds, Beasts and Relatives,* and you'll discover courage and faith by living through Joni Eareckson's recovery after a diving accident that left her paralyzed in *Joni.*

Nonfiction exposes us to people and to facts. Everything that is not fiction (except poetry) falls in this category. We have not made lengthy nonfiction listings in our bibliography inasmuch as these books are perhaps the easiest kind of good reading to find.

Sing a Word-song

Poetry is verbal music. It is more than doggerel that rhymes. It gives us the feel and shape of words. We understand the purpose and feel of metaphors and see things we never saw before.

Many people first met poetry in nursery rhymes, most of which seem nonsensical, but when they were first written, many nursery rhymes had political implications.

> Sing a song of sixpence,
> A pocketful of rye,
> Four and twenty blackbirds
> Baked in a pie.

It doesn't make much sense, but its singing-ness and rhyme make it fun to say. Dr. Seuss has written books full of outrageous rhymes and adventures that have probably delighted you as much as me.

Poems are meant to be read aloud because of the way that words rise and fall and flow and pause and echo. We soon leave the world of nursery rhymes, but we can move on in our experience with poetry—maybe to humorous poems.

It is fun to read aloud the story poems by Henry Wadsworth Longfellow about Hiawatha and Paul Revere.

> Listen my children, and you shall hear
> Of the midnight ride of Paul Revere,
> On the eighteenth of April, in Seventy-five;
> Hardly a man is now alive
> That remembers that famous day and year.

Later, perhaps in an English class, many students encounter Edna St. Vincent Millay's descriptive poetry:

> O world, I cannot hold thee close enough!
> Thy winds, thy wide gray skies!
> Thy mists that roll and rise!
> Thy woods, this autumn day, that ache and sag
> And all but cry with color!

Or the wonder that Sara Teasdale captures,

> And children's faces looking up
> Holding wonder like a cup.

Robert Frost is almost everyone's favorite. A book of his poems for your own family library is a good investment.

> Whose woods are these I think I know
> His house is in the village, though;
> He will not see me stopping here
> To watch his woods fill up with snow.

A word of caution about reading poetry. Read it for fun; don't kill it with a deep search for hidden meanings. We had a woods exactly like the one Robert Frost describes above in his poem, "Stopping by Woods on a Snowy Evening." When we drove from our farm into the village on snowy evenings, our son, Mark, would chant "Whose woods are these I think I know . . ." Then he studied the poem in a literature class and was told there were all sorts of hidden meanings. It reminds me of a poem Jean Little wrote called After English Class:

> I used to like "Stopping by Woods on a Snowy Evening."
> I liked the coming darkness,
> The jingle of harness bells, breaking—and adding to—the
>   stillness,
> The gentle drift of snow . . .
>
> But today, the teacher told us what everything stood for.
> The woods, the horse, the miles to go, the sleep—
> They all have "hidden meanings."
>
> It's grown so complicated now that,
> Next time I drive by,
> I don't think I'll bother to stop.[2]

On Easter morning older teens will enjoy reading John Updike's *Seven Stanzas at Easter*. Here are some of the stanzas from the poem:

Make no mistake if he rose at all
it was as his body;
if the cells' dissolution did not reverse, the molecules reknit,
    the amino acids rekindle,
the church will fall . . .

Let us not mock God with metaphor
analogy, sidestepping transcendence;
making of the event a parable, a sign painted in the faded
    credulity of earlier ages:
let us walk through the door.

The stone is rolled back, not papier-mâché,
not a stone in a story,
but the vast rock of materiality that in the slow grinding
    of time will eclipse for each of us
the wide light of day.

It's unlikely that a family will check poetry out of the library to read. Poetry is better left just sitting around the room waiting for someone to pick it up. Don't be too macho or too sophisticated to do it—and listen to your own voice reading it.

I suggest that among the books that you begin to put in your personal library or on your birthday lists, the first should be books of poetry. There are many to choose from, but here are some suggestions:

The Concise Columbia Book of Poetry, edited by William Harmon. (Columbia University Press, 1989). It contains one hundred outstanding poems, and is a good beginner.

The Best Loved Poems of the American People, selected by Hazel Felleman. (Doubleday, 1936) is a thick book, full of favorites of all kinds—serious, humorous, and classic.

The Oxford Book of Children's Verse (Oxford University Press, 1973) is still one of my favorites, and I don't know why it has the word "children's" in it inasmuch as the book is an anthology that anyone would enjoy.

A favorite, now in paperback and called the book for poetry

haters, is *Reflections on a Gift of a Watermelon Pickle.* One from the collection, written by black poet, Langston Hughes, is called "Dreams":

> Hold fast to dreams
> For if dreams die
> Life is a broken-winged bird
> That cannot fly.
>
> Hold fast to dreams
> For when dreams go
> Life is a barren field
> Frozen with snow.

I would add to my collection *Polishing the Petoskey Stone* (Harold Shaw Publishing, 1990), a collection of contemporary Christian poetry by Luci Shaw.

Of course, I'd add a book of humorous poetry by Edward Lear or an Ogden Nash collection, so I could chuckle over:

> Behold the duck.
> It does not cluck.
> A cluck it lacks.
> It quacks.
> It is specially fond
> Of a puddle or pond.
> When it dines or sups
> It bottoms up.

If you've learned to like poetry earlier in life, you will probably have *Where the Sidewalk Ends* by Shel Silverstein, (Harper Collins, 1974) and some of Paul Fleischman's wonderful poetry books, along with a collection or two edited by Nancy Larrick.

Words, words, words—wonderful words. May your heart be fed with the richness of "a word fitly spoken."

Notes

1. Katherine Paterson, "Words," in *Gates of Excellence* (Elsevier/Nelson Books, 1981), 17.
2. Jean Little, "After English Class," from *Hey World, Here I Am!* (Harper & Row, 1989).

9

A Word for the College-Bound

I am the very model of a modern
Major-General,
I've information vegetable, animal
and mineral,
I know the kings of England,
and I quote the fights historical,
From Marathon to Waterloo, in order
categorical;
I'm very well acquainted too with
matters mathematical,
I understand equations, both the
simple and quadratical,
About binomial theorem I'm teeming
with a lot o' news—
With many cheerful facts about
the square of the hypotenuse.

Thus sings the Major-General in Gilbert and Sullivan's comic opera *The Pirates of Penzance* about the excessive information he has collected. He later finds "these cheerful facts" are void of military strategy for the battle. Military strategy may well depend, however, on the cheerful facts he knows.

Today's university students seem to want the details of military strategy. They want to learn quickly all they need to know to get a good job and get on with it. Once upon a time students went to college to get an education instead of a job. The result of this change in purpose makes for some amusing and amazing stories coming from universities.

One professor said that he had not found a single student in the Los Angeles area, whether in college or high school, who could tell him when World War II was fought. Few knew how many senators Nevada or Oregon have in Congress. A college junior thought Toronto must be in Italy; and another junior at the University of California thought that Washington, D.C., must be in Washington state. Only two could identify the place in history held by people like Thomas Jefferson or Ben Franklin. On and on it goes.

These students know a great deal; they share a lot of information among themselves. The problem is that what they know doesn't seem to relate to history or literature or any kind of intergenerational information.

There is a body of information that every person in the land ought to know because it is good and because other people know it. That is called *cultural literacy*. It is a body of information that allows people to communicate with each other. The information is assumed. Newspapers and books are written on the basis of this body of information. For instance, a casual reference may be made to the meeting of Ulysses S. Grant and Robert E. Lee in Appomattox Courthouse, Virginia, in 1865. Who these men are and why they are meeting should be part of your store of information as a teenager. Everything doesn't always have to be explained when people have this common body of information.

Professor E. D. Hirsch has tried to organize what should be included in "that body of knowledge." At the back of his book *Cultural Literacy: What Every American Needs to Know,* Hirsch has a list of 5,000 essential names, phrases, dates, and concepts. This, he claims, is background information that writers and speakers assume their audience already has. Even if a student has good reading skills, he or she has little chance of entering the

American mainstream, says Hirsch, without knowing what a silicon chip is, or when the Civil War was fought.

Test your cultural literacy. What do you know about the following:

Alamo
1492
Billy the Kid
carpetbagger
El Greco
lame duck
gamma rays
nom de plume

There are 5,000 more items in Hirsch's list, enough to intimidate those who assume that they are literate. Why do I mention this? Because cultural literacy is related to *reading,* and that is what we have been encouraging young adults—and their parents—to do. Not so that you can spout off a list of information like an egocentric prig but so that you and your family can understand and communicate with the larger world in which you live.

Cultural literacy is especially important for college-bound teenagers (whom I would like to address specifically in this chapter), though, hopefully, not limited to them. The crux of the matter is not whether people go to college but whether they read. Many college graduates are essentially culturally illiterate by Hirsch's definition; others who read but have never entered the door of a college, are not. People who read put into their lives more understanding than they realize. If you are serious about your life, I urge you to make picking up a book and reading for pleasure (and for information) one of your regular habits—even when your school assignments seem to weigh you down.

What Should Be in Your "Reservoir"?

No two people include exactly the same titles when listing books that all young people should know. Many colleges and universities have their own lists made up for incoming freshmen. The National Council of Teachers of English publishes an enormous book called *The College and Adult Reading List,* covering 700 titles or more, an overwhelming volume to encounter. The American Library Association prints a short pamphlet of books for college-bound students. I caution you, however, not to take some of these long lists too seriously. It could be that even the people who put them together have not read everything on the list.

Let me cull the most often mentioned from the accumulated lists. These books make up a good place to start some catch-up reading, or you may find yourself responding with pleasure that you have already read them.[1]

(1) *The Mother Goose Rhymes.* It seems a strange beginning to a list, but can you imagine someone who wouldn't know that "Mary had a little lamb"? It's part of our heritage.

(2) *The basic fairy tales.* "Cinderella," "Little Red Riding Hood," "Sleeping Beauty," "Puss in Boots," "Jack and the Beanstalk," "The Three Bears," "Chicken Little," and more.

(3) *Aesop's Fables.* These animal fables are almost universally known in western culture. Remember "The Boy Who Cried Wolf"?

(4) *The Bible.* Certainly you should know the more familiar stories—Abraham, Moses, David, Isaac, Ruth, Esther, the parables, etc. Robert Carlsen of the University of Iowa writes, "These stories are all inextricably woven through Western literature and philosophy. Furthermore, the rhythm of biblical language has had a significant impact on the rhythm of our language as a whole."

(5) *The Greek myths.* These are terribly confusing—all these gods and goddesses and their relationships. As a quick introduction to what mythology is about, I recommend an old book that is still in print: *The Golden Fleece and the Heroes Who Lived Before Achilles* by Padraic Colum.

(6) *The Iliad* and *The Odyssey.* These are stories of the Trojan War and Ulysses and of his long voyage home. You should know at least the plot line but remember the Katherine Paterson quote at the beginning of Chapter **9**.

(7) *Oedipus Rex* by Sophocles is one of the best-remembered Greek tragedies. Most of the lists have Greek tragedies on them, and you may want to look this one up sometime.

(8) *Alice in Wonderland.* Yes, it's one of the foundational

books. It was intended as a children's book, but many say it is not meant to be read until you are at least a senior in high school.

(9) *Robinson Crusoe.* This is the most enduring of the survival stories. Tourists still are shown around his island.

(10) *Little Women.* An enduring family story. Syracuse University held an "Invincible Louisa" conference in May 1984, celebrating its one hundredth anniversary. One of the speakers gave a paper on "The Spirit of Jo March," heroine of *Little Women.*

(11) *Pilgrim's Progress.* You must read this either in the original or in a simplified edition so that you will know about the Slough of Despond, Vanity Fair, the Straight Road, or the Narrow Gate. And besides, it will surprise you with pleasure.

(12) *Don Quixote.* An abridged version of this will do. This erratic knight has become so firmly embedded in Western culture that he has even given the word *quixotic* to the English language.

(13) *Gulliver's Travels.* The two most important of Gulliver's four voyages are *Voyage to the Land of the Lilliputians* and *The Voyage to the Land of the Brobdingnags.*

(14) *Shakespeare.* By the time you are a senior, you are probably familiar with *A Midsummer Night's Dream, Romeo and Juliet,* and *The Merchant of Venice.* The tragedies you will want to read are *Julius Caesar, Macbeth, Hamlet,* and *King Lear.* If Shakespeare scares you off, get Charles and Mary Lamb's book, *Tales of Shakespeare* and read the simplified plots so that you know where the plays are going when you later read the original. Many good videos of Shakespeare's plays are also available.

(15) *Uncle Tom's Cabin.* This book was the match that ignited the Civil War and is still widely read.

(16) *Nineteenth century British novels.* Read *David Copperfield* or *The Tale of Two Cities, Wuthering Heights, Jane Eyre,* or *Pride and Prejudice.*

(17) *Selected works by Mark Twain.* At least *Tom Sawyer, Huckleberry Finn, The Prince and the Pauper.*

(18) *Nineteenth century American novels* like *The Scarlet Letter, Moby Dick, The Red Badge of Courage,* and *Ethan Frome.*

(19) Some European and Russian goodies like *Les Miserables* or *Crime and Punishment.*

(20) *Twentieth century novels* like the ones we have talked about in this book.

You may surprise yourself by noting how many of these you are already familiar with, and that's to your credit. Lists like these should not bully anyone; they are simply a guide composed by mortal men and women. You do with it what you want. Sprinkled in among reading like this should be some shoot-em-up spy stories or a romantic love story, just for sheer fun and relaxation.

Your Mental Attitude

The biggest asset for the college-bound is the right mental attitude: Learning is fun. Studying may not be, but learning is.

With that attitude, be quick to use the dictionary. Make sure you have a good one. "Look it up" ought to be your first response when you meet something you don't know. We keep a dictionary near the table where we eat our meals. It is amazing how often something comes up that needs to be checked out.

Your most important mental attitude involves your conviction about your own value. *You* are special because you are *you;* no one else can be who you are. You have your own contribution to make to the world because of who you are.

*   *   *

In urging you to read books, it is *not* that books are so important that you must read them. It is rather because *you* are so *important* that you *must* read them, because we want to make your life as rich as possible.

*   *   *

Notes

1. I have been most influenced by the list composed by G. Robert Carlsen, Professor and Head of English at the University of Iowa and author of *Books and the Teen-Age Reader,* (New York: Harper & Row, 1971). He has made the list manageable and comprehensive without its being overwhelming.

Illustration by W. T. Benda for Willa Cather's *My Antonia*, reprinted by permission of Houghton Mifflin Company. For description of this book, see page 214.

BOOKS:
TO HELP YOU CHOOSE

How to Use the Book Annotations

We've tried to make the book evaluations user-friendly. Each review is followed by symbols that indicate the age for which the book is intended.

> E.T. —Early Teens (middle school)
> M.T. —Mid Teens (early high school)
> L.T. —Late Teens (senior high to college)
> A.A. —All Ages (good family read-alouds)

Remember, however, that many young teens read books beyond what "experts" think is their ability, and many older teens continue to reread old favorites, bringing greater maturity and insight to what they are reading.

I feel that way about *The Wind in the Willows*. I find new things in it every time I read it.

If an asterisk (*) follows a book annotation, it means that we feel that this book should belong in a basic collection for any school library, whether it is a private, parochial, or public school library

We didn't put recommendations with the Tried and True titles or the Nonfiction titles. The Tried and True have already stood the test of time in ways that the books in the remaining categories have not and, you will notice, we don't predict that all of them will. If you can't find the book or author you are looking for, use the index.

Happy reading!

ADVENTURE

AUTHOR: **Frances Hodgson Burnett**
TITLE: *The Lost Prince (1915)*
DESCRIPTION: Marco Loristan and his desperately poor but proud and self-educated father, crisscross Europe, working always for the redemption of their beautiful but savage country, Samavia, kept in the grip of wicked rulers for 500 years. For those 500 years also a legend has circulated about Samavia's Lost Prince. Would he ever be found? With Samavia embroiled in yet another civil war, he is needed more than ever. Marco and his London street-beggar friend, the crippled Rat, are entrusted to be Bearers of the Sign of the Prince's return to the Forgers of the Sword, hidden all through Europe.
RECOMMENDATION: When Rat and his gang of street urchins first heard the story of the Lost Prince from Marco, "it made them think they saw things; it fired their blood; it set them wanting to fight for ideals they knew nothing about—adventurous things, for instance, and high and noble young princes who were full of the possibility of great and good deeds." *The Lost Prince* is that kind of book. You may find it having that same effect on you! E.T.*

AUTHOR: **Michael Chrichton**
TITLE: *The Great Train Robbery (1975)*
DESCRIPTION: Chrichton, the author of *The Andromeda Strain*, reconstructs in minute and fascinating detail the preparations Edward Pierce made to rob the invulnerable safe containing the gold to pay Her Majesty's soldiers fighting bravely in the Crimea.
RECOMMENDATION: The Great Train Robbery, as it became known to the proper Victorians hungry for scandal, provided Chrichton not only an

opportunity to look into an intriguing criminal's mind and methods but also a chance to examine the society in which Pierce and his accomplices worked. L.T.

AUTHOR: **Ann Holm**
TITLE: *North to Freedom (1974)*
DESCRIPTION: Twelve-year-old David cannot figure out why the guard at the prison camp where he has lived his whole life has engineered his escape. Now he is free and must make his way from there to Italy, then north to Denmark, with only a water bottle, a piece of soap, a loaf of bread, a compass, matches, and his unchildlike wariness. His fierce honesty and desire for freedom are softened by tasting the sweetness of beauty, faith, and even love. They leave this splendid boy more human but more vulnerable when his freedom is threatened again.
RECOMMENDATION: Though Holm carefully expands David's thoughts only as his vocabulary expands on his learning journey, many significant ideas crowd the pages of David's wonderful story. Among them are the importance of individual freedom of conscience and self-determination; the necessity of having a childhood if one is to grow up healthy; the foundational significance of both faith and the acceptance of God's unconditional love. But more than these themes, David himself—the courageous boy with the eyes of an old man searching for his mother, whose "eyes look as if she'd known a great deal, and yet she's still smiling"—will capture you and haunt you and encourage you and give you hope. This is a wonderful book to read aloud as a family or class. E.T., M.T.*

AUTHOR: **Jack London**
TITLE: *The Call of the Wild (1903)*
DESCRIPTION: Long a favorite of young men, *The Call of the Wild* is the story of Buck, a domesticated dog transported to Alaska during the territory's gold rush days, where he learned to adapt to the harsh environment and harsh treatment and arduous work of pulling sleds. He makes a human friend but finally, after Thornton is killed, succumbs to the "call of the wild," to run with a wolf pack.
RECOMMENDATION: London's love of animals and nature is apparent on these pages. M.T.*

AUTHOR: **Robin McKinley**
TITLE: *The Outlaws of Sherwood (1988)*

DESCRIPTION: In this splendid retelling of the Robin Hood legend, McKinley brings the famous merry outlaws and their not-so-famous companions to life with all their strengths and weaknesses, joys and discontents. From when you first meet the forester, Robin, on his way to the fair at Nottingham, musing that his friend Marian is a better archer than he—to the ending, which King Richard the Lionheart himself engineers to the surprise of them all, you'll be entranced by the adventures of these twelve outlaws.

RECOMMENDATION: Don't miss the afterword in which McKinley discusses her search for the historical Robin Hood. She quotes one source who says that the Robin Hood stories "have always reflected what the teller and the audience needed him to be *at the time of the telling.*" Then you might ask yourself what need of yours McKinley's most flesh-and-blood Robin meets as you encounter him on these pages. Look also for McKinley's retelling of the Beauty and the Beast fairytale, *Beauty*, and for her fantasy *The Hero and the Crown*. E.T., M.T.*

AUTHOR: **John L. Moore**
TITLE: *The Breaking of Ezra Riley (1990)*
DESCRIPTION: The prairies of eastern Montana are an unforgiving environment, but for Ezra their harshness is compounded by an aloof, unforgiving rancher-father and cowboy uncles who do not comprehend what is happening to him. He runs away, but when his father dies and someone must take over the ranch, he returns with his wife and baby. There he must face what, in the first place, caused him to flee as he tries to make the ranch profitable.

RECOMMENDATION: The biblical messages of freedom and forgiveness are woven so carefully and subtly and truly into this splendid western that they will surprise you with their inevitable rightness as they did Ezra Riley. This is a book that boys especially will not want to miss. It is published by Lion, so you may have to ask your library to get it for you. L.T. *

AUTHOR: **Baroness Orczy**
TITLE: *The Scarlet Pimpernel (1884)*
DESCRIPTION: In Paris during September, 1792, aristocratic Frenchmen were losing their lives on the guillotine unless the mysterious British Scarlet Pimpernel manages to contrive dangerous escapes for them right under the eyes of the authorities.

RECOMMENDATION: The story of one such escape full of "turmoil, passion and intrigues" is told in this book from a decidedly aristocratic and antirepublican point of view. M.T., L.T.

Gary Paulsen, the person, is found in all of his writing for young people. You are the right audience for him, he believes, because adults "have created the mess we are struggling to outlive." He has hunted, trapped, driven dogsleds, soldiered, worked as a migrant farmhand, thirsted after knowledge, meditated, and—perhaps most important for his stories— experienced that piercingly beautiful oneness with an animal and its natural environment, which he tried to recapture again and again. It is probably not quite accurate to call him a pantheist, for he never indicates that nature is to be worshiped, but it does seem to be Everything for him. (He never, for example, refers to a possible Creator for it.) Also, his writing is a seamless whole into which people can and should be absorbed, spiritually if not physically. No wonder, then, that he also is a vigorous campaigner for nuclear disarmament (apparent in *The Sentries,* another book of Paulsen's)—nothing would be unaffected if a nuclear weapon were to explode! Paulsen writes with a songlike, deceptively simple beauty and has earned the right for young people to consider his ideas seriously.

AUTHOR: **Gary Paulsen**
TITLE: *Tracker (1984)*
DESCRIPTION: John must hunt the deer alone this year for he and his grandparents depend on the meat, but his grandfather is dying of cancer. The doe captivates John with her beauty, and John feels deep in his poetic soul that if only he can touch her, he can cheat death. For two days he tracks her, alone in the frozen swamp.
RECOMMENDATION: In this lyrical, extended short story, Gary Paulsen takes you into the mind and heart of a young boy who longs to prevent the changes he knows are coming to both his beloved grandfather and the splendid deer. There is nothing beyond the physical for either of them even though their lives have been beautiful, joyful, and meaningful. But can a mere boy halt that inevitable change? E.T.

AUTHOR: **Gary Paulsen**
TITLE: *Dogsong (1985)*
DESCRIPTION: Newbery Honor, 1986. Russel is disturbed by the destruction that accompanies modern inroads into Eskimo culture. He leaves his father (who at least gave up drinking because he loved the Jesus that Russel can't understand) to live with the oldest man in the winter settlement, who in a trance passes on to him some of the old wisdom the villagers had lost. He sends Russel out alone on a dogsled run to survive in the Arctic winter, to find his song by merging into his dogs, the

snow, a prehistoric man and in the process, also finding a very modern girl who, in the end, needs civilization's help.

RECOMMENDATION: Gary Paulsen understands the almost animistic Eskimo mindset and can take you deep inside Russel's experience until you, too, feel that you are part of the dogs, part of the past, and part of the wild Arctic environment. You'll find yourself wondering if Russel is right to reject modern ways. And are the missionaries right to make the Eskimos give up their songs? M.T.

AUTHOR: **Gary Paulsen**
TITLE: *The Crossing (1987)*
DESCRIPTION: Fourteen-year-old Manny, a street kid existing by his wits in Juarez, Mexico, wants nothing more than to cross into the United States, the land of milk and honey. Sgt. Robert Locke, the perfect Army officer, wants nothing more than to kill the voices of his dead Vietnam buddies with the most powerful liquor he can find. They chance to meet behind a Juarez bar, there learning something about truth and companionship.

RECOMMENDATION: Paulsen sustains his lyric style even in this book, which is not about oneness with nature but about a boy and a man out of joint with themselves and their environment. Your heart will ache for Manny and Robert both, and you will puzzle for a long time about whether Paulsen means you to think that Locke's death was necessary for his crossing into the kind of humanity that helps the dying. Or, having offered help to Manny, does his death show that any such acts are as meaningless as the ones in the bullring? E.T., M.T.

AUTHOR: **Gary Paulsen**
TITLE: *Hatchet (1987)*
DESCRIPTION: Newbery Honor, 1988. Brian's parents have recently divorced, and he is flying up to spend his first summer with his father on a Canadian oil field. After the pilot of the private plane dies of a heart attack, Brian crashes the plane into a lake. With only the hatchet his mother gave him, he must survive in the isolated wilderness alone.

RECOMMENDATION: This is a different kind of survival story from Ivan Southall's *To The Wild Sky*, though they have superficial similarities. The Canadian wilderness, though not friendly, is not hostile to Brian if only he can learn to be a part of it and so discover its secrets of food, work, and patience. It's nature he must get along with, not people. The city boy toughens and so gains the hope he needs to continue. When rescue comes, it is almost anticlimactic. E.T., M.T.

AUTHOR: **Joan Phipson**
TITLE: *Hit and Run (1985)*
DESCRIPTION: Roland's wealthy father has always been able to protect him from the consequences of his actions, yet Roland is unnaturally afraid of him. At least that's what Constable Gordon Sutton thinks. Then, taunted about his driving ability, Roland impulsively steals a Ferrari, hits a baby pram, and flees from town with Sutton not far behind. Alone in the dangerous Australian bush together for a long 24 hours and unexpectedly needing each other, they learn there is more to Roland than his father would have believed.
RECOMMENDATION: Roland, the main character of this unforgettable story, had always taken the easy way out but had paid the price of losing his father's respect and his own self-respect. Out in the bush, even before he is discovered by the policeman, he has the chance to do the difficult and begin to gain that respect back. Sutton helps as he can, but it is from within that Roland must find the needed moral courage to assume responsibility for his own actions. E.T., M.T.*

AUTHOR: **Jack Schaefer**
TITLE: *Shane (1949)*
DESCRIPTION: This old-fashioned western has many of the ingredients of that genre, including the beleaguered farmers vs. the land-hungry cattlemen and a climactic shootout. But in *Shane*, the good guy wears black and has a mysterious past though he does come riding unannounced into young Bob's life at a crucial moment. How Shane physically helps Bob and his father and other farmers wrest a new living from the raw prairie and how he more significantly helps Bob "stay clean inside through the muddled, dirtied years of growing up" make up the taut pages of this exciting book.
RECOMMENDATION: If you never read any other westerns, you will be glad to have read this one. M.T., L.T.*

Ivan Southall is one of Australia's most respected novelists, one who deserves to be read more in North America. (See other titles listed under "Contemporary Fiction.") He puts his characters in extreme situations, and so his stories are thrilling adventures of human endurance. More important, he explores how young people respond, react, and grow in those situations. He exults in people—varied, fascinating people. Almost all of his characters believe rather matter-of-factly in God, though rarely is he, to them, a personal friend. In fact, Gerald, who had to fly the Egret after Jim's heart attack, remembered that his father sometimes said, "Praying's all right for parsons, [but] speaking for myself I'd rather roll up my sleeves and rely on my own sweat." Gerald thought, "That was all right to a point, but it didn't seem to cover situations like this. Perhaps his father had never been in a situation like this." And so for some of Southall's characters—not all—their growth is a growth toward a first kind of foxhole faith as well as maturity.

AUTHOR: **Ivan Southall**
TITLE: *Ash Road (1965)*
DESCRIPTION: Three teenage boys camping in the Australian bush accidently start a fire that ravages a whole district. They and the residents left on Ash Road—youngsters and two old men—must discover in themselves reserves of strength, courage, and forgiveness to help each other stay alive.
RECOMMENDATION: Peter finds his manhood; Lorna, love for her dour father; Graham, the ability to admit his guilt; Pippa, the strength to do what must be done; Gramps, compassion for a neighbor; and Grandpa Tanner, the humility not to shake his fist at God in fury but to forget about himself and pray for little children. This fine novel pits ordinary people against an extraordinary fire before which they can only humbly acknowledge their finiteness. E.T., M.T.*

AUTHOR: **Ivan Southall**
TITLE: *To the Wild Sky (1969)*
DESCRIPTION: The pilot flying six children to Gerald's birthday party on a ranch in Australia dies of a heart attack. Gerald takes over the plane, but a dust storm and strong headwinds prevent him from crashlanding it near his home. Crash, they do—on the shore of a deserted island. The children must bury the pilot and figure out how to stay alive until help arrives, if indeed it will.
RECOMMENDATION: As always, Southall puts his children in an extreme situation to explore how they respond, and as always, his children grow closer to maturity, finding reserves of courage, resourcefulness, strength—and even faith. (This is in contrast to how the children act in *Lord of the Flies*, to which the book is often compared.) In *To the Wild Sky*, it is left to the reader to complete the novel. After all they have been through, after all they have learned, will Colin and Mark, Bruce and Jan, Gerald and Carol be rescued or will they, as Jan has a premonition, die one by one? M.T., L.T.

AUTHOR: **Ivan Southall**
TITLE: *What About Tomorrow (1977)*

DESCRIPTION: Sam's family desperately needs his paper route money during the Depression in Melbourne, Australia, but on the day he was 14 years, 4 months, and 8 days, he crashes his brakeless bike into a tram and scatters his 64 papers to the wind. Rather than face the consequences, he runs away, and from that day his life is profoundly different, as we see during flash-forwards to one of his missions as a fighter pilot during World War II.

RECOMMENDATION: If you have ever marveled at the unique circumstances that make up *you*, you will thrill to Sam's discovery that God has worked overtime to engineer the days just after his accident so that he could manage a job big enough for a man—growing up. M.T., L.T. *

AUTHOR: **Robert Louis Stevenson**
TITLE: *Kidnapped (1886)*
DESCRIPTION: David Balfour receives a letter of introduction to his Uncle Ebenezer of the great Scottish family, the Shaws, as an inheritance from his father. But Uncle Ebenezer tries to have David killed and then later tricks him into going on a ship that is headed with its prisoners to slavery in the New World. Find out how David escapes this condition, helps a new friend, Alan Stewart, who is part of a scheme to overthrow King George, and regains his rightful inheritance.

RECOMMENDATION: If you are looking for an exciting adventure, *Kidnapped* may be your book. Reading this book will reaffirm your values of perseverance and loyalty. Look for the edition with the wonderful N. C. Wyeth illustrations. A.A.*

AUTHOR: **Robert Louis Stevenson**
TITLE: *Treasure Island (1883)*
DESCRIPTION: If you don't have to read *Treasure Island* for school, you may want to try it on your own. Jim Hawkins is the boy hero of this fast-paced story of a mysterious treasure map, a mutinous crew, battles between adventurers and pirates—the most infamous being Long John Silver—and, at last, rewards for all who survive, even the pirate.

RECOMMENDATION: This Stevenson novel is also illustrated by N. C. Wyeth, making it an edition worth owning. A.A. *

ANIMALS

AUTHOR: **Richard Adams**
TITLE: ***Watership Down (1972)***
DESCRIPTION: Warned by a farsighted rabbit that their warren is going to be destroyed by an encroaching housing development, a group of rabbits flees into the unknown. After confronting both danger and temptation to an easy life, they find a new home but then must find female rabbits to join them. A nearby overcrowded warren might be glad to let some does go, but its dictatorial leader prevents it. The rabbits must succeed in this conflict or die out even though they have been sustained thus far by faith in their mythical god, have developed the necessary leadership qualities, and even have evolved to adapt to their dire circumstances.
RECOMMENDATION: This terrific story reads like a suspenseful epic. The rabbits are not thinly disguised humans although each has his or her own vividly drawn personality as well as a shared myth-based religion, a government, and a history. You can also read *Watership Down* as an allegory for our civilization threatened by decay, and, if you do, you will find many parallels to familiar items from Western culture, from Brer Rabbit, to the Creation story, to totalitarian dictators. M.T., L.T.*

AUTHOR: **Colin Dann**
TITLE: ***The Animals of Farthing Wood (1979)***
DESCRIPTION: When their home in Farthing Wood is threatened by a new housing development, the animals (some of whom are natural enemies and some of whom move so slowly they would endanger the community) take the Oath of Common Safety so that they can travel together to a wildlife refuge Toad has heard about. Toad is their guide, but Fox and Badger provide the leadership; and Owl and Kestral, the protection by scouting.

"Jody Find the Fawn"—illustration by N. C. Wyeth for Marjorie Kinnan Rawlings' *The Yearling* (1939); reprinted with permission of Charles Scribner's Sons. For description of this book, see pages 106–107.

They face natural dangers such as a forest fire, and man-made dangers such as highways and fox hunts, paying the high-but-necessary price to achieve their goal.

RECOMMENDATION: This is a wonderful and heartwarming story you might enjoy sharing aloud with your family. Its sequel is *In the Grip of Winter.* E.T., M.T.*

AUTHOR: **Allan Eckert**
TITLE: *Incident at Hawk's Hill (1971)*
DESCRIPTION: Based on an event in 1870 near Winnipeg, Canada, *Incident at Hawk's Hill* is a moving account of a reclusive little boy, more attuned to animals than people, who gets lost on the vast Canadian prairie and for two months lives with an injured mother badger until his family finds him at last. The visiting archbishop tells the MacDonalds that the return of their son, Ben, is a modern parable of the faithfulness of God.
RECOMMENDATION: Eckert has an uncanny ability to get right inside the lives of lonely Ben, his anxious father, their cruel trapper neighbor, and the mother badger herself. This is a story worth reading aloud with your family. E.T., M.T.*

AUTHOR: **James Herriot**
TITLE: *All Creatures Great and Small (1972)*
DESCRIPTION: You'll be delighted to meet James Herriot, who in the 1930s was a young vet apprenticed to Siegfried Farnon, a bachelor Yorkshire vet extraordinaire with "ideas both brilliant and barmy," which "came in . . . a constant torrent." You'll meet the dour and hardworking farmers; rich eccentric landowners (Mrs. Pumphrey, who indulges her Tricky Woo, is the classic example); Siegfried's Casanova younger brother, Tristan; gentle Helen with whom James falls in love; and a wide assortment of animals whose personalities are as distinctive as those of their owners.
RECOMMENDATION: Herriot is a master storyteller whose tongue-in-cheek style is just right to tell these marvelous tales. You'll cheer to know there are four wonderfully long "All Creatures" volumes to laugh and cry over; the other three are *All Things Bright and Beautiful, All Things Wise and Wonderful,* and *The Lord God Made Them All.* The PBS series that recreated them is very faithful to the books, but nothing will substitute for the pleasure of reading them. M.T., L.T.*

AUTHOR: **Brian Jacques**
TITLE: *Redwall (1986)*

DESCRIPTION: Redwall is a peaceful Abbey where the brother mice dedicate their lives (not to God—no worship here, just the cultural reverberations of a true monastic community) to preserving their pastoral environment and to healing any who need it. However, the evil rat, Cluny, and his hordes want to destroy the Abbey and its way of life. How will the nonviolent mice fight back? It is a young novice, Matthias, who—in outgrowing his bumbling habits—leads the way; first, to preparedness and, finally, to a full scale defense. But even Matthias needs a symbol of the righteousness of their cause, and with the help of the ancient recorder Methuselah, the love of a fieldmouse named Cornflower, and the tactical skills of other woodland folk—Constance, the Badger, in particular—he sets off on a quest to recover the lost sword of the Abbey's long-dead hero, Martin. Besides, the sword could come in handy for a final confrontation with Cluny.

RECOMMENDATION: This delightful story, the middle volume of a trilogy that also includes *Mossflower* and *Mattimeo*, is a combination talking-animal story, tale of medieval courtly love and adventure, and exciting struggle between good and evil almost on the fantasy scale. You can enjoy this book on several levels, even reading into it, if you wish, how we as a society ought to confront the evil that threatens us. E.T., M.T.

AUTHOR: **Farley Mowat**
TITLE: *The Dog Who Wouldn't Be (1957)*
DESCRIPTION: Farley Mowat was a boy lucky enough to grow up on the edge of a Canadian prairie with a mutt and various wildlife as his companions, a tolerant mother, and a father full of schemes that took them camping, hunting, and sailing (miles from any water!).

RECOMMENDATION: You can share Farley's luck if you read this gently humorous account of his boyhood, focused primarily around the escapades of his dog, Mutt, who regards himself as too good for a dog's station in life—in fact, he believes he is nearly human. M.T., L.T.

AUTHOR: **Marjorie Kinnan Rawlings**
TITLE: *The Yearling (1938)*
DESCRIPTION: Pulitzer Prize, 1939. As an only child, Jody longs for a pet as much as he longs to grow up. When his father kills a doe to acquire an antidote for a deadly rattlesnake bite, he is allowed to keep the fawn. They have an enchanted year together, but Flag, as a yearling, begins to destroy their crops. Jody must relinquish the pet that fed his need to share the love his taciturn family has difficulty expressing.

RECOMMENDATION: Perhaps you will be surprised that your emotions can be so deeply touched by a story so full of "masculine" action as this one about Jody Baxter, his father, Penny, and his mother, Ory, as they struggle against marauding wolves and bears, natural disasters, and sometimes even their untamed hard-drinking neighbors, so that they can carve out a living from the Florida scrub. E.T., M.T.*

AUTHOR: **Wilson Rawls**
TITLE: *Where the Red Fern Grows (1961)*
DESCRIPTION: Billy, a ten-year-old boy who lives far back in the Ozark hills, is pining away for a hunting dog. How he makes his wishes—indeed, his prayers—come true and how Little Ann and Old Dan change his life, bringing deep joy, button-popping pride, and great sorrow, is the never-to-be-forgotten story, *Where the Red Fern Grows*. It resonates with the author's deepfelt love for family, for nature, and for God.
RECOMMENDATION: Many classroom teachers read this book to their upper elementary students, and even "reluctant readers" have often gotten caught up in Billy's bittersweet pleasures. Rawls has written another Ozark boy-loves-animal book, *The Summer of the Monkeys*. E.T., M.T.*

AUTHOR: **Robert Siegel**
TITLE: *Whalesong (1981)*
DESCRIPTION: Hruna is a humpback whale whose size and courage mark him for a great destiny among the sea creatures. Humbly he submits to a visit to the Great Whale at the ocean's bottom, where he learns his place in the scheme of the universe as well as his true name. Skirmishes with man, the polluter of the oceans and the whale's most fierce enemy, prepare him to lead a final climactic battle for the survival of his pod.
RECOMMENDATION: Even those of you who know little about the life of sea animals will be fascinated by the lyrical (music is the primary motif) story of one humpback whale. You may read it as an absorbing adventure and as a fable about the need of all creatures—human, included—to find their proper niches in the whole fragile and enchanted structure of the created ecology. Crossway first published this book. A.A.*

AUTHOR: **Patricia Wrightson**
TITLE: *Moon Dark (1987)*
DESCRIPTION: Blue, Mort the fisherman's dog, knows that the Australian wildlife—the bush rats, bandicoots, koalas, kangaroos, flying foxes, and wild dingos—with whom he shares nocturnal adventures, are uneasy and

hungry. Since building had begun in their backwater scrub, there doesn't seem to be enough food for everyone. Now the bush rats and the bandicoots are openly at war. With the help of Keeting (Whom do you think this ancient magical singer is?) and by dint of the animals' own exhausting efforts, the ecological balance is restored.

RECOMMENDATION: *Moon Dark* may well become one of your favorite stories; perhaps you will want to share it aloud with your family. Without humanizing the animals, Patricia Wrightson has captured their distinctive—memorable—personalities. She has woven Australian myths throughout, as in all her books, enriching the story's action and meaning. And the very lack of stridency in her ecological message underscores its urgency. E.T.

CONTEMPORARY

AUTHOR: **Clayton Bess**
TITLE: *Story for a Black Night (1982)*
DESCRIPTION: This disturbing little book is a modern "Who is my neighbor?" story. In the middle of a black night comes a knock on the door on a farm in the Liberian bush. Ma lets in a grandmother, mother, and baby. In the morning only the baby is left but is discovered to have the deadly smallpox. How the strangers had come there and how Ma and her family treat the baby and what kind of goodness and evil motivate the various people—make up this tale.
RECOMMENDATION: Your expectations will be set on end just as they would have been had you been in Jesus' audience as he told the parable of the Good Samaritan. Nevertheless, is it bitterness or forgiveness that controls the heart of the narrator? You will have to decide if he is his Ma's son. M.T.

AUTHOR: **Sue Ellen Bridgers**
TITLE: *All Together Now (1979)*
DESCRIPTION: Casey must spend her twelfth summer with her grandparents while her father is in the Korean War and her mother is working. An odd assortment of people combine to make her time there unforgettable: Dwayne, a 33-year-old retarded baseball fanatic; Hazard, a charming but unemployed dancing-man-waiter who is still courting grandmother's friend, Pansy, after 25 years; and Uncle Taylor who would rather race cars and flirt with Gwen than work in grandfather's lumberyard.
RECOMMENDATION: Casey senses that this will be the only time she will be able to deceive Dwayne into believing that she is the boy-companion he longs for. In doing so, she gets caught up in the small but significant battles

in the empty lot, on the racetrack, and in the courthouse, to preserve for him the space he needs to be himself when his brother wants to commit him to an institution. This is a book about what people can do—even to determine by sheer will that others get well as the polio epidemic touches their small town—if only they will take the responsibility for each other. E.T., M.T.

AUTHOR: **Sue Ellen Bridgers**
TITLE: *Permanent Connections (1987)*
DESCRIPTION: Rob is 17, sullen, withdrawn, and getting high with drugs and sex and alcohol. All of a sudden he finds himself stuck at his grandfather's home in the hills of North Carolina, helping take care of an uncle who broke his hip and an aunt afraid to go out of the house. His father, though he had fled the same home himself years before, hopes that Rob will be helped in the process. But Rob, rebuffed by Ellery, who has her own pain, gets high, wrecks his uncle's truck, and finds himself in trouble with the law. Through it all Rob also discovers that "something . . . had stretched through his life, holding him against all odds until this moment of need" and that he is loved and can love in return.
RECOMMENDATION: Sue Ellen Bridgers explores that old theme, "No man is an island." Rob, Ellery, and the grown-ups, Ginny and Coralee, all seem to want to go it alone in their individual pains but find that the griefs are lessened when they allow others, through both space and time, to minister to them. Rob is caught and held safe by his knowledge of the ancient Book of Common Prayer. While you may question the orthodoxy of the priest as he tells Rob to pray to the God within him, there is nothing contrived about the miracles of redemption that take place in this most realistic book. M.T., L.T.

AUTHOR: **Bruce Brooks**
TITLE: *Midnight Hour Encores (1986)*
DESCRIPTION: Sibilance T. Spooner was born 16 years ago as Esalen Starness Blue, child of two Berkeley hippies. Her mother wanted her freedom, so, when Sib was 20 hours old, her father took his daughter East to become a musical prodigy—a cellist who wins every world-class competition going. Because she wants to meet her mother (or so she says—this brash egotist has ulterior motives), her father takes her cross-country in an old VW bus, giving her "lessons" on the morning of the Age of Aquarius as they go. After they arrive in San Francisco, Sib has to make a critical choice.

RECOMMENDATION: At one level the vivid descriptions in *Midnight Hour Encores* are tinged with nostalgia for the hang-loose days of the '60s, but at a deeper level the story is a biting satire about people who sang of freedom and love but refused responsibility and commitment. You may be startled by Sib's sassy irreverence at times, but you will also find most satisfying just how she discovers that she has only developed her incredible talent because of her father's love. M.T.

AUTHOR: **Bruce Brooks**
TITLE: *No Kidding (1989)*
DESCRIPTION: In the 21st century, 69 percent of the population is alcoholic, alcohol-related sterility has reduced the number of children, and most government money is spent on alcohol education and rehabilitation. Families, even religion, are destroyed by the situation. Sam is a 13-year-old AO—Alcoholic Offspring—who has exercised his power to commit his mother to a rehab center, and his younger brother, Ollie, to a foster home. Now his mother is getting out and he wants to re-create a family. Does his control extend that far or is control an AO illusion?
RECOMMENDATION: You may not immediately understand what the author intends in this strangely disjointed book, but he will make you feel an incredible sadness by his implication that even today children of alcoholics have been robbed of their childhoods because they have reversed roles with their parents. The title, *No Kidding*, has this secondary, literal meaning. Sam tells his mother, "This *is* a childhood. How do you think it feels to have everybody telling you you're pitiful, when you're just living?" And what a high price the two have to pay for their love to work for at least themselves! M.T.

AUTHOR: **Brock Cole**
TITLE: *The Goats (1987)*
DESCRIPTION: A boy and a girl are this year's camp goats, stripped by the others and left on an island for the night. They decide that they will never go back to the camp and so they escape, for three days eluding the defensive camp officials and the girl's worried mother, and for three days discovering that their "socially retarded" selves have great dignity and integrity. They emerge as Howie and Laura, perhaps not so socially retarded after all.
RECOMMENDATION: You may think, "Yuck! How could a book about such a horrid prank be anything but horrid itself," but Brock Cole's first novel is surprisingly tender and sensitive, with some intriguing scenes— particularly when the boy and girl are taken under the wings of some black

inner city kids at another camp and when they realize that what they do affects others. For them the essence of personhood is that connectedness. Cole, however, does not live up to the promise of this book in *Celine*, which seems to pander to our negative media environment. E.T., M.T.

Robert Cormier, though he is very controversial in the young-adult literature field, is thought by many critics to be its finest writer. He certainly succeeds in getting you to care about his characters. He has said that teens write to him with two messages: (1) Please change your endings to happy ones since writers have the power to do that, and (2) You have created characters like us. What would you ask or tell Cormier if you had the chance? Do you wonder if his unremitting nihilism (there is no meaning or purpose to life, even in the noblest resistance to the evil around us) is truly realistic, truly the way the world is? Is there never any triumph of good? Is suffering never redemptive or worth it for a good cause? Is every person like Archie or Obie or Jerry or Adam or Kate?

AUTHOR: **Robert Cormier**
TITLE: *After the First Death (1979)*
DESCRIPTION: Three teenagers—Miro, the terrorist-kidnapper who must kill his first victim; Kate, the substitute driver of the bus full of day-camp children; and Ben, the son of the general in charge of the secret rescue unit—must all face death one summer day on a bridge in New England.
RECOMMENDATION: Like all of Cormier's books, this one, too, has an ending of shattering despair, but the context surrounding the terrorist incident in which he explores the notion that innocence can cause evil seems better to justify the inevitable end. Cormier says that though he would love to write happy endings, realism must deny them. Do you agree? M.T., L.T.

AUTHOR: **Robert Cormier**
TITLE: *Beyond the Chocolate War (1985)*
DESCRIPTION: When Obie's single-minded devotion to the Vigils is divided by his passion for Laura Gundarson, he sees himself as only another of Archie Costello's victims. He plots revenge on Archie by using a new student's homemade guillotine but instead finds himself confronting Archie's evil in himself.
RECOMMENDATION: The individual's ability to freely choose good instead of evil is Cormier's theme in this devastating sequel to *The Chocolate War*, but do you think that it rings true in the purposeless,

totally-depraved characters he has created at Trinity School? How can they choose good, and what will it mean if they do? Other questions may occur to you: Is Jerry strong enough to return to school? Is Goober a good enough friend to support Jerry? And is Obie really just another face of Archie? M.T., L.T.

AUTHOR: **Robert Cormier**
TITLE: *The Bumblebee Flies Anyway (1983)*
DESCRIPTION: Barney doesn't recall volunteering for these frightening experiments on his memory at The Complex, but he does cling to the fact that he is different from the terminally ill teens around who are also receiving experimental treatments. To defeat the boredom of hospital routine; to give excitement to Billy, Allie, and Mazzo; and to win the admiration of Cassie, Mazzo's beautiful twin, Barney builds "The Bumble-bee." Determined to give it one flight, he learns that the act of building has been everything, his one gesture of defiant authenticity in a world of despair.
RECOMMENDATION: You'll want to cheer for Barney when he breaks out of his emotional compartment to touch the people around him. Like Cassie, you realize that he is one of the good guys. Yet you'll want to rage at The Handyman who gives him the mind-altering drugs, and at the fatalistic circumstances that make life "turn out lousy all the time," and that turn prayer into "In the Name of The Tempo and the Rhythm . . ." M.T., L.T.

AUTHOR: **Robert Cormier**
TITLE: *The Chocolate War (1974)*
DESCRIPTION: Though he just wants to fit in, play football, and forget his mother's death, Jerry Renault nevertheless refuses to sell chocolates to raise money for Trinity, his Catholic prep school, defying the cruel clique that controls the place. In so doing he has disturbed the universe as the poster in his locker had dared him to. Ultimately, though, he pays a staggering price to confirm the Vigils' creed: that everyone is cruel and greedy; that everyone is either a victim or a victimizer.
RECOMMENDATION: Everyone at Trinity is evil to the core, including the Brother-teachers. Everyone is either a delighted victimizer or frightened victim whose very status contributes to the victory of evil. This book that vaulted Cormier to fame can be described as "nihilistic," because there is no meaning even to the seemingly "good" acts of Jerry and Brother Jacques and Goober. Cormier says students tell him all the time that what

he writes is mild in comparison to what goes on in their schools. How does Jerry's experience at Trinity compare to your school? M.T., L.T.

AUTHOR: **Robert Cormier**
TITLE: *I Am the Cheese (1977)*
DESCRIPTION: Under interrogation and without his medication, Adam Farmer begins to put pieces of his strange childhood together, but those pieces lead him to the horrible truth about his loving family and his own identity—"I am the cheese."
RECOMMENDATION: Despite the warm scenes between mother and son and father and son, Adam had to face the fact that "he was surrounded by nothingness." Be prepared for yet another Cormier heart-wrenching trip into nihilism. L.T.

AUTHOR: **Margaret Craven**
TITLE: *I Heard the Owl Call My Name (1973)*
DESCRIPTION: When the bishop learns that his young priest, Mark Brian, only has two years to live, he sends Mark, who is ignorant of his condition, to live and work in his most difficult parish, among a vanishing tribe of Kwakiutl Indians in the wilds of British Columbia. There "where death waited behind every tree," his faith had to make a wall to support him as he "made friends with loneliness, death and deprivation"—and with many of the Indians. There also is realized the bishop's desire for Mark to learn so much about life that he not fear death.
RECOMMENDATION: You will find yourself deeply moved by this sensitive yet not sentimental book, and you may want to share it with your family. M.T., L.T.*

AUTHOR: **Clyde Edgerton**
TITLE: *Walking Across Egypt (1987)*
DESCRIPTION: Mattie Rigsbee is slowing down a bit at age 78, but she doesn't want to burden her unmarried son and daughter—in fact, her sense of humor is as good as ever, thank you. What she really wants is to follow her Lord's commandment to "do unto the least of these," including a stray dog and the dogcatcher. Then there is the "very least," the dogcatcher's nephew, Wesley, who might just respond to some good, Southern home cooking and a taste of Sunday school.
RECOMMENDATION: Even teens who don't particularly enjoy reading have loved *Walking Across Egypt* with its natural story-telling style and humor and its deep commitment to homespun, even biblical, values. Be

prepared for the characters' language to fit them, from proper Baptist to juvenile delinquent. M.T., L.T.*

AUTHOR: **Sarah Ellis**
TITLE: *Next-Door Neighbors (1989)*
DESCRIPTION: Peggy must move into the city when her father, a minister, takes a church there. A lie slips out of her lips as she tries to impress the girls at her new school, a lie that only opens the gulf between them. Only the younger Russian refugee son of the church janitor and the old Chinese gardener for the rich widow parishioner seem to accept Peggy as she is. Finally, with George and Sing as next-door neighbors, Peggy finds her own niche, true to her best self.
RECOMMENDATION: You will find Peggy a girl and George a boy whom you wouldn't mind being friends with yourself. E.T.

AUTHOR: **Paul Fleischman**
TITLE: *Rear-View Mirrors (1986)*
DESCRIPTION: Olivia comes east to rural New Hampshire from Berkeley after her high school graduation to continue the ritual of her dead father's annual, daylong, bike trip. Through what she sees along the course, she reflects on her first meeting with him the previous summer. Despite his taunts then about her radical mother's beliefs, she wants to earn the right to be considered worthy of his inheritance.
RECOMMENDATION: Olivia discovers that she is neither like her social activist mother ("I make appointments, therefore I am," ridiculed her father) nor like her recluse father ("No wonder he was worried about death [with] no vision of family and friends keeping his memory alive," she thinks), but is nonetheless firmly connected to both of them. E.T., M.T.

Paula Fox is considered one of America's best writers for young people. Her books are not particularly fast-paced, so reading them rewards patience. Her themes of separation, communication, guilt, and love are all important ones, and her careful, controlled words convey them with power. You will not find her sympathetic to God-given solutions; rather, her characters must work out their own painful choices and thus find their humanity—if it is findable.

AUTHOR: **Paula Fox**
TITLE: *The Slave Dancer (1973)*
DESCRIPTION: Newbery Award, 1974. Jessie is kidnapped from New Orleans onto a slave ship going to Africa to pick up cargo. His job will be to play his flute so that the slaves can dance and therefore get the exercise

they need to stay alive. Though white, he is little more than a slave himself, and through him you can realize secondhand the horrors of slavery.

RECOMMENDATION: This is Paula Fox's most famous and most controversial book. Many feel that it is racist—demeaning to black people—and others think it is among the best books ever written for youth. If you let yourself go into Jessie's life, you may experience some little bit of what it meant to be a slave, and that may change you. Though the book does not have a hopeful ending—Jessie cannot ever listen to music again—ask yourself what hope any slave can have—then or now. E.T., M.T.*

AUTHOR: **Paula Fox**
TITLE: *Lily and the Lost Boy (1987)*
DESCRIPTION: Lily and Paul, 11 and 13, explore the almost idyllic Greek island of Thasos during their father's sabbatical there, enjoying each other's company as well as the natural beauty, the villagers, and the ever-present ancient history and myth, until they meet Jack, another American boy with unimagined freedom to do as he wants. What he wants is to thrill young Greek boys with dangerous bike-rides along the cliffs.

RECOMMENDATION: This book explores the idea that total freedom results in lostness—an important idea in our world where fewer and fewer teens are given limits. However, it is not preachy; you will be caught up in Lily and Paul's vivid experiences. E.T.

AUTHOR: **Paula Fox**
TITLE: *The Moonlight Man (1986)*
DESCRIPTION: Catherine, 15, has long anticipated a vacation with her divorced father, an unreliable alcoholic and witty though failing writer, in an isolated Nova Scotia cottage. During their month together, her daydreams about "dear Papa," the moonlight man, are shattered with the reality of his dreadful binges, yet she must learn to temper her disillusionment with love and hope for happiness.

RECOMMENDATION: As in several of Fox's books, there is a religionless minister who plays a secondary role—this time helping Catherine when her father has passed out in the middle of the night from a drinking binge. Reverend Ross does not speak of his faith to Catherine but does put Christ's love into action for her though her father had thought him superficial and hypocritical. Fox seems to need a religious figure of some sort when she expresses her ideas of guilt and forgiveness and love, but is she just saying here that the only victory people can have is their honest facing up to their own deaths? M.T.

AUTHOR: **Paula Fox**
TITLE: *One-Eyed Cat (1984)*
DESCRIPTION: Newbery Honor, 1985. Ned Wallis, the only child of a village minister and an invalid mother, receives a blowgun for his 11th birthday from his uncle but is forbidden to use it. He disobeys, however, and believes that he shot out the eye of a wild cat. Ned must be freed from the guilt that consumes him and his loving-though-isolated family.
RECOMMENDATION: Paula Fox's recurring themes of isolation, guilt, and love are apparent in this award-winning book. There is not much action, and so it may be hard to get into, but reading it carefully will give you much to think about. It's interesting that Ned can only connect with people when he has confessed his guilt. What do you think about Ned's minister-father's goodness? Does it smother his family or does it help Ned and his mother confess and be welcomed home? E.T.

AUTHOR: **Paula Fox**
TITLE: *The Village By the Sea (1988)*
DESCRIPTION: Ten-year-old Emma must stay at an isolated beach cottage with her Aunt Bea and Uncle Crispin while her father has open-heart surgery. To escape the sharp tongue of her unhappy aunt, Emma flees to the beach where she builds an elaborate miniature village with a newfound companion. Her joy in its creation is dashed by Aunt Bea, but then Emma learns a secret that helps her to forgive her aunt.
RECOMMENDATION: Don't be deceived by Emma's age. The book, like many of Paula Fox's, is deceptively simple but profound. Any teen who wonders how to create (or maintain) love and significance in the middle of anger and humiliation will appreciate Emma's dilemma. Loving support of family, the ability we have to know and create (as God's creatures, though Fox does not say it), and the help that comes from art—all figure into her solution. E.T.

AUTHOR: **Sheila Garrigue**
TITLE: *The Eternal Spring of Mr. Ito (1985)*
DESCRIPTION: Sara had been evacuated from London to Vancouver, British Columbia, to escape the World War II bombings. She is anticipating her cousin's wedding and learning how to care for bonsai plants from the Japanese gardener, when Pearl Harbor is attacked. With death and alienation surrounding her, Sara tends her plants in secret and finds a daring way to help Mr. Ito and his now-interned family.
RECOMMENDATION: The quiet and effective message of this book is that "All over the world people were weeping because of the war—Russian

mothers and Italian wives and Japanese children" (p. 95). Buddhist Mr. Ito goes on to tell Christian Sara that essentially all religions are the same as well, just different roads to the same God. You will have to decide if this message is as persuasive. E.T.

AUTHOR: **Elizabeth Gibson**
TITLE: *The Water is Wide: A Novel of Northern Ireland (1990)*
DESCRIPTION: In 1969 Kate Hamilton is returning to her second year at a new university in Londonderry, Northern Ireland, where she has been studying English literature and seeking fellowship with the Christian Union. But this year all her neat categories of good and bad, religious and secular, are shattered by the escalation of the terrorist and counter-terrorist activities in the Catholic-Protestant conflict and by several new friends, Deidre, Colm, Jack, and Liam. With their help she exorcizes an old nightmare and receives opportunities to share mercy, reconciliation, and love.
RECOMMENDATION: This is a wonderful book whose characters are no paperdoll cutouts but real students whose strengths can be taken to negative extremes and whose weaknesses make them vulnerable. You will soon be inside their skins and making your own their struggles for spiritual maturity in a politically terrifying setting. Their love stories are just a bonus! Gibson has written another novel for Zondervan as well, *Men of Kent*, about two families in a remote setting, caught up in the political and religious strife of the 17th century English Civil War. L.T.*

AUTHOR: **Hannah Green**
TITLE: *I Never Promised You a Rose Garden (1964)*
DESCRIPTION: After a suicide attempt, Deborah Blau, 16, is committed to a mental hospital with the initial diagnosis of schizophrenia. Her own fantasy world—complete with its own name, Yri—is more pleasant by far than the brutal "real" world. But because she is courageous, intelligent, and sensitive, Deborah finds within herself resiliency for the struggle to rejoin that real world where, as she is promised, it's not all a rose garden.
RECOMMENDATION: You will find yourself rooting for Deborah all the way and becoming, thereby, more sensitive to those around you who daily struggle with emotional and mental illnesses. L.T.

AUTHOR: **Joanne Greenberg**
TITLE: *In This Sign (1970)*
DESCRIPTION: Though unequipped to do so, two young deaf people at the home for the handicapped, Abel and Janice, leave the insensitive

institution and make their way into the frightening "normal" world. *In This Sign* tells of their fifty years together and the home they make for their hearing daughter, Margaret, who must become a bridge for them to the hearing, bearing the weight of their tentative successes and painful failures, crossings, and crisscrossings.

RECOMMENDATION: Not only does Greenberg make real for you this little-explored world and touch your heart with a desire to become more loving and more understanding, but she also paints a not very flattering picture of our very ordinary society that too often lacks that love and understanding. L.T.

AUTHOR: **Jean Harmeling**
TITLE: *The Potter of Charles Street (1990)*
DESCRIPTION: As a sixth grader, Eve is not too young to realize that her friendship with Bobby Muscovi is special; that her boy-crazy older sister, Chantel, is seeking happiness the wrong way; and that her father's war injuries have transformed him into a bitter man. After tragedy forces Bobby to leave their seaside town, Eve goes into Boston with Chantel and there meets Mike, a young hippie potter. Across the years, Mike teaches her how to use the potter's wheel and how to find love, a love that frees her to become her true self through losing herself to those who have hurt her.
RECOMMENDATION: Eve's is a tender "first love" story with an ending that may surprise you but will surely satisfy you. It is published by Crossway. E.T., M.T.*

AUTHOR: **Jamake Highwater**
TITLE: *Eyes of Darkness (1985)*
DESCRIPTION: As this story opens, you meet a young Indian doctor who is helpless to prevent the Wounded Knee massacre of his people by the government he works for. How did Alexander East come to be in such a predicament? You recollect with him the nearly golden days of his youth as Hakadah in Minnesota, his days of refugee wanderings in and out of Canada as Yesa, the days of the spiritual training by his wise grandmother, the physical training by his warrior uncle, and the unexpected "resurrection" of his long-thought-dead father who had become a Christian while in federal prison. It is his father who insists that his son get the white man's schooling, and so he becomes Alexander. Caught between conflicting views of the world, Alexander determines to "use the white man's wisdom to keep his Indian heritage alive."
RECOMMENDATION: Though the 19th century Indian way of life is not totally romanticized in this fiction-based-on-fact account—you do see the

Indians warring against each other and getting drunk—the teachings of the spiritually wise grandmother are presented in an attractive form that highlights the bankruptcy of the materialistic whites. Uncheedah had once told Yesa, "You must welcome the person you are becoming instead of wanting to be someone else. Only in that way can you win a place in the world." Yesa was unable to follow this advice and so represents all those people caught between two worlds. M.T.

AUTHOR: **Felice Holman**
TITLE: *Slake's Limbo (1974)*
DESCRIPTION: Aremis Slake was a castaway kid who made a home for himself in a hole in the side of a New York subway station, managing to live there for 121 days until an accident caused him to lose his "nest" and to desire a "resurrection" above ground. Or was it he who caused the events that led to the new Slake?
RECOMMENDATION: This book explores the notions of personhood and chance or determination in a very simple yet layered and powerful story about a haunting boy. Even reluctant readers have been known to value this book. E.T., M.T.

AUTHOR: **Felice Holman**
TITLE: *The Wild Children (1983)*
DESCRIPTION: Twelve-year-old Alex does not live comfortably in post-revolutionary Russia, for no one does. But he does have his family, some food, a tiny room of his own, and a wonderful math teacher on whom he has a crush. One morning his family is taken away like so many others. At his teacher's advice, he heads to Moscow, where he begins a desperate existence in a gang of *bezprizorni*, wild, starving, homeless children who gather in packs, almost like animals. Alex maintains his humanity even as he becomes a thief and a vagrant and a friend to the unlikely group he is forced to live with.
RECOMMENDATION: Always maintaining hope for a better life, Alex will give you hope, too, even as you get angry about such conditions ever existing for children anywhere. E.T., M.T.*

AUTHOR: **Irene Hunt**
TITLE: *Up a Road Slowly (1966)*
DESCRIPTION: At 7, Julie went to live with her spinster schoolteacher aunt and her ne'er-do-well alcoholic uncle because her mother had died. With them and the other country schoolchildren, she begins to walk "up a

road slowly'' toward life in all its joys and sorrows, choosing its wisdom and love.

RECOMMENDATION: Many consider this to be a classic coming-of-age love story. Especially if you are introspective, you may find Julie's growing awareness of her values paralleling your own. E.T., M.T.*

AUTHOR: **Mollie Hunter** (See author overview in the Historical section.)

TITLE: *Cat, Herself (1985)*

DESCRIPTION: Cat is a traveler, the Scottish equivalent of a gypsy, who lives as independently of society as she and her small band can. They are homeless by choice, misunderstood and persecuted by the locals, and victimized sometimes by their own alcoholism as well. Cat is searching for her place within the travelers, or possibly without them, but certainly for her place in God's Creation as she grows to maturity.

RECOMMENDATION: Cat is a typical Mollie Hunter heroine: fiercely independent yet also part of a loving family. She is typical, too, because she represents Hunter's interests in Scotland's rich and varied cultures and history, yet she is not a paper-flat type but a living teen who faces some of the same growing up dilemmas as you. M.T.

AUTHOR: **Bel Kaufman**

TITLE: *Up the Down Staircase (1964)*

DESCRIPTION: This is a hilarious look at a not-so-hilarious subject, the impossible conditions under which students had to learn and teachers had to teach in a large New York City high school a generation ago. Sylvia Barrett is an idealistic and beautiful young teacher of English who drowns in bureaucratic memos, discovers that her students are contending with more than the mysteries of grammar, and who must decide whether she can make any positive difference in their lives.

RECOMMENDATION: You will find yourself comparing this to your own high school experiences. M.T., L.T.

M. E. Kerr is a highly praised author who says she writes of teenage experiences for preteens. Many of her books have received "Notable" commendations from the American Library Association, hailed for their honest, non-preachy way of capturing bittersweet teenage experiences. If love in its many aspects (including the all-pervasive sexual) and money (who has it and who doesn't and what possessions it can buy) are what overwhelm your life, then you may agree that these accolades are deserved. However, if you cannot tell whether Kerr is examining the upper-middle-class hypocrisies concerning love and money with a critical eye, or if she has really bought into the materialistic life (with a dash of churchiness thrown in to guarantee social status) and is just recording it as she sees and believes it, then you may have severe reservations about the value and honesty of her stories.

AUTHOR: **M. E. Kerr**
TITLE: *If I Love You, Am I Trapped Forever? (1973)*
DESCRIPTION: Alan Bennett thinks he's the hottest thing going at his high school and has a steady, Leah, to prove it. Yet along comes balding, bespectacled, half-Jewish Duncan Stein, who preaches the doctrine of one-date relationships, to prove him wrong.
RECOMMENDATION: No one around Alan—his parents, Duncan's parents, his teachers—seems to be able to keep commitments, so why is it that the boy who was in for the short haul—Duncan—gets the girl for keeps, while Alan, who wants permanency—well, at least a steady for his senior year—is left alone fantasizing about someone else's mother? Do you think Alan, the future writer, succeeds in doing what he says that writers must do—understand people enough to "get through to the real facts"? M.T.

AUTHOR: **M. E. Kerr**
TITLE: *Love Is a Missing Person (1975)*
DESCRIPTION: Suzy Slade, 15-year-old daughter of wealthy, divorced parents, thinks the romance of her black friends, Nan and Roger, sets the standard for love; thinks librarian Miss Gwendolyn Spring's off-limits erotica collection and her friendship are significant; and thinks her sister Chicago is lucky for getting to choose how she wants to live. But then Chicago, in an act of pseudo-liberal defiance, steals a picture from the collection and runs off with Roger, while Miss Spring's old World War II heartthrob shows up just to use her, so Suzy is more confused than ever about what love really is.
RECOMMENDATION: Is this book's hollowness just an accurate reflection of the hollowness of the affluent uncommitted lifestyle it depicts, or is it because the author did not write with a moral weight equal to its subject matter? For example, when Suzy asks Miss Spring for a definition of right and wrong, the librarian tells her, "Someone said that right is what you feel good after and wrong is what you feel bad after." M.T.

AUTHOR: **M. E. Kerr**
TITLE: *Gentlehands (1978)*

DESCRIPTION: Buddy falls for a rich summer girl, Skye Pennington. Therefore, he feels he needs quick lessons in sophistication that his local-policeman-and-housewife family cannot provide. He brings Skye to meet his German immigrant grandfather, long estranged from his mother. There they get well-cooked meals, opera on tape, and lessons in wildflower and bird identification—culture on every hand. Soon, however, a journalist hanger-on at the Pennington's beach home reveals that he's looking for a Nazi death camp guard. Could it be Buddy's grandfather?

RECOMMENDATION: *Gentlehands,* which broadens Kerr's typical subject matter of boy-meets-rich-girl to include Nazi Germany, may leave a nagging question in your mind: Why would Buddy's grandfather tell him during one of his lessons on the good life that ''Once you know something is wrong, you're responsible, whether you see it, or hear about it, and most particularly when you're part of it,'' and yet not seem to take his own advice? After all, he seems to be aware that his death-camp murdering was wrong. If the answer is as Skye (unwittingly—she never says anything deliberately intelligent) quotes: ''An answer is always a form of death,'' then isn't there the strong implication that their materialistic way of life is spiritually dead? Is Kerr's irony only unwitting as well? M.T.

AUTHOR: **Daniel Keyes**
TITLE: ***Flowers for Algernon (1966)***
DESCRIPTION: Keyes expanded into this full-length book his moving short story about a young retarded man who is operated on to increase his intelligence but, like the experimental mouse before him, all too soon loses what he has so longed for. The book also explores Charlie's previously suppressed memories of his difficult childhood and his desires for a normal emotional and sexual life as well.

RECOMMENDATION: What you will find so powerful about Charlie's story is that it is all written by him, from his first stumbling attempts at English to his masterful insights that surpass even his experimenters' and then poignantly back again—for Charlie, unlike Algernon, realizes what he is losing. If you can find the short story in a collection somewhere, you will probably like it even better than the book. L.T.

AUTHOR: **Madeleine L'Engle** (See author overview in the Fantasy section.)
TITLE: ***Meet the Austins (1960)***
DESCRIPTION: First in the Austin Family series (which, like the Times Quartet, grows increasingly complex). A country doctor, his wife, and four

children must accept the death of a family friend and the intrusion of a disturbed orphan into their happy family. E.T.*

AUTHOR: **Madeleine L'Engle**
TITLE: *Moon by Night (1963)*
DESCRIPTION: Second in the Austin series. The Austins, minus orphan Maggy, take a cross-country camping trip. Fourteen-year-old Vicky meets two boys, Zachary and Andy. Zachary leads her into physical danger during an earthquake, when they question the goodness of God to allow such a natural disaster and they compare it to the man-made one that engulfed Anne Frank. E.T.*

AUTHOR: **Madeleine L'Engle**
TITLE: *The Young Unicorns (1968)*
DESCRIPTION: Third in the Austin series. The Austins have moved to New York for their father to do research on medical uses of the laser. There they meet a piano prodigy (blinded by that laser), a bitter former gang member, and various characters associated with the great cathedral of St. John the Divine. Has the evil so pervaded the city, as the Bishop seems to have decided, that people need help choosing good? Free choice and the redeeming qualities of music overcome the threat to the Austins and New York. E.T., M.T.*

AUTHOR: **Madeleine L'Engle**
TITLE: *A Ring of Endless Light (1980)*
DESCRIPTION: Fourth in the Austin series. Newbery Honor, 1980. Vicky's story continues the following summer. Her minister grandfather is dying; thoughtless, suicidal Zachary reappears, causing the death of a family friend who rescued him; she meets Adam who needs her to help in his experiment with dolphins and grieves over the serious accident of his boss. Death is everywhere, and Vicky must decide if eternity is, indeed—as her grandfather's favorite poet declared—"a great ring of pure and endless light," or if God is just a "deep and dazzling darkness." In typical L'Engle style she receives the help she needs from literature and nature as well as people. E.T., M.T.*

AUTHOR: **Madeleine L'Engle**
TITLE: *Arm of a Starfish (1965)*
DESCRIPTION: First in a quartet about Meg Murry and Calvin O'Keefe's daughter, Polyhymnia. 12-year-old Poly is kidnapped while under the care of marine biology student, Adam Eddington, by people who want the

results of her father's experiments in regeneration of starfish. Adam must decide between beautiful Kali and the kidnappers or the O'Keefes and their Embassy friend, Joshua, just who has the best interests of America at heart. His choice does not come in time to save Joshua but in time to understand that even enemies are under the care of a loving Father. M.T.*

AUTHOR: **Madeleine L'Engle**
TITLE: *Dragons in the Waters (1976)*
DESCRIPTION: Second in the O'Keefe series. Poly, Charles, and their father are traveling to Venezuela on a freighter to see what can be done there about the spreading pollution. They meet 13-year-old Simon Renier who, with a distant cousin, is returning a family heirloom portrait of Bolivar to a museum. When the cousin is killed and the portrait is stolen, Poly, Charles, and Simon must dig deeply into Simon's link with the Quinzano Indians. Their seemingly small battle to preserve the Quinzano's environment, to absolve Simon of his idolatrous illusions about his ancestors, and solve the mystery have cosmic implications. M.T.*

AUTHOR: **Madeleine L'Engle**
TITLE: *A House Like a Lotus (1984)*
DESCRIPTION: Third in the O'Keefe series. The title is from the Hindu scriptures, the Upanishads. Poly is now 16, a brilliant misfit in her regional high school, who blossoms under the tutelage of dying lesbian Maximiliana Horne. Max has arranged for Poly to be a gofer at a conference on Crete, but just before she is to leave, Max makes a drunken pass at her. Destroyed by her fallen idol, Poly assuages her pain in the arms of her boyfriend. However, healing and forgiveness are not hers until after she encounters troubled Zachary (*Moon* and *Ring*) in Athens, and the innocent friendship of a married Polynesian delegate in Crete, and finds refuge in the monastery and music of the conference.
RECOMMENDATION: Though many of the themes and eclectic philosophical conversations resemble L'Engle's other books, Poly's insistence that her sexual encounter with her shamed boyfriend was wonderful betrays a wavering from biblical truth. Even by secular standards, how her boyfriend took advantage of Poly would be called date rape or sexual abuse. Perhaps L'Engle's warning not to idolize others can be applied to herself in this instance! M.T., L.T.

AUTHOR: **Madeleine L'Engle**
TITLE: *An Acceptable Time (1989)*

DESCRIPTION: L'Engle's "realistic" Poly O'Keefe stories and her "fantasy" Murry ones merge in this sequel to both series. See annotation with her fantasy titles. M.T., L.T.

AUTHOR: **Ursula LeGuin**
TITLE: *Very Far Away from Anything Else (1976)*
DESCRIPTION: Owen and Natalie, both misfits in the high school scene, he—because he's compelled by science and she—because she's devoted to classical music, discover each other and also discover that what their culture sells as love isn't really love after all. Best of all, they discover it before it is too late to remain committed to the ideals of their friendship.
RECOMMENDATION: This slim book, written in LeGuin's unmistakable style, says without preaching that our culture is selling us a lie when it proclaims on every side that sex is the most important ingredient in a relationship. M.T.

AUTHOR: **William Lederer and Eugene Burdick**
TITLE: *The Ugly American (1958)*
DESCRIPTION: In this pre-Vietnam collection of short stories loosely woven into a novel about the Americans who live and work in the imaginary Southeast Asian country of Sarkhan, Lederer and Burdick have sought to expose the mistaken attitudes that have guided American foreign service. Unlike the Russians, recruits were not required to learn the language of their country, they lived in luxury apart from the people they were meant to serve, and they often worked on projects having nothing to do with the needs of the natives.
RECOMMENDATION: Does what you know about our foreign policy since the late '50s lead you to believe that significant changes have taken place, or are we still making the same mistakes? L.T.

AUTHOR: **Robert Lipsite**
TITLE: *The Contender (1967)*
DESCRIPTION: A dropout on the edge of involvement in ghetto drugs and despair, Alfred impulsively joins a boxing gym and discovers the inner discipline that he needs to choose what is best for his future.
RECOMMENDATION: Though realistic in its dialogue and the violence it depicts, this book is hopeful at the same time. The physical action parallels the moral crises of the book well. E.T., M.T.

Margaret Mahy, a New Zealander, has taken the young-adult literature world by storm, winning two Carnegie Medals (the British equivalent of the

Newbery) in the 1980s. Part of her fascination is her ability to create eccentric characters who talk about off-the-wall, intriguing ideas. Part, too, is her matter-of-fact portrayal of the supernatural (occult) world side by side with the ordinary routines of daily life. Spooky! Though many, even most, of her characters make what Christians would consider right or good choices, they do not do so for Christian reasons. Though Mahy is not preoccupied with sex, which is casually accepted as part of teenage life, nearly all of her characters are changing over from "innocent" childhood to knowledgeable adulthood through some sort of sexual initiation. But is it true that sex makes us knowing, grown up? (Other books of hers are listed under "Mystery.")

AUTHOR: **Margaret Mahy**
TITLE: *The Catalogue of the Universe (1986)*
DESCRIPTION: Angela, the beautiful illegitimate daughter of loving Dido, is searching for her father. Tycho, short, ugly, and stuffed full of scientific and philosophical tidbits, is searching for Angela's love and the meaning of life. Events, "the stuff of the world," according to Tycho, force both of them to take great leaps of faith to find in each other the happiness they know is not guaranteed by the universe, for happiness is, after all, not even mentioned in The Catalogue of the Universe, the book Angela gave to Tycho.
RECOMMENDATION: The scientific and philosophical references here are reminiscent of L'Engle's (though without the theological ones), yet somehow the way Mahy plays with them is more deliberately clever. If you're laughing, maybe the implications of the despair built into a universe without God won't hurt so much. Tycho and Angela do create meaning for themselves by their love for each other, both emotional and physical, though they know others' loves have not lasted. The plays on words and ideas are fascinating, the philosophy brave but inadequate. M.T., L.T.

AUTHOR: **Margaret Mahy**
TITLE: *Memory (1988)*
DESCRIPTION: Nineteen-year-old Jonny Dart, plagued by guilt and his vivid memory of his sister Janine's death five years before, searches for the only other witness to the accident—Bonny, her best friend. Instead, he finds Sophie, a senile, dirty, memoryless old woman. In helping her, Jonny discovers some truth about the death, friendship, and himself.
RECOMMENDATION: To become part of Jonny's story is to get inside the skin of a sensitive existentialist who, in the surrealistic setting of a senile woman's filthy home, must come to grips with life, love, death, and guilt.

The story itself is compelling, as are the array of characters. Jonny makes brave and good choices at almost every turn, yet his journey toward goodness and forgiveness stops tantalizingly short of its destination. M.T., L.T.

AUTHOR: **Catherine Marshall**
TITLE: *Christy (1967)*
DESCRIPTION: Christy Huddleston, a sheltered 19-year-old girl seeking "life piled on life" comes to the mountains of Cutter Gap, Tennessee, in 1912 to teach school for the American Inland Mission. It's life she finds, but life in its rawest forms—poverty, disease, ignorance, revenge shootings, drunkenness—enough to disillusion the most idealistic and shake the faith of the most genteelly religious of girls. But she also finds among the people and her co-workers deep longings for beauty and truth, steadfast loyalty, and self-sacrificial love, all coming to a head during a typhoid epidemic.
RECOMMENDATION: Marshall wrote this story based on her mother's first year in the Smoky Mountain Mission. It truly teems with life, the "life piled on life" that Christy found because she gave hers away. Fairlight, Opal and Tom, Bird's Eye, Lundy, David, Miss Alice, and Dr. Neil all will become your friends, too, on this marvelous adventure of faith. If you liked *Christy*, you will probably also enjoy *Julie* by Marshall. M.T., L.T.*

AUTHOR: **Harry Mazer**
TITLE: *The Girl of His Dreams (1987)*
DESCRIPTION: In what the flyleaf calls an "urban fairy tale—a realistic story with a happy ending," Willis Pierce has put the pain of Villa Street (*The War on Villa Street*) behind him, living on his own in a university town, working at a factory, running, wondering if life is more than "work and sleep and eat and eat some more." Then he meets Sophie, the newsstand girl who has just moved into town from her brother's farm. Though she's not the beauty queen type the guys at the plant go out with and that he sometimes dreams of, they strike up a friendship. Despite bumps and setbacks, it is strong enough to help Willis realize his improbable dream of running against Aaron Hill, the college all-star, and to bring Sophie back off the farm for good.
RECOMMENDATION: As either an urban fairy tale or as a romance (Mazer's classification), this book is surely more honest than the typical young adult fare. You will no doubt find both Willis and Sophie appealing. As in most love stories written for teens, sex is a given (though Willis and Sophie come to it more cautiously than, say, M.E. Kerr's characters).

Though they find sex is not enough to keep them together, they don't give up on each other until they find out what can give their love a surer basis. Compare this to Le Guin's *Very Far Away from Anything Else* where the teens make this discovery in time to maintain their purity. L.T.

AUTHOR: **Harry Mazer**
TITLE: *The Last Mission (1979)*
DESCRIPTION: Jack Raab is 15 in 1944 when he sneaks his brother's birth certificate and enlists in the Air Corps in order to fulfill his daydream of killing Hitler, who had killed all the Jews, his people. He quickly discovers that war isn't as glamorous as he had thought, but still he and his bomber crew complete 25 missions unscathed. In late April 1945, with rumors of the war's end circulating, they make an unusual run over Czechoslovakia and are hit. Jack survives to be taken prisoner by the retreating Germans.
RECOMMENDATION: While not as profound as *No Hero for the Kaiser*, also about a too-young boy in combat, *The Last Mission* has a high degree of adventure and a standard anti-war theme. There is a sprinkling of the predictable barracks language as well as a sense of naiveté that clings to Jack all through his incredible experiences, based on Mazer's own. E.T., M.T.

AUTHOR: **Elva McAllaster**
TITLE: *Strettam (1972, out of print)*
DESCRIPTION: Strettam is an ordinary—very ordinary—small American town off Highway 37. Nevertheless, the Seven Deadlies are seeking the allegiance of Strettam's very ordinary citizens and people just like you. The battle is petty and at the same time cosmic; McAllaster's writing about it is cutting and insightful. Though sin is exposed as you may perhaps have never thought of it, hope is not far distant.
RECOMMENDATION: It may take you a bit of effort to get into this book, but once you do you will not be able to put it down. (If you can find it, that is, because unfortunately it is out of print. It was published by Zondervan. Try the inter-library loan at your public library or the shelves of your church library.) It invites comparison to two other books you have probably heard of, *This Present Darkness* by Frank Peretti and *Screwtape Letters* by C. S. Lewis. Which of the small town American battles seems more genuine to you? More likely? In which are the people more responsible for their actions? Peretti's or McAllaster's? Let *Strettam* lead you to *Screwtape Letters* if you have not already read it. L.T.*

AUTHOR: **Lucy Maud Montgomery**
TITLE: *Anne of Green Gables (1908)*
DESCRIPTION: No girl, or for that matter, no boy should grow up without meeting Anne Shirley, the carrot-haired, imaginative, accident-prone, talkative orphan who wins over the hearts of a spinster sister and bachelor brother, Marilla and Matthew, who run a small farm outside Avonlea on Prince Edward Island. They'd hoped to get a boy to help them but instead take in Anne, who was sent to them by mistake. Avonlea, as Diana and Gilbert can testify, was never the same afterward.
RECOMMENDATION: You'll be glad to know that many other books follow in the series that takes Anne's story right through her children's life. And if you still do not tire of these genuine PEI folks, Montgomery has also written the Emily of New Moon series. E.T., M.T.*

AUTHOR: **Walter Dean Myers**
TITLE: *Fallen Angels (1988)*
DESCRIPTION: Richie Perry is only 17 when he leaves Harlem for the army and is sent to Vietnam. He and the other soldiers have a lot of learning and growing and figuring out to do: Why are they in Vietnam? Are they ready to die? Will they become such different people by their devastating experiences that they won't know themselves when they get back to the world? Are the Vietnamese human like themselves? In fact, to the Army, are the blacks fully human?
RECOMMENDATION: You may be shocked by the raw, Army vocabulary, but it probably was impossible for Myers to write this account (in memory of his brother who died in Vietnam in 1968) accurately with cleaned-up language. Through it all you will feel compassion for young—very young—men struggling to maintain their dignity and integrity, and, for one of the bunkmates at least, his faith, in the complex circumstances of a war that they had not been prepared to understand. M.T., L.T.

AUTHOR: **Zibby O'Neal**
TITLE: *In Summer Light (1980)*
DESCRIPTION: Kate must spend the summer at her island home to recover from mono and therefore must confront her ambivalent feelings about her famous and domineering artist-father. It is Ian, a graduate student cataloging her father's work for a museum show, who helps her to value her own loving self and her artistic ability as well as to achieve a reconciliation with her father.

RECOMMENDATION: The paper that Kate is writing on Shakespeare's *The Tempest* provides an effective backdrop to the themes of love and forgiveness that O'Neal touches on so lightly. E.T., M.T.

Katherine Paterson is a prolific and much-honored writer of both historical fiction and "realistic" novels for preteens and their older brothers and sisters. Brought up on the mission field in China and having returned to Japan to work in Christian education as an adult, Paterson brings a Christian vision to bear on her fiction, from novels about gospel singers to members of a 19th-century political-religious sect. But that does not mean that everything works out "happily ever after" for her characters, nor that her most overtly religious characters are especially attractive. In fact, she tells about a professor who once told her that he doubted that a writer could describe the Christian experience effectively except by fantasy or science fiction (*Gates of Excellence*, 60). Family relationships for Paterson remain the most problematic; it is in the family scene that redemption can be found but also where separation and lack of communication bring the most pain. Nevertheless, she always holds out lifelines of hope to her readers, declaring that she will "not write a book that closes in despair" (*Gates*, 38). See titles under Historical Fiction as well.

AUTHOR: **Katherine Paterson**
TITLE: *Angels and Other Strangers (1979)*
DESCRIPTION: Even if your family no longer reads aloud together, demand that they include a story or two from this wonderful collection as part of your Christmas rituals. You will find your own understanding of the Christ-event enriched as "Woodrow Kennington Works Practically a Miracle" to coax his bratty sister back into the circle of his family's love; or as lonely Japanese Pastor Nagai, considered a traitor to his country during World War II for worshiping the Westerners' God, holds a Christmas Eve service for two "guests," one a beggar girl and the other a spying policeman; or as black Jacob looms out of a snowstorm to become a fearsome angel to Julia and her tiny children, stranded on an errand she feared would ruin the perfect Christmas she had planned.
RECOMMENDATION: Paterson wrote these nine stories to be read aloud during the Christmas Eve service of the Presbyterian church her husband pastored. With little Elizabeth, finally assured that she hadn't killed her 3-day-old brother and that Jesus did love her, you'll find yourself saying, "Happy Birthday, Jesus, and many happy returns of the day." A.A.*

AUTHOR: **Katherine Paterson**
TITLE: *Bridge to Terabithia (1978)*
DESCRIPTION: Newbery Award, 1978. Jesse was, in his own words, "a stupid, weird little kid who drew funny pictures and chased around a cowfield trying to act big" when Leslie Burke arrived in his country school. Together these improbable friends create a secret kingdom, Terabithia, with which Leslie tries "to push back the walls of his mind and make him see beyond to the shining world—huge and terrible and beautiful and very fragile." A tragedy precipitates Jesse's and Leslie's premature "moving out" from their Terabithia.
RECOMMENDATION: If you enter into Jesse's experience, as Paterson allows you to do, the walls of your mind will be pushed back as well to see the shining world both terrible and beautiful. You will rejoice and you will mourn and you, too, will move out beyond. Be glad, however, that Paterson doesn't ask you to make an either/or choice about her story, which she seems to be suggesting that Jesse and Leslie have to make about the Easter story: a hated truth or a beautiful myth. E.T.*

AUTHOR: **Katherine Paterson**
TITLE: *The Great Gilly Hopkins (1978)*
DESCRIPTION: "God help the children of the flower children," Gilly Hopkins' social worker sighed when gutsy Gilly had gotten herself into her biggest fix yet. Abandoned by her mother years before, shuttled from one foster home to the next, she had now landed with hippo-sized Maime Trotter, scared William Ernest, and their blind and black neighbor, Mr. Randolph. Determined to outwit both them and cool Ms. Harris, her new school teacher, Gilly finds herself being made soft by their unconditional love, when toughness was what she needed for survival. However, when her "softness" was strong enough to withstand a broken heart, she set forth once more to be "Galadriel Hopkins, come into her own."
RECOMMENDATION: There isn't a caricature among this odd mix of characters, and you will come to love them all as you share in their pain and triumphs. E.T.*

AUTHOR: **Katherine Paterson**
TITLE: *Jacob Have I Loved (1981)*
DESCRIPTION: Newbery Award, 1981. Louise is the elder and less favored twin of fragile, musically gifted Caroline. Isolated on a small island in the Chesapeake Bay, where the villagers wrest a living from crab and oyster fishing and where educational opportunities are limited and a wrathful Methodism seems to dominate, Louise watches her sister gain

favors from everyone she cares about—the only good teacher, the mysterious Captain Wallace who returned to Rass after a 30-year absence, and steady Call who has crabbed with her until World War II takes him away. How Louise slowly decides to root out her own bitter spirit and choose a good life for herself—off the island—is the climax to this story.

RECOMMENDATION: "Jacob have I loved, but Esau have I hated," bitter, Bible-spouting Grandma whispers to Louise, and Louise believes she is the God-hated elder Esau. Whether her own hardened heart has prevented her from hearing it or whether it was never emphasized, teenaged Louise cannot seem to respond to the grace of God that Caroline sang about in the folk-carol, "I Wonder as I Wander." Ultimately that grace triumphs as Louise chooses not to become what her vindictive (crazy?) grandmother is, but in so doing she must slough off the shell of self and of Rass Island. You will rejoice in her final choice but be saddened that she earlier missed so many opportunities for redemption. M.T.

AUTHOR: **Katherine Paterson**
TITLE: *Park's Quest (1988)*
DESCRIPTION: Though 11-year-old Park lives in a fantasy world of knights in shining armor, questing for the Holy Grail, a real-life quest overwhelms his dreams: He wants to find out about his father who died in the Vietnam war, but his mother is not talking. Reading his father's books, sneaking away to the Memorial in Washington, D.C., and finally spending two weeks at his father's boyhood farm where he meets his grandfather (who cannot speak due to a stroke), his Uncle Frank, and a Vietnamese girl named Thanh, are all paths he must travel to successfully complete the quest and drink from the cup of Holy Grail.
RECOMMENDATION: Even if Park's acceptance of the circumstances of his father's death and his mother's sorrow seems a little too easy, you will nonetheless acknowledge with him that truth has begun to make him free. The blending of the Arthurian legend with the realities of a boy in a single-parent home is especially meaningful. E.T.

AUTHOR: **Gary Paulsen** (See author overview in Adventure section.)
TITLE: *The Island (1988)*
DESCRIPTION: Wil's parents move him abruptly from Madison, Wisconsin to a tiny town far north. At first he is disgruntled, but soon, out exploring, he comes on an island, where he begins to feel a harmony with the herons and frogs he observes. He also feels an obsessive thirst to know about the creatures of the island and himself, so he camps out there. His parents, the

shrink they send after him, the town bully, its nicest girl, and finally the media all succeed in varying degrees to figure out Wil as he tries to figure out his world.

RECOMMENDATION: Paulsen explores his theme about oneness with the natural world once again in this beautiful story about a boy's self-imposed exile that is really a journey for understanding. However, the flaws in Wil's pantheism (surely it is also Paulsen's) are most apparent here, as well as its great emotional appeal to those who are sensitive to the natural world. When Wil becomes the predator turtle as he attacks Ray, he knows that somehow he is wrong but has no basis for saying that—everything in nature just is; nature has no moral code. Wil, as a moral boy, has appealed to a standard outside of nature, outside of the All. If you have felt a great thirst to learn, you will also be fascinated by Paulsen's ideas about how we learn, how we can know (in several ways), and how the various arts help us know. E.T., M.T.

Richard Peck has told an interviewer that he believes teens want "supernatural powers, escape, all kinds of strange romance and . . . 'gore'." It's hard to put all his books together—the slapstick humor of the Blossom ones in which the supernatural—that is, ghosts—comes in for its share of spoofing, and the "realistic" novels that explore the pain of teens' lonely predicaments. (See titles under both Contemporary and Fantasy categories.) He wants to give you what he thinks you want. Is it? And it is enough?

AUTHOR: **Richard Peck**
TITLE: *Remembering the Good Times (1985)*
DESCRIPTION: Buck, Kate, and Trav have an unusual friendship that crosses the cliques of junior and senior high school, but it is not strong enough to save the driven Trav from self-destruction.
RECOMMENDATION: Peck's portraits of contemporary junior and senior high school ring true but at times verge on stereotypes. Kate's great-grandmother puts her finger on the hollowness of the community's "community" after Trav's death, but is diagnosis enough? Trav had said time and again that there are no solutions to life's problems. The book begins with a birth and ends with death—and you will ache for Buck and Kate who have nothing but the good times to remember. M.T.

AUTHOR: **Richard Peck**
TITLE: *Father Figure (1978)*

DESCRIPTION: Jim must give up his role as a father figure for his 8-year-old brother, Byron, after their mother's suicide, when their grandmother sends them to their father, who had walked out on them years ago.

RECOMMENDATION: Since Jim must contend with his mother's suicide, his brother's mugging, and falling in love with his father's girlfriend, you can imagine that this book is filled with pain and with unanswered questions. The closest Jim can get to comfort at his mother's funeral is a quote from "Sampson Agonistes" about noble death from a "yellow-pages" minister who didn't know she'd committed suicide. However, what you must determine is if Peck has painted an honest picture of what these experiences might mean for someone who doesn't believe in God. M.T., L.T.

AUTHOR: **Robert Newton Peck**
TITLE: *A Day No Pigs Would Die (1972)*
DESCRIPTION: Rob was a 12-year-old boy in April when he cut school, helped his neighbor's distressed cow give birth, and got mauled in the process. He was a man a year later, the day no pigs would die, after he had raised the newborn pig he had received as a thank-you from the neighbor, absorbed from his taciturn pig-butchering Shaker father not only the bone-deep values of hard work but also hard faith, had a joyous day at the Rutland Fair, and made the sacrifice necessary for manhood, "just doing what's got to be done."

RECOMMENDATION: This book may stir you like no other father-son book has. Rob's father, who cannot read or write and has difficulty expressing his profound love for his son, nevertheless has built so much of his deep faith in God and in his Vermont land into Rob that you will be richer for having met them both. E.T.

K. M. Peyton's subject—and her strength—is people, whether it is their emotional dilemmas in growing up or their opportunity to shape history. "Everything's about people in the end," Pennington told Marion. Because God at least figures into her characters' lives, if only on the edges and with little power (even miracles are brought about by people), her books are more deistic than merely humanistic. Perhaps that's what allows her very real characters to retain their hope and dignity.

AUTHOR: **K. M. Peyton**
TITLE: *Pennington's Last Term (1971)*
DESCRIPTION: In this first of the Pennington series, we meet 17-year-old Penn, whose awesome temper is often triggered by the hypocrisies of his

schoolteachers and whose awesome musical ability is developed by his shrewd music master.

RECOMMENDATION: Though the schoolmasters may seem exaggerated, Pennington's own intriguing contradictions keep the book from stereotypes. M.T.

AUTHOR: **K. M. Peyton**
TITLE: *The Beethoven Medal (1972)*
DESCRIPTION: Ordinary yet determined, Ruth falls hard for enigmatic, moody, talented Patrick Pennington. She experiences the heights and depths of life, learning as in Beethoven's "Moonlight Sonata," that "nothing is pure moonlight." Penn himself, as a person and as a pianist, becomes more disciplined through her love for him.

RECOMMENDATION: Better than the first volume, especially if you like music. M.T.

AUTHOR: **K. M. Peyton**
TITLE: *Pennington's Heir (1973)*
DESCRIPTION: Pat and Ruth get married because they are going to have a baby. Their first year together as a family struggling to survive as Pat tries to break into the musical world is chronicled in this honest, loving book to which music provides a rich counterpoint.

RECOMMENDATION: Watching Pat and Ruth realize what commitment they have made is satisfying even though—or maybe *because* it happens so infrequently in our world—they started out with two strikes against them caused by their initial sexual encounter. M.T., L.T.

AUTHOR: **K. M. Peyton**
TITLE: *Marion's Angels (1979)*
DESCRIPTION: Lonely Marion inherits from her dead mother, a history buff, her intense love for the local medieval church and its twelve carved angels. When her prayer for a rich American to help save it from destruction is miraculously answered, she learns that miracles are "never simple . . . inevitably causing repercussions"; these for Patrick Pennington, whose concerts help raise the restoration fund; for Ruth, who feels left out of Pat's musical life; and for Marion's lonely widower father, Geoff.

RECOMMENDATION: The Pennington books are among the most refreshing, honest recreations of first love, especially in their exploration of the lovers' realization of their many-sided personalities and of the growth the commitment fosters. And if you like music, they are extra-special. However, in the last book in which Pat and Ruth are only minor characters pulled into Marion's miracle, the whole series is deepened. With Marion you will wonder when coincidences edge over into miracles and whether miracles can be manipulated. But you may wonder also, as she does not, what role God plays in miracles: Are they about people, as Pat says, and made by people, as Marion believes of herself; or is God really in control? E.T., M.T.

AUTHOR: **Joan Phipson**
TITLE: *The Watcher in the Garden (1982)*
DESCRIPTION: Catherine is an irritable girl who finds herself drawn to the lovely garden of an old blind man, there slowly learning to quell the bad in her nature and to nurture the good, with the help of Mr. Lovett and the garden itself. Terry is a bitter, vengeful boy who feels the world—and Mr. Lovett in particular—owes him something, and he's determined to take it from the garden. How they come to read each other's minds and accept—or reject—the healing of the garden makes up the action of this compelling story.
RECOMMENDATION: Instead of good vs. evil being played out on a cosmic scale as happens in so many books, in *The Watcher in the Garden* it is played out on a simple personal scale in a way with which you might identify. The only artificial note in this otherwise so genuine story about human attempts to improve a flawed character is that it takes extra-sensory perception for Catherine and Terry to meet. Their confrontation had been inevitable and could have been as natural as the rest of this near-masterpiece. M.T.

AUTHOR: **Chaim Potok**
TITLE: *The Chosen (1960)*
DESCRIPTION: Reuven's and Danny's friendship began with a play-for-blood softball game between their two yeshiva high schools, though Jewish boys in Brooklyn during World War II were known more for their scholarship than their athletic prowess. Brilliant Danny is being groomed to take his Hasidic rabbi father's place but is compelled to master forbidden "secular" ideas as well. Reuven's father secretly helps him find the books he desires. This most wonderful of stories is about father-son relationships and about faith-knowledge relationships.
RECOMMENDATION: If you have grown up in any kind of subculture (religious or ethnic, or, as with Hasidic Judaism, both), you will feel this book and most others by Chaim Potok echoing marvelously in your heart and mind. If you haven't, you will feel like a member of one before you

reach the last page. *The Promise* continues Danny and Reuven's story into their post-college days. L.T.*

AUTHOR: **Chaim Potok**
TITLE: *My Name is Asher Lev (1972)*
DESCRIPTION: Asher Lev is a young Hasidic Jew with a gift, the ability to paint, who, in his compelling need to exercise that gift, breaks the commandments of his faith, "Thou shalt make no graven image." Not only that, he paints crucifixes, the symbol of the people who have attempted to destroy the Jews. And so Asher grows up with a tension that finally must explode, learning that his gifted hands hold power both demonic and divine, able both to destroy and to create.
RECOMMENDATION: Like all of Potok's books, this one is about family and faith and their roles in the meaning of the life young people must construct for themselves. Eighteen years later, Potok published a sequel about Asher as an adult, *The Gift of Asher Lev,* in which he comes home to Brooklyn from his European exile when his uncle dies and finds the ties just as binding and just as demanding of choice and sacrifice. L.T.*

AUTHOR: **Cynthia Rylant**
TITLE: *A Kindness (1988)*
DESCRIPTION: This is not a book that is as "young" or "easy" as its slim spine and larger print might indicate. Instead, it is a complex book about family and responsibility and love in the context of a single artist-mother happily raising Chip, her 15-year-old son. Anne, one night only, sleeps with a man whom she has always loved from a distance, and, unknown to him, becomes pregnant. Much to Chip's horror, she decides to keep the child. Chip, for his part, must relinquish his need to control his mother and, surprisingly, his new baby sister.
RECOMMENDATION: Probably because they make choices, you will think moral for reasons outside the familiar framework of biblical morality, you may find this book both moving and disturbing. For example, Anne chooses not to get an abortion because keeping the baby was consistent with the value she placed on the life of an endangered species, a sea turtle. M.T.

AUTHOR: **J. D. Salinger**
TITLE: *The Catcher in the Rye (1945)*
DESCRIPTION: This book has the dubious honor of launching the movement toward "socially realistic" young-adult literature even though it was published for adults. For years it was on "forbidden" lists, though today its first-person narrator, flat "real" vocabulary laced with swear

words, and an urban-rich-troubled-misunderstood protagonist are standard fare.

RECOMMENDATION: Do you feel sorry for Holden Caufield, kicked out of yet another prep school where all things phoney get on his nerves, victim perhaps of his parents' indifference, or do you feel a good swift kick in the pants might do him some good? Or do you have yet another, more complex, response to him? Why do you think this book is so famous? More important, does his experience enrich your own? L.T.

AUTHOR: **Ivan Southall**
TITLE: *Let the Balloon Go (1968)*
DESCRIPTION: A fiercely independent boy is trapped inside John's body, though he is plagued by cerebral palsy and by an overprotective mother. The first day that he is left alone he decides that he must climb a tree.
RECOMMENDATION: The saying, "A balloon that would never be a balloon until someone cut it free," provides the context to John's struggle to become an ordinary but free boy. (But then, John could be any child seeking to cut the restraints of childhood and so grow up.) Southall has a real knack for putting you right inside the skin of his heroes. Oh, how you want John to succeed and to "say 'Hi-ya' to God!" Afterward, his chastened parents have a word of wisdom about the true nature and price of freedom. E.T.*

AUTHOR: **Ivan Southall**
TITLE: *Josh (1972)*
DESCRIPTION: Josh visits his aunt Clara in a small Australian bush village that his great-grandfather founded and for three days contends with the foreignness of the place and the jealousy and animosity of the kids there.
RECOMMENDATION: This story is told completely inside Josh's head, ideas tumbling one after the other, and so it is difficult for readers to maintain their own perspective. Josh must make peace with his roots and fit together his tolerant big city upbringing ("Of course we've got a Bible, and we've got other books too. The Talmud and the Koran and all sorts of scriptures from China and India and everywhere else. We respect what other people think") with the actions of the people in this town who so obviously respect his charitable aunt but scorn him. Does he do that finally or does he walk away from the contradictions in them and himself? E.T., M.T.

AUTHOR: **Suzanne Fisher Staples**
TITLE: *Shabanu: Daughter of the Wind (1989)*

DESCRIPTION: At 11, Shabanu, the younger daughter of a nomadic Muslim camel herder in the Pakistani desert of Cholistan, is old enough to know that her childhood freedoms are ending. Her sister, Phulan, will soon marry Hamir, and that means her own wedding will surely follow. Tragedy—when Hamir is shot due to Shabanu's unthinking disregard of Islamic cultural customs—precipitates a critical choice for Shabanu. Should she accept her family's choice of a husband for her and so protect their precarious existence, or should she follow the dictates of her heart and so put them in jeopardy?

RECOMMENDATION: This wonderful Newbery Honor book reveals the heart of a young member of a culture distant from your own on two accounts—it is both Muslim and Pakistani—and compels you both into Shabanu's way of life and her individual dilemma. E.T., M.T.*

AUTHOR: **Mildred Taylor**
TITLE: *The Road to Memphis (1990)*
DESCRIPTION: "Powerful" is the best word to describe this latest book by Mildred Taylor about the Logan family. Perhaps you read *Roll of Thunder, Hear My Cry* and *Let the Circle Be Unbroken* when you were younger. Cassie and her brothers and friends are themselves older now, on the verge of adulthood. Cassie is in her last year of high school in Jackson and looking forward to college and law school. Stacey, Clarence, and Moe are aware that, with a war economy gearing up, they might do better than work in the box factory, and Sissy wants only for Clarence to marry her. They have changed by the fall of 1941, but their Southern community does not seem to have changed at all.

RECOMMENDATION: If you want to experience prejudice secondhand (yet powerfully), then become part of what happened in three explosive days to Cassie, her friends, and the white boy, Jeremy, with whom they have always shared an uneasy friendship. Feel your personhood demeaned, trust a hurting white person with your very life, learn what your own responses might be as you move outside the strong protection of your loving family, and yet stand for one last time in the closed circle of that family united in prayer. M.T.

AUTHOR: **Yoshiko Uchida**
TITLE: *A Jar of Dreams (1982)*
DESCRIPTION: Rinko, 11 years old during that Depression summer when Aunt Waka came to visit them from Japan, is struggling like the rest of her family to survive, not just in body but in spirit. It is not easy to be the outsider when times are tough for everyone—you're likely to get blamed

for all sorts of troubles. But Aunt Waka brings a fresh and spirited perspective, just as they are about to give up, that helps Rinko and her family keep their jar of dreams full.

RECOMMENDATION: Uchida makes the Japanese American experience come alive for younger readers. E.T.

AUTHOR: **Betty Vander Els**
TITLE: *Leaving Point (1987)*
DESCRIPTION: Ruth, the heroine of *The Bomber's Moon*, and her younger brothers had looked forward to spending the 1950 Christmas holiday with their parents back on the mission compound in Chengtu. But when they finally get there, their parents are frantically dealing with the sensitive political situation of the new Communist regime and with dozens of guest missionaries trying to get exit visas. As the days turn into weeks and then into months, Ruth takes refuge in their makeshift school lessons with Mr. Hilary and in clandestine meetings with a young Communist, Chuin-mei. Then she learns that her growing friendship with the Chinese girl may put both Chuin-mei and her own parents in grave danger.

RECOMMENDATION: If you have ever wondered which political systems are best for people, you will appreciate Ruth's struggles to make sense of both Communism and Christianity in a very real setting, the setting of the author's own girlhood. E.T., M.T.*

Cynthia Voigt writes most frequently about the Tillermans, one of the most interesting families in fiction. The doers do fiercely and the thinkers think loudly, so there is much to involve most any kind of reader—those who like physical action and those who like mental puzzles. All of her characters are, in one way or another, with or without religious dress, existentialists. This means that they believe that each person's short existence on earth is meaningless in the long span of earth's history, but despite this reality, each person can create meaning for him or herself by choosing to live with integrity and to relate with love to other people, particularly family members. When you stop to think that most of her Crisfield characters had horrid things happen to them—usually abandonment of some kind—you may be astonished that they have the inner moral resources to make the choices you so often want to applaud. In each book there is at least one love-giver who enables the good in Voigt's characters to grow and function, though only in *Come a Stranger* can you see how that good may be grounded in an absolute moral standard. You will be glad that Cynthia Voigt has seen writing as a way that young people can look into her mind to see her "essential ideas, which in fact govern choices and action"

(Newbery Award acceptance speech, Horn Book, 403). If you have loved all the Tillerman books, go looking for other Voigt titles, especially *Jackaroo* and others set in the Middle Ages.

AUTHOR: **Cynthia Voigt**
TITLE: *Come a Stranger (1986)*
DESCRIPTION: Mina Smiths is such an exceptional dancer that, although black, she wins a scholarship to a New England summer dance camp, where she learns about the world of music and ideas outside her own isolated Crisfield, Maryland. Coming home, she doesn't fit in again, but more devastating, she does not fit in again at the camp the next summer. After two weeks, she is sent home. Is it because she is black or because her maturing body can no longer dance? With Tamer Shipp, her minister-father's summer replacement, she first begins to sort out her feelings of rejection. Over the years to come it is with Tamer, and later with Dicey Tillerman, and always with her secure loving family, that Mina learns the many meanings of love, courage, faith, and truth.
RECOMMENDATION: If you want to set the Tillermans' brave existential-ism in the context of Christianity, it is Mina's story that will allow you to do so. Even so, Cynthia Voigt's most overtly religious characters either don't seem to think about their faith (as Mina's father does not) or are in the throes of doubt (as are Brother Thomas or Tamer Shipp). There is nothing much of God's love in Voigt's portrayal, either, unless it is through Mina's Momma. On another level, *Come a Stranger* is also a touching story of a young teen's crush on an unavailable older—good—man, and here it resolves as truly and satisfactorily as it could possibly do. If you want to read more about Tamer and Bullet, Dicey's uncle, you may wish to find *The Runner*. M.T.

AUTHOR: **Cynthia Voigt**
TITLE: *Dicey's Song (1982)*
DESCRIPTION: Newbery Award, 1983. Having gained her family a home with their grandmother (*Homecoming*), Dicey must now get on with the business of growing up on the farm, at her part-time job, and in school. This she does by learning—sometimes painfully—to juggle the sometimes contradictory tasks of holding on to her family, reaching out for new friends, and letting go of her dying momma.
RECOMMENDATION: Those who admire the plucky Dicey will be glad to know how her new life develops. Though in the larger context, her Gram cannot provide her with any certitudes ("Was that the right thing to do?" Dicey asks and Gram's reply is, "How should I know? It feels right and

that's about all I have to go by."), she does provide love and much practical wisdom. For Dicey, life becomes a song well worth singing. E.T., M.T.*

AUTHOR: **Cynthia Voigt**
TITLE: *Homecoming (1981)*
DESCRIPTION: Thirteen-year-old Dicey and her three younger siblings are abandoned in a shopping mall by their emotionally ill mother and must make their way on foot to their great-aunt Cilla's home in Bridgeport, Connecticut. When it becomes apparent that they will not be able to stay there, Dicey, James, Maybeth, and Sammy begin the trek again, this time to Maryland and their unknown grandmother Tillerman, who might well be crazy. With her is their last chance to have a home and family.
RECOMMENDATION: *Homecoming* is the first of Cynthia Voigt's splendid companion books about the young teens who live around Crisfield, Maryland. Dicey is the determined character who holds all the others together, quite literally in this first book. Like the hero in the ageless Greek epic tale, *The Odyssey*, *Homecoming*'s children face dangers and hardships but meet people who help them on their way until at last their hearts' longing is fulfilled. You may be intrigued to discover the parallels to *The Odyssey* as you read as well as be stimulated by Dicey and James' discussions about the ultimate questions of life and death and eternity. Where is their true home? What kind of people should they be as they search? Is personal integrity the highest good? Is Someone looking out for them or are they truly on their own? E.T., M.T.*

AUTHOR: **Cynthia Voigt**
TITLE: *Seventeen Against the Dealer (1989)*
DESCRIPTION: This story completes the Tillerman saga with Dicey, now 21, again the Odysseus figure, venturing out on uncharted waters, determined to make a go of her dream, to make a living as an independent boat builder. However, burying herself in the work, Dicey makes several mistakes not only about the business but about people—her grandmother, whose illness she underestimates, Jeff Greene, whose love she takes for granted, and an itinerant talker named Cisco whom she trusts. Having seemingly lost everything, Dicey learns—again—what it is that matters most in a world where there are no guarantees.
RECOMMENDATION: Dicey is a doer like Sammy, not a thinker, so *Seventeen* is not as rich in ideas as is *Sons from Afar*. Yet her story, and Jeff's, deserves this completion as she, too, chooses a moral and honest and loving life even though she does not believe that these attributes are built into the universe. M.T., L.T.

AUTHOR: **Cynthia Voigt**
TITLE: *A Solitary Blue (1983)*
DESCRIPTION: Newbery Honor, 1984. Abandoned by his beautiful mother, Melody, when he was seven and living with his ineffectual professor father, Jeff grows up silent and withdrawn, coming totally alive only when he spends a summer with Melody. But the second summer, when he was 13, Melody makes clear that she loves Jeff only selfishly, and he withdraws completely. The Professor is alarmed into action and together, with the help of his father's friend, Brother Thomas, and a healing move to the blue-heron marshes of Crisfield, Maryland, they reach out to each other in love and forgiveness.
RECOMMENDATION: Jeff and his father stumble through their days saying, "I'm sorry. It doesn't make any difference, really." But the theme of *A Solitary Blue*—and probably all of Voigt's writings—is that love—or at least what you do with love when it strikes you—makes all the difference in the world. Father and son learn that they don't have to be solitary, that they make a difference to each other, and that they don't have to apologize for who they are. They are people whom you will be most grateful to make your friends. M.T.

AUTHOR: **Cynthia Voigt**
TITLE: *Sons from Afar (1987)*
DESCRIPTION: James Tillerman is a thinker and Sammy Tillerman a doer, as different as two brothers could be. But Sammy helps James search for the father who had abandoned them twelve years ago, a search that takes them to schools, courthouses, and libraries around Maryland and ends in a decrepit waterfront bar in Baltimore. They had sought the truth about the man but discover some truths about themselves, truths strong enough to live by.
RECOMMENDATION: If *The Odyssey* and *Hansel and Gretel* are the stories that haunt *The Homecoming*, then the Greek myth of a father and son, Daedalus and Icarus, and the essay by the French existentialist, Camus, "The Myth of Sisyphus," undergird *Sons from Afar*. James decides, in defiance of the evidence that each individual, brief life is essentially meaningless. He can create meaning for his own life primarily by his commitment to be himself and by his strong bonds of love to his family whose meaning and significance he knows, even if Truth cannot be known. If you are intrigued by ideas and have already been captured by the Tillermans, then you will cheer James' and Sammy's choices while longing for them to discover that life really is meaningful. M.T.

FANTASY

AUTHOR: **Natalie Babbitt**
TITLE: *The Eyes of the Amaryllis (1977)*
DESCRIPTION: Jenny must stay with her Gran, a widow who is waiting for a message from her long-dead ship-captain husband. Unlike her father, who saw his father's ship swallowed by a hurricane, Jenny is drawn to the sea and so helps her grandmother search for the message and, during another violent storm, learns that it's "amazing what people will do for love."
RECOMMENDATION: Because she had loved her husband so much and longed to hear from him once more, Jenny's Gran is convinced "that all the things we can touch and see in this world, are only one part of what's there, and that there's another world around us all the time that's mostly hidden from us." But is that spiritual world hateful or loving? A storm gives Jenny the evidence she needs to decide for herself. E.T.

AUTHOR: **Natalie Babbitt,**
TITLE: *Tuck Everlasting (1975)*
DESCRIPTION: When Winnie meets the wonderful Tucks, who had unintentionally drunk from a certain spring and are suspended forever in time, she is tempted to accept what each believes about life: Ma, that things just *are* and must be lived with; Pa, that life is a never-ending cycle of which death is a natural and good part; Jesse, that life is meant to be enjoyed; and Miles, that people must do something useful to be alive.
RECOMMENDATION: There are bits of Christian truth mixed in all that the Tucks say, though some of it, like Pa's Eastern mystical view of life is not at all biblical. Like Winnie, you will probably be intrigued by these kindly people's dilemma and the choice she must make. Even college students

The Mountain-path

"The Mountain Path"—one of J. R. R. Tolkien's own illustrations for his book *The Hobbit*, reprinted by permission of Houghton Mifflin Company. For description of Tolkien's *Lord of the Rings* trilogy, see pages 158–59.

enjoy discussing this book, which can be read by quite young children.
E.T.*

AUTHOR: **John Bibee**
TITLE: *The Magic Bicycle (1983)*
DESCRIPTION: *The Toy Campaign* and *The Only Game in Town* are the
next two sequels in a projected seven-volume series published by
InterVarsity Press. John is an orphan who lives with his uncle, the sheriff of
Centerville, his aunt, and three cousins. He wants to win the bicycle
contest being promoted in town by the strange Horace Grinsby of Goliath
Toys, but his bike had been run over in the driveway where he had
carelessly left it. He uncovers an old-fashioned battered Spirit Flyer in the
town dump and, in fixing it up for the race, discovers its magical powers.
Grinsby knows them, too, and will stop at nothing to destroy the bike.
RECOMMENDATION: If you are familiar with Christian doctrine, you will
enjoy finding the parallels between the exciting circumstances of this story
and biblical truths. If you aren't, the story itself will easily capture your
interest. The last line delightfully promises sequels, for while his family was
learning about the magic that had captured him, "John was flying on the
Spirit Flyer on a new adventure known only to the kings." E.T.*

AUTHOR: **Nancy Bond**
TITLE: *A String in the Harp (1976)*
DESCRIPTION: Newbery Honor, 1977. Soon after their mother's unexpected death, Peter, Becky, and Jen's father takes them off to a bleak
corner of Wales so that he can teach at the university in Aberystwyth. Each
is isolated in his or her own grief until Peter—perhaps the most miserable
of them all—discovers an ancient harp tuning key that slowly draws him
into the sixth-century world of the bard, Taliesin. His sisters slowly get
drawn into the everyday worlds of their Welsh neighbors, a lonely bird-
loving boy, Gwilym, and a down-to-earth farm girl, Rhian. Together all of
them explore the surrounding land and their newly discovered feelings
about life and the ancient magic.
RECOMMENDATION: You may find this to be one of the most satisfying
books of fantasy you have read, as the events in Taliesin's life converge to
heal the Morgans of their grief at the same time that Peter emerges from
his grief-shell to save Taliesin for the land. Two themes are subtly woven
throughout, one spoken by the Welsh language scholar, Dr. Rhys: "If we
think a thing is impossible, does that truly make it so? Who are we, after
all? Why should there not be forces that we do not understand?" Peter
fumbles to the other: "The pattern was right, it was working itself out.

People spent their lives weaving patterns, borrowing bits from one another. . ." Ask your family to read this one together. E.T.*

AUTHOR: **Eleanor Cameron**
TITLE: *Beyond Silence (1980)*
DESCRIPTION: Andrew, still grieving over the accidental death of his brother, goes to the Scottish castle-home of his father's boyhood. There he is intrigued by visions and voices of his great-aunt when she was young—explained as "hypnagogic"—and plagued by nightmares of the accident and an irritating, nosey houseguest. As he discovers that "the future enters into us, in order to transform itself in us," he also discovers that his grief is mixed with a guilt that he had suppressed.
RECOMMENDATION: This book has been described as a "psychological science fiction," but you may find it more like a fantasy. Cameron is exploring the notion that all of life is connected throughout time as well as space (rather like L'Engle in this respect). Do you agree that Andrew is justified in thinking that "maybe [things are] going to be okay after all"? M.T.

Susan Cooper has been compared to C. S. Lewis and J. R. R. Tolkein, both of whom she studied under at Oxford. Her fantasy series has high seriousness and terrific command of images and language, great for reading aloud. You can't help but long for Good to defeat Evil when you read her stories. Yet they are not an allegory for the Christian story of Jesus' defeating Satan even though they contain many allusions to the Bible as well as to myth. In the Dark is Rising sequence, good and evil have equal powers and exist independently of the older natural world—a belief often labeled "dualism." (In the Christian story, God created everything good, and evil is a corruption of the good that Christ proved is stronger and will ultimately triumph.) Even though Cooper thinks that all of human history shows the eternal struggle between good and evil, it is those equal forces in our human hearts that are more real than the spiritual world we cannot see. And because she didn't write about the Eternal battle, all the children have to hang on to is their "fierce caring [which] can fan [hope] into a fire to warm the world" and their promise to try their best to fight for good.

AUTHOR: **Susan Cooper**
TITLE: *Over Seas, Under Stone (1965)*
DESCRIPTION: Barney, Jane, and Simon Drew are caught up into the timeless battle between good and evil when they find an ancient map in their rented holiday house in Cornwall. Following its clues, they search

"over sea and under stone" for King Arthur's grail, but so do sinister forces disguised as innocent villagers and tourists.

RECOMMENDATION: Susan Cooper thinks with Great-Uncle Merry that all "once upon a time" stories are "underneath all the bits people have added . . . about one thing—good against evil." *Over Seas, Under Stone* is the first in her marvelous contemporary Once Upon a Time series, and the bits she has added all echo the oldest stories of England and Wales, especially the King Arthur legends. E.T., M.T.*

AUTHOR: **Susan Cooper**
TITLE: *The Dark is Rising (1973)*
DESCRIPTION: Newbery Honor, 1974. On his eleventh birthday, Will Stanton discovers his role in the cosmic battle of Light and Dark, as the last of the immortal Old Ones. His quest is to find the six signs of a cross inside a circle, made of wood, bronze, iron, water, fire, and stone. He must join them together because "the dark is rising," threatening to quench the power of light.

RECOMMENDATION: In this second novel from which her Dark is Rising series takes its name, Susan Cooper deepens the layers of her story. Will Stanton is no ordinary child like the Drews, who are drawn to the good. He is an immortal, chosen like Merriman Lyon, (the Drews' Great-Uncle Merry and also Merlin) from before time to fulfill a destiny that the Law demands, to serve the Light in its gripping battle with the Dark. E.T., M.T.*

AUTHOR: **Susan Cooper**
TITLE: *Greenwitch (1974)*
DESCRIPTION: Will Stanton meets Jane, Barney, and Simon Drew on an Easter holiday back in Cornwall. Jane witnesses the women of the village in their traditional making of a Greenwitch that they offer as a sacrifice to the sea. Jane's unselfish wish for the lonely Greenwitch is crucial to the continuing battle between the Dark and the Light.

RECOMMENDATION: This is the least of the books in the series, yet it, too, extends Cooper's mythical world, focusing this time through the old Cornwall sea-creature legends on the timeless natural world that has its own Wild Magic, beyond good and evil. E.T., M.T.*

AUTHOR: **Susan Cooper**
TITLE: *The Grey King (1975)*
DESCRIPTION: Newbery Award, 1976. To recover from a serious illness, Will is sent to his aunt's farm in Wales where he meets a lonely albino boy, Bran, and his dog, Cafall, who also have dual identities. In the shadow of

the mountain controlled by the Dark's Grey King, Will and Bran continue the battle against the Dark, rescuing the gold harp and awakening the sleepers, who are necessary for the Light to gain the strength it needs for the final coming conflict.

RECOMMENDATION: Again, Cooper twists the strong threads of her story into more complex patterns. Bran is particularly compelling as he comes to terms with his human and his legendary identity. The particular issues that are highlighted against the larger pattern of Light vs. Dark are the free will of human beings, and the sacrifices that must be made when we serve absolute principles. E.T., M.T.*

AUTHOR: **Susan Cooper**
TITLE: *Silver on the Tree (1977)*
DESCRIPTION: The final confrontation of Light and Dark is at hand, drawing all five of the children and their protector, Merriman Lyon, into the conflict. To find the one last weapon, the crystal sword that alone can defeat the Dark, Will and Bran journey into the Lost Land, a visionary country that echoes of all the myths of Britain as well as the Apocalypse of the Bible. But for all their high adventure, in the end, the simple human bonds of love prove to be most crucial against the annihilating evil of the Dark.

RECOMMENDATION: The brilliant kaleidoscope turns again as Cooper's young heroes shift in and out of time and space. This fifth and final volume of the Dark Is Rising series has at the same time the strangest visual images and the most direct message: "We have delivered you from evil, but the evil that is inside of men is at the last a matter for men to control." You may want to puzzle out whether or not it is better for the children to forget all their otherworldly adventures and to wonder whether Uncle Merry's ascension doesn't promise the second coming that he said would never happen. E.T., M.T.*

AUTHOR: **Pauline Fisk**
TITLE: *Midnight Blue (1990)*
DESCRIPTION: Bonnie has just moved into a flat with her mother, Maybelle, near Highholly Hill after living with her vindictive grandmother who is still bent on destroying their emerging happiness. Running from Grandbag through the holly hedge, Bonnie glimpses a man, a shadowy boy, a hot air balloon, and a chance to escape to another world. Though it mirrors her own world, families are happy there, and her family—Mum, Dad, Arabella, and the baby—accept her with no questions asked. But even here a mirror of Grandbag pursues her. Will the ancient gods of

Highholly Hill help her? Will Shadowboy? Or is the evil within, her own feelings of hatred? In making a quiet, ordinary sacrifice of herself, Bonnie learns that it is possible to run from hate and that things can change. RECOMMENDATION: The writing of this complex fantasy is excellent (it may remind you of Susan Cooper), with characters drawn so surely that they will seem as real to you as the grubby girl in your class or the intense boy watching your soccer game. The moral dilemma of the story is resolved in a convincing way, yet the biblical truth that underlies it is not preachy. Lion published Fisk's book. E.T., M.T.*

Alan Garner is a difficult—or challenging—author, depending on which critic you read. Some say he is the best young adults' author living, while others see fatal flaws in what could be masterpieces. He himself says that "there are no original stories," meaning that from prehistory, people have explored the same inexhaustible themes of love and courage, betrayal and death, time and eternity, justice and truth. Most of his novels take their shape from old Celtic and Norse myths because he believes that "fantasy is the intensification of reality." *Red Shift* ends on a totally negative note— "not really not now any more"—which is softened in his later, more warmly human *Stone Quartet* (which you will find under Historical Fiction). Even if you cannot stay in Garner's ever-expanding, god-abandoned yet god-haunted universe for very long, you will be rewarded by the effort you put into understanding his books.

AUTHOR: **Alan Garner**
TITLE: *The Weirdstone of Brisingamen (1969)*
DESCRIPTION: Susan discovers that her heirloom bracelet is really the lost weirdstone of Brisingamen, and many are the powers—both good and evil—who want it. She and her brother, Colin, lose and then find it and must, with the help of dwarves and the Lady of the Lake, set out on a quest to restore it to the good wizard Cadellin.
RECOMMENDATION: Garner has dug deeply into Celtic mythology to tell this contemporary good and evil story (which will remind you of Susan Cooper's and Lloyd Alexander's—even some of the names are the same). If you ever feel as though you are in a battle with principalities and powers, the good dwarf Durathror's description of courage in such circumstances may give you heart. E.T., M.T.

AUTHOR: **Alan Garner**
TITLE: *The Moon of Gomrath (1963)*

DESCRIPTION: Susan and Colin once again seek to be part of the battle between good and evil, this time sacrificing their own protection to lend Susan's magic bracelet to the elves, ill from the "smoke-sickness" created by man. The High Magic of wizards and spells is powerless to help vulnerable Susan, so the more elemental, more natural Old Magic (of the moon), which is neither good nor evil but not fitted to modern civilization, must be let loose.

RECOMMENDATION: Two very interesting ideas keep appearing in this sequel to *Weirdstone*. One is the notion that man's progress has negative side-effects, from "smoke-sickness" to impersonal warfare, yet man's thoughts are powerless to correct them. The other is the feeling that Susan and Colin have—that people need to be part of a victory for their actions to have any meaning. Do you agree with them? E.T., M.T.

AUTHOR: **Alan Garner**
TITLE: *Elidor (1965)*

DESCRIPTION: As with other of Garner's novels, contemporary British children are caught up in ancient stories of good and evil. This one echoes "Childe Rowland" as Roland and his brothers and sister are drawn into the wasteland kingdom of Elidor through a church being razed in a Manchester slum. Its evil follows them back home to destroy the gifts the king has given them and so prevent the prophesies of restoration from being fulfilled.

RECOMMENDATION: Roland's family believes that there has to be a rational explanation for everything, but he keeps faith with what he knows to be true and real even though it means that the unicorn Findhorn must die and that Roland be left standing in a slum with only his memories. E.T., M.T.

AUTHOR: **Alan Garner**
TITLE: *The Owl Service (1968)*

DESCRIPTION: Carnegie Medal, 1967. Alison's mother and Roger's father have just married. The new family vacations at the Welsh cottage that had been Alison's dead father's. Gwyn and his mother come from Aberystwyth to do the housework. There the three teenagers discover old dishes with an owl pattern and are drawn into a triangle of love and jealousy that reenacts the ancient Welsh legend of Lleu, Gronw and Blodeuwedd, of flowers and owls, and passion and death, which had its roots in their very valley.

RECOMMENDATION: This splendid modern story uses a timeless myth to probe the notions of the intertwining of love and jealousy, as well as possessive parental control and human freedom. Alison, Gwyn, and Roger "together are destroying each other" and must discover within themselves the key to break the ancient pattern of destruction. The words, the images, the characters, and the powerful brooding valley will all reverberate in your expanded understanding long after you finish the book. M.T.

AUTHOR: **Alan Garner**
TITLE: *The Red Shift (1973)*
DESCRIPTION: The hills of Cheshire, a prehistoric stone axe, and the girls who love and protect them unite three boys otherwise separated by 2000 years. Garner's difficult-to-penetrate novel shifts from brilliant but bitter Tom in the 20th century, lost without his girlfriend, Jan, who must study in London; to sentry, Thomas, in the 17th, who must put aside fear to protect the village from the King's marauders; and to deserter, Macey, in the second century, who tries to "go native" but stumbles onto a local priestess. By the end these three profoundly sad stories merge into one.
RECOMMENDATION: A red shift is a paradoxical astronomical phenomenon associated with a retreating light source that implies that the passage of time is an illusion and that the galaxies are drifting apart. Are Macey and Thomas then inside the head of Tom? Can individuals ever really connect? If you are able to get into Tom's life—not an easy task in this difficult book—you will mourn with him his loss of love and trust. L.T.

Madeleine L'Engle is a rare author, one who is both openly Christian and fully accepted in the secular publishing world. Not only does she weave biblical references into her books but at a deeper level alludes to mystics, theologians, writings from other faiths that echo Christianity, and to scientists who share her concerns: faith, hope, and love; the singular importance of the individual; and how his or her choices affect the whole of creation. The universe is the setting for a battle between good and evil; all characters in L'Engle's books, whether they are "fantasy" or "real," must throw in their lot with one side or the other—usually at a personal cost. Nor is right or wrong easy to discern from the externals of intelligence, beauty, wealth, or even religious trappings. L'Engle affirms created life and the ultimate, if not immediate, triumph of good. Her books are richly layered, surprisingly and challengingly eclectic, and with one exception (*House Like a Lotus*), uncompromisingly true. They reward careful reading and rereading. (You'll find L'Engle's books listed under both categories, and—although they're not—some of her contemporary books could also be listed as mysteries.) Countless families and classrooms have shared these books by reading them aloud together.

AUTHOR: **Madeleine L'Engle**
TITLE: *A Wrinkle in Time (1962)*
DESCRIPTION: First in the Times Quartet, Newbery Award, 1963. Meg Murry tesseracts to another planet to battle the IT for control of her little brother Charles Wallace's mind, her only weapon powerful enough being love. E.T., M.T.*

AUTHOR: **Madeleine L'Engle**
TITLE: *A Wind in the Door (1973)*
DESCRIPTION: Second in the Times Quartet. Meg and Charles Wallace are a year older. Meg, with the help of a cherub, must travel into the mitochondria of Charles' ill body to name a farandola. Thereby she can not only save his life but add to the underlying harmonies of the universe and defeat the evil Echthroi. E.T., M.T.*

AUTHOR: **Madeleine L'Engle**
TITLE: *A Swiftly Tilting Planet (1978)*
DESCRIPTION: Third in the Times Quartet. A teenaged Charles Wallace, with the help of his grown sister and a unicorn named Gaudior, travels through both time and space to several critical "might-have beens" of history where small choices for good may prevent a nuclear holocaust in his own time.
RECOMMENDATION: These first three books of the series are worth coming back to again and again. E.T., M.T.*

AUTHOR: **Madeleine L'Engle**
TITLE: *Many Waters (1986)*
DESCRIPTION: Fourth in the Times Quartet. The 15-year-old Murry twins, Sandy and Dennys, finally get their chance at time travel when they ask their father's computer to take them to a warm, dry place. They land in Noah's oasis before the Flood. Like Charles Wallace and Meg, they must discern good from evil, gain help from celestial creatures, make choices that will affect the history of their planet, and believe that El (God) has a pattern—not chaos—that will work out "in beauty in the end."
RECOMMENDATION: You may have to suspend your disbelief to enter a story you know so well from Sunday school through the medium of fantasy. E.T., M.T., L.T.

AUTHOR: **Madeleine L'Engle**
TITLE: *An Acceptable Time* (1989). (See this book also in the Contemporary section.)

DESCRIPTION: L'Engle's "realistic" Poly O'Keefe stories and her "fantasy" Murry ones merge in this sequel to both series. Poly, visiting her Murry grandparents, is pulled into a 3,000 year-old American Indian/British Druid society, along with her neighbor, Bishop Columbra, and the heartless Zachary (A Moon by Night and House Like a Lotus). There she discovers that two warring tribes consider her a goddess with magical powers. One of them decides to sacrifice her to bring the much-needed rain. Poly must determine whether she is willing to die for the people—and for the selfish Zachary who also believes that her death would heal his diseased heart. RECOMMENDATION: All of L'Engle's themes are repeated here—the meaning of time, the crucial importance of love, and the necessity of sacrifice and forgiveness. She intersperses orthodox Christian doctrine with Druid and animistic beliefs and practices. Perhaps you will find that one of the most telling theological exchanges comes at the climax of the crisis when Poly refuses to take credit for doing what only God can do but does not give him the credit for it either, saying, "It just happened." M.T., L.T.

AUTHOR: **Ursula LeGuin**
TITLE: *A Wizard of Earthsea (1968)*
DESCRIPTION: Series continued in The Tombs of Atuan and The Farthest Shore. On an adult level, the series concludes with Tehanu. Because he saved his village from marauders, it is discovered that Sparrowhawk has magical powers. Sent to study with the sorcerers, he learns quickly, particularly the true name of things, but he uses his newly discovered power against a jealous fellow student. As a result, Ged—for that is Sparrowhawk's true name—disturbs the balance of the world by releasing a fearsome evil shadow. It takes three confrontations before Ged can be freed of his terrible quest to undo the harm he has begun. By the last volume, Ged is the Archmage, but the wells of magic are running dry and with it the Earthsea peoples' joy in living. With the young prince of Erlad, Arren, he seeks out the source of this wasting and despair but not without great cost to himself and the prince.
RECOMMENDATION: This lyrical fantasy series explores the ageless themes of good and evil, being and nonbeing, humility and arrogance. It affirms the good we all desire without denying the evil that resides in the hearts of all humans. Its stirring phrases and uncompromising integrity will etch Ged into your heart; it may disturb the balance of your own universe, but only for the good. E.T., M.T.*

AUTHOR: **Harold Myra**
TITLE: *Children in the Night (1991)*
DESCRIPTION: Harold Myra has created a totally "fantastic" yet believable world, an underground civilization where there is total darkness but where some people long for the light their religious myths have promised. An angry, young orphan boy, Yosha, who is the butt of the other boys' jokes; a talented young girl, Asel, who rises to the pinnacle of priestess's powers; and Auret, a horribly crippled man who mysteriously and disruptively joins them are the key characters in this classic battle of good vs. evil, which rages not only in the dark world of Aliare but in their own hearts as well.
RECOMMENDATION: Be prepared to experience a strange lightless world with all your senses heightened by Myra's sensuous writing. Your fingers, your nose, your ears, these will help you "see" what is hidden in this subterranean world. Be prepared also to discern many parallels between Aliare and our own world by Myra's carefully layered writing. Your mind and your heart both will be deeply touched by this fantasy that tells such powerful truth. Zondervan is the publisher of this book, so you may have to ask your library to get it for you. M.T., L.T.*

AUTHOR: **Ruth Nichols**
TITLE: *The Marrow of the World (1972)*
DESCRIPTION: Philip and his adopted-as-a-foundling cousin Linda are taken from their Canadian summer cottage to a sometimes desolate world where the wicked witch Ygerna (really Linda's half sister. The mythical Morgan is their mother) orders Linda to get for her the marrow of the world, which will guarantee her immortality. Philip, Herne the huntsman, the dwarves, and Leo the kindly wizard can only protect Linda to a degree. She must finally decide whether she wants to be a witch or a human being.
RECOMMENDATION: Nichols, in this early fantasy, explores themes of psychological wholeness and human choice, by way of myth and legend, which will later flower in complexity in her *Song of the Pearl*. E.T., M.T.

AUTHOR: **Ruth Nichols**
TITLE: *Song of the Pearl (1976)*
DESCRIPTION: Seventeen-year-old Margaret is happy to die of asthma and melancholy, happy to give up her love-hate relationship with her Uncle Matt. But both love and hate follow her to her life after death where, under the tutelage of a strange Chinese man named Paul, she journeys back through all her previous existences—as Elizabeth, wife of a 16th-century shipmaster; Zawumatec, an abused slave of the Iroquois Indians; and as

Tirigan, a Sumerian warrior in 2100 B.C.—to discover the source of her hatred and so be freed of its ancient burden; and then to be reincarnated once again, this time to a life of love alone.

RECOMMENDATION: Ruth Nichols has skillfully blended the religious mythology of many cultures to tell a strange but hauntingly beautiful story of the triumph of love over hatred. In doing so she undermines any claims to truth that any of them (including Christianity) may have. Instead, her Margaret's eternal life story is one in which the young woman comes to the psychological understanding that "past actions had woven into her future." This means that she could also understand that she, like all people, is (or could be) herself a god. Though she wrote this long before there was a "New Age Movement," many of the ideas in Nichols' book are the stuff of New Age thinking. M.T., L.T.

AUTHOR: **Pat O'Shea**
TITLE: *The Hounds of the Morrigan (1985)*
DESCRIPTION: Pidge and Bridget are just ordinary Irish children, but they have been chosen by the creator-god, The Dagda, to thwart the Morrigan, the three-in-one goddess of death and destruction, by preventing her from regaining her ancient power from a bloody pebble and a hideous snake. On their quest they are pursued by the Morrigan's hounds and helped by the oddest, most enchanting assortment of creatures ever to take a life of their own on paper. Even Pidge and Bridget's smallest, seemingly insignificant actions in the "real" world become freighted with significance in the fairy world that hovers just out of sight of those who refuse to see that even natural apples coming from pink blossoms is miraculous.

RECOMMENDATION: More than in most good-versus-evil fantasies, you can catch glimpses of the parallels between Christianity and the old myths in this imaginative weaving of Irish myth into contemporary reality. Another wonderful distinctive is its celebration of the goodness of created life. Though he is beginning to be aware of the dangers that he and Bridget face, Pidge thinks, "In my heart I'm glad that I'm mixed up with [these supernatural events]. Not everyone gets this kind of chance." E.T., M.T.*

AUTHOR: **Richard Peck** (See author overview in the Contemporary section.)
TITLE: *The Ghost Belongs To Me (1975)*
DESCRIPTION: ALA Notable Book. There are more laughs than shivers in this first farce, à la Mark Twain, about the ghosts that haunt Bluff City in 1913, Alexander Armsworth and Blossom Culp in particular. The pretentious get their comeuppance and swindlers their just deserts thanks to

them, saucy great-uncle Miles, and a ghost that just wants to be laid to rest properly.

RECOMMENDATION: Alexander comments that ghosts were falling out of fashion in the 20th century as much as Victorian gingerbread architecture and his sister's ample figure. Peck is also a 20th century unbeliever who uses these vaudeville characters and slapstick comedy to poke fun at human frailties. Among its sequels are *Ghosts I Have Been* and *The Dreadful Future of Blossom Culp*. E.T.

AUTHOR: **Robert Siegel**
TITLE: *Alpha Centauri (1980)*
DESCRIPTION: Becky is vacationing on an English farm, where she meets the horse, Rebecca, who in the middle of the night takes her off through the Eye of the Fog into prehistoric Britain. There the vicious Earth Movers are attempting to destroy the remnant band of peace-loving centaurs. After being captured and made a slave by the Earth Movers, escaping and making a perilous visit to the First Ones, Becky discovers that her arrival fulfilled an ancient prophecy predicting the salvation of the centaurs through the Path to the Stars—if only she is willing to make a sacrifice at great personal cost.

RECOMMENDATION: If you loved Lewis's Narnia Chronicles, L'Engle's Time Quartet, and Cooper's Dark Is Rising series, you will be delighted to discover *Alpha Centauri*, which echoes with the harmonies of both Celtic myth and biblical narrative. E.T.*

AUTHOR: **J. R. R. Tolkien**
TITLE: *The Lord of the Rings (1954, 1955)*
DESCRIPTION: The trilogy consists of *The Fellowship of the Ring*, *The Two Towers*, and *The Return of the Ring*. The publication of *The Hobbit* and *The Lord of the Rings* in the 1950s hailed the contemporary revival of the fantasy or epic romance. Many firmly believe that none of those books that have followed it can match it for the consistency and believability of the setting—Middle Earth—and the characters—the hobbits, wizards, elves, ents, dwarves, orcs, trolls, and other creatures of "faerie." They are involved in an epic struggle between good and evil symbolized by the lost ring that Sauron, the Dark Lord, had made. The wizard, Gandalf, and the hobbits are attempting to destroy the ring before it destroys them. All must make choices as to which force he or she will serve, choices that shape who they are and what will become of the lands they inhabit.

RECOMMENDATION: The plight and the quest of these so-human creatures with their full range of emotions will become your own as you come under the spell of enchantment that Tolkien so skillfully weaves by his language that borders on poetry. You should become better yourself for having journeyed with Frodo through Middle Earth. M.T., L.T.*

AUTHOR: **Walter Wangerin, Jr.**
TITLE: *The Book of the Dun Cow (1978)*
DESCRIPTION: Chauntecleer the Rooster gives the barnyard world he rules over "direction and meaning and a proper soul" in part by his daily canonical crows. He knows his own importance. What he does not know is that this proper soul is keeping the diabolical Wyrm imprisoned beneath the earth as well. In a neighboring land, a prideful rooster reaches for more power than is rightfully his and in so doing gives birth to the monster-Rooster, Cockatrice. The Wyrm exploits that situation to break away. The battle lines are drawn, but Chauntecleer learns that, though he can win a fearsome battle, yet without the mysterious Dun Cow and the ordinary Mundo Cani (the barnyard mutt), he cannot win the war.
RECOMMENDATION: You will recognize many people you know—in all their mixture of gracious loveliness and frustrating faults (dare you think, sins?)—in the delightfully endearing animals that people this fantasy-fable. Perhaps you will also recognize the biblical account of proper living, of real lostness, and of undeserved salvation in it as well, and hold its truths more dear for recognizing them in this form. L.T.*

AUTHOR: **John White**
TITLE: *The Tower of Geburah (1978)*
DESCRIPTION: Sequels in the Archives of Anthropos series published by InterVarsity Press are *The Iron Sceptre, The Sword Bearer,* and *Gaal the Conqueror.* In the C. S. Lewis tradition, John White has created three children who enter another land, Anthropos, through an object, a TV, in their own world. There they discover that the rightful king, Kardia, is imprisoned; that the drought-stricken land is under the control of evil powers; and that the Shepherd, Gaal, is rumored to be near. Wesley, Lisa, and Kurt are drawn into the battle but must choose which side to aid and, in their very stubborn humanity, do not automatically make the best choices. It's good for them and for Anthropos that Gaal is near.
RECOMMENDATION: As one of Gaal's servants tells the children, "True wisdom cannot be seen from the outside, only from within." This book allows you to get on the inside of both wisdom and some very exciting adventures. You will be glad that the last line of the first volume promises more. E.T., M.T.*

AUTHOR: **Charles Williams**
TITLE: *All Hallows Eve (1945)*
DESCRIPTION: Charles Williams explores familiar themes of substitutionary love and the coequal realities of the natural and the supernatural. After World War II no more terror should fall from the sky, but even so a pedestrian, Lester Furnival, is killed in a plane accident. From her position in purgatory, Lester goes about unfinished business on earth, appearing to her husband Richard, asking forgiveness of old friends, and, most particularly, helping to unshackle Betty from the grasp of the greedy spiritualist, Simon the Clerk, whose magic he is matched against Lester's love. The climax comes on a rainy London Halloween, "All Hallows Eve," when Williams shows again that the only wholeness people can have is through love.
RECOMMENDATION: Williams will reward your efforts if you attempt to read and understand him. L.T.

AUTHOR: **Charles Williams**
TITLE: *Descent into Hell (1937)*
DESCRIPTION: Peter Stanhope has written a play, which his neighbors decide to put on. Only Pauline Anstruther understands its significance, but she is terrorized by ghostly fears. Stanhope encourages her to let him "substitute" for her; he will take over her burden of fear through love. Relieved of that burden, Pauline can now bear the burdens of others by the other actors. Some of them grow in grace with her and others refuse to.
RECOMMENDATION: Charles Williams, a friend of C. S. Lewis and J. R. R. Tolkien, did not write a typical fantasy by which his characters and you, his readers, are transported to another world that those with less spiritual insight cannot see. Rather, you see the supernatural invading the natural, for according to Williams's Christian theology, the two always coexist, either easily or uneasily, either for good or for evil. It may seem surrealistic or spooky, but it makes theological sense. L.T.

AUTHOR: **Paul J. Willis**
TITLE: *No Clock in the Forest: An Alpine Tale (1991)*
DESCRIPTION: Impeccably outfitted, William wonders why he has agreed to go hiking among the peaks of The Three Queens with Garth who has only an odd old ax. Nearby, Grace wonders why she has agreed to go on the "You-Can-Do-It Expedition" with all its deprivations and none of its advertised pleasures. She decides to leave in the middle of the night and— after the road has disappeared—meets William. Each is propelled into a Narnia-like world where they must determine their allegiances and use a

poem, a key, and Garth's old ax to defeat Lady Lira's schemes. The "real" world is never far away as they each receive from others gifts of grace and mercy and love that they hadn't even imagined that they had needed. RECOMMENDATION: This "eco-fantasy," so called because it is so carefully rooted in the natural—endangered—environment, yet so other-worldly in the tradition of Lewis and Tolkein, may start a new tradition in fantasy writing. You will probably appreciate the modern touches, the very warty characters and the humor laced throughout, especially if you're not already a fantasy fan. M.T., L.T.*

AUTHOR: **Patricia Wrightson**
TITLE: *The Ice is Coming (1977)*
DESCRIPTION: Series continued in *The Dark Bright Water* and *Journey Behind the Wind*. The Ninya are threatening the Australian land with a new ice age. Wirrun, a young Abo, answering the call of the land and providing the care that only People can give, must find the Eldest Nargun, the oldest, most powerful spirit who controls fire, before the Ninya freeze it. Along the way he is given power by Ko-in, helped by a lost Mimi, and in the end is assisted by other Aborigines—even one Inlander, though the white Happy Folk are too busy pursuing their gilded happiness to care. The evil that threatens in the last volume is man-made, a wooden idol that claims men's spirits and judges them beyond death. Once again, Wirrun, the hero who knows the cost of being a hero, is called upon to save the land. As long as he is accompanied by his water-spirit wife, Murra, he has courage for this, his most dangerous journey. But Murra is stolen back by her sisters and Wirrun loses heart. Wirrun must meet Death himself before he can defeat the enemy of the land.
RECOMMENDATION: The Aborigines are to Australia what Native Americans are to the United States and Canada. Patricia Wrightson has used their myths, foreign to most Westerners, to structure her fantasies. Perhaps their very animistic foreignness, with its land and water spirits that talk and fly, and its dark shapeless evils, will heighten your awareness of the universal themes of good and evil. There is no familiar elevated language of European fantasy; nevertheless, a deep reverence for life and passion for goodness pervade these pages. Even in such a strange form you will discern the rockbottom truths of the necessity of self-sacrifice and of devotion to the good. Perhaps you will wonder what Wirrun meant when he assured the idol Wulgaru with "I am," for in the biblical tradition, that name can be claimed by God alone. M.T.

HISTORICAL

AUTHOR: **Margot Benary-Isbert**
TITLE: *The Ark (1953)*
DESCRIPTION: In devastated Germany after World War II, the refugee Lechow family—or what was left of it, for Margret's twin had been killed and Father was in a camp in Russia—was ordered to reconstruct their lives at 13 Parsley Street in Mrs. Verduz's two attic rooms. Across the hard months from October 1946 to December 1947, the Lechows do come back to life by sharing their meager stores, watching them multiply with love. They open their hearts to other refugees, including Matthias' musical friend, Dieter, and impish Joey's orphan friend, Hans Ulrich. Only Margret does not have someone special, but she does have the offer of a job as kennel maid for Mrs. Almut. She and Matthias rebuild an old railway car into an Ark for their family and are renewed and restored by working on the land. Margret and Matthias' story continues in *Rowan Farm*.
RECOMMENDATION: Never a book to shy away from the harsh realities of war, *The Ark* is even more a book about the greater realities of love and courage and faith. You will be blessed to find these qualities so real among the people you may have thought of as the enemy. E.T., M.T.*

AUTHOR: **Gillian Bradshaw**
TITLE: *A Beacon at Alexandria (1986)*
DESCRIPTION: Charis's father engages her to Ephesus' cruel new governor. In order to escape, she disguises herself as a eunuch, Chariton, and goes to Alexandria to study medicine. No one will take her on except an old Jewish doctor, but from him she learns not only the Hippocratic skills and theories but also compassion for her patients. Alexandria is the most intellectually exciting city in the Roman Empire, where all ideas clash,

including the doctrines of various Christian factions. Because she has caught the keen eye of the godly Archbishop Athanasios, she is engulfed in the riots that follow his death and has to escape once more, this time to Thrace, at the northern border of the Empire. There she is assigned to be an army doctor, while the Goths begin to harass and finally to conquer the once invincible Romans. Though she feared she would have to wait until heaven, it is in Thrace that Charis can at last become whole: a Roman, a doctor, and a woman.

RECOMMENDATION: Gillian Bradshaw's vivid panorama captures both the splendor and the squalor of a little-known period of history—the declining years of the Roman Empire. It does so through the eyes of a most unusual heroine, a brilliant young girl who longs against all possible reason to become a doctor. Many philosophies clash in idea-obssessed Alexandria, but the ones that allow Charis and her love, Athanaric, to be true to their own best selves come from a humble Jewish doctor and an archbishop who loves God more than he loves power. Reading *A Beacon at Alexandria* is a wonderful way to be swept up in their struggle, for it is yours, too. Another book by Bradshaw set in this time period is *The Bearkeeper's Daughter*. L.T.*

AUTHOR: **Lloyd C. Douglas**
TITLE: *The Robe (1942)*
DESCRIPTION: Marcellus, son of a Roman senator, is banished to the edge of the Roman empire, where he is in charge of soldiers performing a crucifixion. It has left him with a bad taste in his mouth and the victim's robe in his possession. That robe, with its unusual power to affect its handler's mind, causes Marcellus's mental sickness and then his recovery so that he—and his Greek slave, Demitrius, and eventually his beloved, Diana, a favorite of two cruel emperors—is led to discover the truth about Jesus. M.T., L.T.*

AUTHOR: **Esther Forbes**
TITLE: *Johnny Tremain (1943)*
DESCRIPTION: Newbery Award, 1944. If Johnny's story were not exciting enough—he is a young but skilled silversmith's apprentice whose hand is burned in molten silver because the other apprentices resent his pride and ability—it gets mixed up in Boston's 1773 struggle to force the issue of taxation with the British. Both Johnny and America learn what it means to "stand up" in freedom and responsibility.

RECOMMENDATION: Everyday citizens and famous people from your history textbooks come alive on these pages that some teens have been known to read again and again. E.T., M.T.*

AUTHOR: **Kathryn Forbes**
TITLE: *Mama's Bank Account (1943)*
DESCRIPTION: Mama dips into her Little Bank at home to keep her Norwegian immigrant family solvent so that she doesn't have to go to the Big Bank in downtown San Francisco. Only after her daughter Katrin sells her first story twenty years later and gives the money to her mother, does she learn that Mama had invented the Big Bank so that her children would not worry.
RECOMMENDATION: Your entire family will enjoy this account of Katrin's growing up years. A.A.*

AUTHOR: **Rudolf Frank**
TITLE: *No Hero for the Kaiser (1983)*
DESCRIPTION: On Jan's 14th birthday, September 14, 1914, a German artillery unit destroys his Polish village on its way to a "quick" victory over Russia. Having nowhere to go, Jan and a dog named Flox become mascots to the unit and with the common soldiers learn the common horrors and camaraderies of war. The men soon regard their quick-witted "Panie" as good luck. After fighting with him on both the eastern and western fronts, they want to reward him with German citizenship, knowing that it would make good war propaganda as well. How Jan responds to this honor is the moving conclusion to this powerful novel.
RECOMMENDATION: The story of what happened to this book is as stirring as Jan's story itself. Published in Germany in 1931, it was widely praised, but when Hitler came to power in 1933 it was publicly burned and Rudolf Frank was put in jail. After it was republished in the '70s, it won many prizes, including the prestigious Heinemann Peace Prize in 1983, the year it was translated into English. The German-speaking Polish boy, Jan, is a boy for all peoples. M.T.

Leon Garfield is a British novelist who has the astounding ability to make the ordinary people of 18th-century London real. As one of his characters so aptly put it: "Everything was described in the sharpest detail, so the reader was forced to believe every word." Because things are not often what they seem in the foggy mists and dark alleys of London, rollicking melodrama, sinister mystery, and sardonic humor are his trademarks. These qualities remind many of Charles Dickens's ability to evoke

Victorian London. People in all their fascinating variety of motives, inventiveness, warts, kindnesses, evils, silliness, and hypocrisies are Garfield's great strength. It's not just because people are his focus that he can be considered a humanist, but because people—in the end—are everything. "For better or worse," conclude the printer's devil from Angel Court and the infatuated bookseller's apprentice, Tom Titmarsh, this world is not God's kingdom, "but ours." It's no wonder then that his characters need "warmth"—human companionship—above all else.

AUTHOR: **Leon Garfield**
TITLE: *Smith (1967)*
DESCRIPTION: Smith, a young free-spirited pickpocket, must contend with a blind judge to whom devils and angels are all one, a swashbuckling highwayman, a sly lawyer, a jail rat, and two mysterious men in brown to solve a murder he witnessed in the alleys around St. Paul's Cathedral and Newgate Gaol in 18th-century London.
RECOMMENDATION: Though spiced with the same surprises and vivid street dialect of Garfield's other rollicking melodramas, *Smith* is considered the best of his early books because the young hero is so alive and complex. You feel for Smith as he must ferret out who's the devil and who's the angel, and determine if cleverness or kindness will yield the most promising clues. E.T., M.T.

AUTHOR: **Leon Garfield**
TITLE: *Footsteps (1980)*
DESCRIPTION: Twelve-year-old William Jones is haunted by the nighttime footsteps of his dying father. Laden with his father's watch and his guilty secret, William runs away to the dark alleys of 18th-century London to right the wrong his father had done. There he is caught in poverty and depravity—as well as humor and care—but most particularly in a mystery that threatens his own life.
RECOMMENDATION: Fast-paced intrigue and adventure, this book is full of surprising twists and tongue-in-cheek humor. Through it all, William puzzles out whether or not human beings are more naturally good or bad. E.T., M.T.

AUTHOR: **Leon Garfield**
TITLE: *The Apprentices (1978)*
DESCRIPTION: This cycle of twelve stories is set in consecutive months of an 18th-century year and is about apprentices to such Covent Garden-area businesses as undertaker, chemist, painter, printer, bookseller,

midwife, basketmaker, clockmaker, wigmaker, and lamplighter. Each turns on a very human interpretation of a biblical text, and most concern the young apprentice's desire for love, often of his master's daughter, for if he could marry her, he would get the business. The vivid descriptions of London street life and human foibles give these stories typical Garfield sardonic humor as do the characters' literal or unknowing interpretations of the texts. Perhaps the most tender (and least funny) story is "Rosy Starling"—about a blind but beautiful basketmaker's apprentice. She is met on May Day by a wigmaker's apprentice, Turtle, who cannot bring himself to trick her out of her hair. The most disturbing is "Tom Titmarsh's Devil" about a bookstore boy, attracted in spite of himself to a printer's "devil" (apprentice) who urges him to read *Thine is the Kingdom*, written by the ragged, intense Mr. Marsh, who is trying to come to terms with all the cruelties he'd seen illuminated one night by a lamplighter's apprentice. RECOMMENDATION: Leon Garfield returns again and again to the themes of light and dark, good and evil, always catching his readers off guard with his humor, sarcasm, and uncanny ability to deflate the most bloated hypocrite. You will laugh and you will puzzle how people saturated in the Bible—which Garfield finds much richer than the Celtic myths so many writers use as their sources—can twist the supernatural into such offbeat human meanings. M.T., L.T.

AUTHOR: **Alan Garner**
TITLE: *The Stone Book (1978)*
DESCRIPTION: (This and the next three books make up The Stone Quartet.) On the day that "changed Mary for the rest of [her] days," she climbs up to the top of the spire her stonemason father is finishing and down to a hidden cave with him to "see and know" the prehistoric markings there. She asks for a book to carry to chapel and he lovingly makes her a stone book whose fossils have "all the stories of the world and the flowers of the flood."

AUTHOR: **Alan Garner**
TITLE: *Granny Reardun (1978)*
DESCRIPTION: Joseph skips the last day of school to help his grandfather build a wall, trying to get up the courage to tell him that he doesn't want to apprentice to him but rather to "get aback" of the dying stonemason's trade to the more necessary, elemental blacksmith's.

AUTHOR: **Alan Garner**
TITLE: *The Aimer Gate (1979)*

DESCRIPTION: Robert, like his father before him, is searching for a trade. He wishes he could be a soldier like his Uncle Charlie, home on leave from World War I, though he also helps care for Faddock Allman, who lost his legs in that war.

AUTHOR: **Alan Garner**
TITLE: *Tom Fobble's Day (1979)*
DESCRIPTION: The sled William made is Tom Fobbled (swiped) by an older neighbor and crashed. Grandfather, a smithie who that day is retiring, makes him a new one with metal and wood from an ancient family loom. Riding farther on it than any of the boys dare and lighted by the searchlights looking for German planes, William feels "a line through hand and eye, block, forge and loom to the hill."
RECOMMENDATION: Each of these exquisite short stories can be savored by itself, yet, as the introduction to each states, "together they form a saga tracing four generations of a working class family in Chosley, a small town in Cheshire, England." Don't be deceived by the large print and simple woodcut illustrations. "Simple" in this case means elemental and deep, like the Greek drama or mythology that influences all of Garner's writing. If you have ever wondered about the origin of the universe or about what you should do with your life or how your ancestors affected you, then your wondering will be enriched by The Stone Quartet. A.A.*

AUTHOR: **Esther Hautzig**
TITLE: *The Endless Steppe (1968)*
DESCRIPTION: A privileged 10-year-old Polish girl is exiled to Rubtsovsk on the steppes of Siberia, with her adored father, her mother, and grandmother. There, unlike other Jews, she survives World War II. There in that cold alien environment she comes to maturity amid deprivation and squalor, supported by the love of her family, the companionship of hard-won friends, a mind ignited by the teaching of other exiles, and the protection of her God. When she can leave at age 16, Esther discovers that Siberia has become her home.
RECOMMENDATION: Esther Hautzig told this story of her girlhood, reminiscent of the way Laura Ingalls Wilder told hers. She will help you discover that the ingredients of surviving teenage years with dignity intact are the same the world over. E.T., M.T.*

AUTHOR: **John Hersey**
TITLE: *A Bell for Adano (1944)*

DESCRIPTION: A U.S. army major, Victor Joppolo, described by his author as "a good man, though weak in certain attractive human ways," is left as the mayor of Adano after the American invasion of Italy in World War II. There he meets many people, most good and all weak, who have been repressed by decades of fascism. He tries, through being a servant, not a dictator, to show them the meaning of democracy.
RECOMMENDATION: A warm, human account. L.T.

AUTHOR: **John Hersey**
TITLE: *The Wall (1950)*
DESCRIPTION: Through the eyes and pen of a nosey little Jewish scholar, Noach Levinson, you share a daily record of Jews forced first to relocate to the Warsaw ghetto in November, 1939, and then to be trapped there behind the wall they were forced to build around it, and finally to be hunted down and exterminated there by May 1943.
RECOMMENDATION: Many consider *The Wall* John Hersey's masterpiece. Noach and a few neighbors around Sienna 17 are not just Jews but Everyman in extreme circumstances. They display not only all the petty vices of jealousy and greed and bitterness but also all the reserves of faith and courage and love. Their defeats and ultimate triumphs of spirit will become your own. L.T.

AUTHOR: **Irene Hunt**
TITLE: *Across Five Aprils (1964)*
DESCRIPTION: Jethro Creighton is 9 in April, 1861, when, on his family's farm in southern Illinois, he receives news that Fort Sumter has been fired on. He is 13 in April 1865, when he learns that his idol, President Lincoln, has been assassinated. In between he grows to an early manhood as his brothers and cousin and schoolteacher go off to fight in the war, one on the side of the Confederacy; his family is attacked for Bill's "disloyalty"; he hides a deserter and writes Lincoln for advice; and he learns the meaning of courage and maturity as he shoulders the work of the farm.
RECOMMENDATION: More than any other novel for young people set in the Civil War era, *Across Five Aprils* brings the war to life and into perspective in all its horrors and significance because you see it through the eyes of Jethro, a fine young man for whom human life is never cheap and decency is never to be mocked. E.T., M.T.*

Mollie Hunter says she has a philosophy of life that compels her to write for young people, and which permeates her historical novels, contemporary novels, and folklore-fantasies, all set in Scotland. She believes in the "triumph of human love over the dark powers of the soul-less ones" and in "a one-to-one contact between man and God, and between man and man." Her splendid storytelling abilities bring these themes to life; they are not preachy bits tacked on. Her books are so varied that whether you like stories about today's teens, fantasy, or historical romance, you will find something of hers to suit you.

AUTHOR: **Mollie Hunter**
TITLE: *A Sound of Chariots (1972)*
DESCRIPTION: Nine-year-old Bridie is devastated by the death of her passionate Socialist father and the grief of her deeply religious mother. Across the years, until she is 15 and must leave home to make her living, she comes to terms with the realization that she, too, will die someday, with her heightened awareness of the beauty of life and the flight of time and with her own opportunity to live for her father and what he believes.
RECOMMENDATION: Though about death, Bridie's story surges with life; though about grief, it is filled with honest hope and sensitive beauty. Bridie is her father's girl, one who would "find it much more exciting to ride to Heaven on [Marx's] coattails than to get there by crossing over from the Sinners to the Saints." However, her mother's Brethren faith is viewed lovingly and honestly, though limited by a child's incomplete understanding. E.T.

AUTHOR: **Mollie Hunter**
TITLE: *Hold on to Love (1984)*
DESCRIPTION: In this sequel to *A Sound of Chariots*, on the brink of World War II, Bridie pursues her dream of being a writer even as she works long hours in her grandfather's Edinburgh flower shop. Bridie learns, as her dying grandmother warns, "Hold on to love!" but will that love be of her passionately chosen craft, or will it be of a fine young man named Peter whose possessiveness may interfere?
RECOMMENDATION: Bridie's story is really Mollie Hunter's own and as honestly told as her retellings of Scottish history and folklore. Bridie has a turning point experience in which she realizes that God exists and, though he may be her antagonist—someone to argue with—he is quite thoroughly mixed up in Bridie's life. E.T., M.T.

AUTHOR: **Stephen Lawhead**
TITLE: *The Pendragon Cycle (1987)*
DESCRIPTION: This trilogy includes *Taliesin, Merlin,* and *Arthur,* published by Crossway Books. The King Arthur saga is one of the foundational epics

of Western culture, and Stephen Lawhead retells it with breathtaking sensitivity and detail. His span reaches back to the lost city of Atlantis from which the beautiful and good Charis escapes with her life only to find herself in the realm of squabbling Celtic chieftains. She meets the fabled bard-prince, Taliesin, who first envisions the righteous Kingdom of Summer where love, justice, and mercy reign; and then bears Merlin. Merlin must bring his father's vision to reality through suffering many strenuous trials that nearly destroy him and by nurturing the young Pendragon, Arthur, to become the High King. Arthur has battles of his own, for the petty chieftains around him value their own skins more than a visionary kingdom that could bring peace to all the peoples of Britain. And lurking in the mists and shadows around Taliesin, Merlin, and Arthur is the hate-filled sorceress, Morgian.

RECOMMENDATION: Many are the retellings of the Arthur story, and deservedly so, for his tale is a wellspring of much that is good in our culture. What sets Lawhead's splendid interpretation apart is his careful integration of Christian faith and truths into the lives of his characters. And why not? What is the Kingdom of Summer, after all, but an attempt to actualize the kingdom of Heaven on earth? If you find that these fire your imagination and spirit and you want to read other Arthur stories, try the romances of Mary Stewart (*The Crystal Cave, The Hollow Hills, The Last Enchantment,* and *The Wicked Day*) or the histories of Rosemary Sutcliffe (*Sword at Sunset,* and the trilogy, *Sword and the Circle, Light Beyond the Forest,* and *Road to Camlann*) or the definitive and best-loved version of them all, based on Mallory's *Morte d' Arthur,* T. H. White's *The Once and Future King.* M.T., L.T.*

AUTHOR: **Sonia Levitin**
TITLE: ***The Return (1987)***
DESCRIPTION: Full of pathos, yet laced with humor, this is the story of Desta, an Ethiopian Jewish teenage girl, who was secretly airlifted from a refugee camp in the Sudan to redemption in Israel during the 1984 Operation Moses rescue mission.
RECOMMENDATION: Because of the richness of Sonia Leviton's re-creation of both Desta's warm Ethiopian family and village life and of her Jewish beliefs, you will enter fully into the girl's profound losses as she escapes her village as well as her gains of freedom, learning, and personal choice. This is a wonderful book! E.T., M.T.*

AUTHOR: **Janet Lunn**
TITLE: ***Shadow in Hawthorn Bay (1986)***

DESCRIPTION: Fifteen-year-old Mary was bound, it seemed from birth, to her dear cousin Duncan. Living in Scotland, with her gift of the second sight, she hears his voice calling her from Canada after four long years of silence, so she makes the difficult journey across the ocean to join him. Devastated to learn that he has died and that his family has returned to Scotland, to earn money for her own passage back she uneasily makes a place for herself in the pioneer community. The settlers are suspicious of her Scottish folk beliefs in fairies and ghosts, and she is haunted by Duncan's voice, as well as disturbed by the needs of the settlers and the attentions of Luke.

RECOMMENDATION: How Mary puts to rest the ghost of Duncan and chooses the course dictated by a new way of seeing, filled with both sadness and joy, is the essence of this excellent early 1800s love story. E.T., M.T.

AUTHOR: **Margaret Mitchell**
TITLE: *Gone with the Wind (1936)*
DESCRIPTION: Has there ever been a novel (or movie) more popular than *Gone with the Wind*? Many think not. Margaret Mitchell drew such strong characters in Scarlett O'Hara, the belle of a plantation devastated when Sherman marched through Georgia; in Ashley Wilkes, the gallant but weak-willed southern gentleman she adored but could not have; Melanie, the sweet girl who married Ashley and could see only good in all people; and Rhett Butler, the charming scoundrel in whom Scarlett met her match, that the actors who played them in the movie were forever identified with them.

RECOMMENDATION: The panorama of the Civil War era will come alive for you on these 1000 pages, but you may also want to compare *Gone with the Wind* to Margaret Walker's *Jubilee* for another point of view about these events for which our country is still paying a price. M.T., L.T.

AUTHOR: **Janette Oke**
TITLE: *Love Comes Softly (1979)*
DESCRIPTION: First of trilogy including *Love's Enduring Promise* and *Love's Long Journey* published by Bethany House. Marty's young husband is killed on their covered wagon journey west. The same day that she buries him, in desperation she marries Clark, a widower with a child—a union in name only that is merely a convenience for both of them. Across the fall and winter months until she can leave Clark on the first wagon train going east, Marty learns to be a pioneer housewife, learns to care for Missie and her own Clem's baby, and learns to love Clark's God and—surprisingly—Clark.

RECOMMENDATION: This simple romance begins a highly popular series that has spawned other series, and you will be charmed by its simple but true values. Janette Oke says that pioneer life appeals to her because in those uncluttered days "only what [was] of true worth was accepted and cherished," including spiritual values. Even if you have had trouble getting into other books, you will probably find Oke's many prairie romances right for you. E.T., M.T.*

AUTHOR: **Ruth Park**
TITLE: *Playing Beatie Bow (1980)*
DESCRIPTION: Fourteen-year-old Abigail watches a neighbor boy play a game called "Beatie Bow" and follows the strange girl, also watching, into her own city of Sydney, Australia, but a century before. There she encounters the Bows and Talliskers, "poor as dirt, but full of vitality," who compel her to stay until she fulfills her role in preserving their family gift of foresight and healing—and until she learns what it is to love.
RECOMMENDATION: The characters in Park's fine slip-time book make Victorian New South Wales come fully alive. How Abby is smitten with love for Judah, whose time she longs to escape, is as well described as any first love. But it is what she comes to realize about sacrificial love and the significance of each human's life that makes her experience worth sharing. E.T.*

AUTHOR: **Katherine Paterson** (See author overview in Contemporary section.)
TITLE: *The Master Puppeteer (1975)*
DESCRIPTION: Jiro hates the exacting work of puppet-making almost as much as he hated to go hungry with his mother and father during the famine in 18th-century Osaka, Japan. He apprentices himself to the puppet theater, where he quickly masters the intricate art of moving the large puppets. He also makes friends with Kinshi, the son of the demanding master puppeteer, and cheers the exploits of the Robin Hood-style bandit, Saburo. Jiro and Kinshi both learn that compassion for the hungry exacts a price, one that must be paid by many members of the Hanaza Puppet Theater.
RECOMMENDATION: Katherine Paterson is something of a master puppeteer herself, bringing to vivid life Jiro, Kinshi, and the family troupe at the Hanaza Puppet Theater in poverty-stricken, riot-torn Osaka, Japan. Though these two genuine boys are true to their times, their appeal lies partly in their universal characteristics of ambition, jealousy, loyalty,

compassion, and humor. Kinshi's self-sacrifice nearly makes him a Christ-figure. E.T., M.T.*

AUTHOR: **Katherine Paterson**
TITLE: *Rebels of the Heavenly Kingdom (1983)*
DESCRIPTION: Wang Lee is kidnapped off his parents' farm by despicable bandits during the drought of 1851. When his freedom is bought by a member of the God-fearers, his fortunes become tangled up with this idealistic Heavenly Kingdom of Great Peace. They are driven by their own versions of pacifist and celibate Christian doctrines but also by a great hatred for the corrupt and unjust Manchu government. Because their leaders believe that they have been given the Mandate of Heaven to inaugurate a new era of righteousness, they take up arms to drive the Manchu out. Wang Lee, and his savior, Mei Lei, and their companions slowly become hardened warriors until they must confront the fact that their ideals have been lost.
RECOMMENDATION: Wang Lee and Mei Lei may seem light years away from your contemporary existence, but Paterson skillfully brings their complex and fascinating (and historically true) situation to life. These young people in a distant time and place face the same dilemmas as all ethical young people—how not to be corrupted when the evil that surrounds you tempts you to use less than noble means to justify noble ends. M.T.*

AUTHOR: **K. M. Peyton** (See author overview in Contemporary section.)
TITLE: *Flambards (1968)*
DESCRIPTION: In 1908 Christina must go to Flambards, a decaying fox hunting estate, where she is repulsed by her cruel hunt-crippled uncle. She is caught between Mark, as obsessed with horses as his father and whom she is expected eventually to marry, and his brother Will, who hates hunting and is secretly learning to build and fly one of the first airplanes in England.
RECOMMENDATION: *Flambards* is about the clash of two ways of life—the old landed gentry and the modern world of technology—more than it is about Mark, Will, and Christina, though she is as lively a heroine as you could wish. The book can help you to see, as Christina did briefly, historical "patterns in life, which proved everything was not quite so inconsequential as sometimes it seemed." Its sequels are *The Edge of the Cloud* and *Flambards in Summer.* M.T.

AUTHOR: **K. M. Peyton**
TITLE: *Flambards Divided (1981)*
DESCRIPTION: World War I was supposed to change the world, but around Flambards social attitudes at least seemed to remain the same, making Christina and Dick's socially improper marriage most difficult. Then Mark arrives back there as well, to convalesce from his dreadful war wounds, complicating matters even further.
RECOMMENDATION: In this last of the Flambards series, written ten years after the others, Christina is less certain of her beliefs, like most young people who had survived World War I. You may find it most interesting to detect how the characters defend their moral choices to themselves and to each other, what they call sin and what they don't, because in Europe that war was the great dividing point between the traditional way of life and our own modern era. Christina, particularly, struggles with the change. M.T., L.T.

AUTHOR: **Eugenia Price**
TITLE: *The Beloved Invader (1965)*
DESCRIPTION: First of a trilogy that includes *New Moon Rising* and *Lighthouse*. The true story of Anson Dodge, a wealthy young New Yorker who gave up a typical career to minister to the forgotten people of St. Simons Island after the Civil War's devastation, is told as a romance. Dodge married two women: his beloved cousin, the joyous and glamorous Ellen whose tragic death he mourns for years, and the Island's own Anna, who kept house for him for many of those years and who with him learns that God makes redemptive use of everything in our lives.
RECOMMENDATION: You'll be glad to know that Price is a prolific writer of historical fiction, all from a Christian perspective. L.T.*

AUTHOR: **Eugenia Price**
TITLE: *Savannah (1983)*
DESCRIPTION: First of a quartet of books that includes *To See Your Face Again, Before the Darkness Falls,* and *Stranger in Savannah.* In 1812 Mark Browning makes his way to Savannah, the raw young town aspiring to gentility that contains the secrets of his birth and—he hopes—the key to his future. He meets the merchant Robert Mackey who invites him into his home and office, and so Mark's life becomes entwined with that prominent family (including its beautiful wife and mother) and all the intrigues and pleasures that come to an astute young businessman with a dark past. Mark's story and that of his descendents continues in the sequels that take you through the Civil War era.

RECOMMENDATION: The setting, both of time and of place, is all-important in this book as it is in any good historical fiction—and Eugenia Price's stories stand with the best. Many of these characters really lived, though you may find some of them too beautiful, too intelligent, and too passionate to seem quite real. The Savannah stories are also loosely tied to Price's Don Juan McQueen series. L.T.*

AUTHOR: **Kenneth Roberts**
TITLE: *Northwest Passage (1937)*
DESCRIPTION: Major Robert Rogers not only led the 1759 expedition against the Indian village of St. Francis but also had a dream to find an overland passage to the Pacific. Pursuing it, he travels to London to find financial backing and then to Michigan, where he becomes governor of Fort Michilimackinac. Roger's story is told through the eyes of his friend, Langdon Town, who has a desire of his own to be able to paint the Indians as they really are.
RECOMMENDATION: There is enough humor, suspense, romance, adventure, and excitement to satisfy the most demanding of readers. Families have been known to enjoy reading this book aloud. Roberts has written other historical fiction books, too. L.T.*

AUTHOR: **Margaret Rostkowski**
TITLE: *After the Dancing Days (1986)*
DESCRIPTION: When 13-year-old Annie's army doctor father comes home from World War I, things don't settle back to normal. How could they? Her mother's beloved brother Paul had been killed. Her mother is determined to forget the war even though her father decides to work at a veteran's hospital. Annie is drawn to a bitter, disfigured soldier there, despite her own misgivings, and despite her mother's disapproval. From Andrew she learns much about courage, about heroism on and off the battlefield, about meaning in the face of senselessness, and about living by her own beliefs.
RECOMMENDATION: Even in a thoughtful, loving family there can be grave disagreements over values. Annie's father and mother choose different ways to put the horrors of WW I behind them—bury the painful memories, or support the veterans who make them remember. Annie must decide her own way and in the process has her shining ideals of heroism shattered. But the truth she gains in the process is worth so much more— it is a truth she can grow and live by. E.T.

AUTHOR: **Mary Stolz**
TITLE: *Pangur Ban (1988)*
DESCRIPTION: In A.D. 913 Cormac is 15 and struggling against the inevitability of becoming a farmer, struggling to find time to draw the woodland creatures he loves even though he'll be beaten for shirking the farm work, struggling to puzzle out the meaning of life and faith. How can he get admitted to the monastery, where he can learn Latin and illuminating when his vocation is not to serve God but to serve his talent? But get there he does, never quite conforming yet always shaping his talents to add to the treasures of words and pictures housed there. And when the Vikings arrive to destroy everything, he finds a way to preserve his best work and so encourage another young seeker of faith two centuries later.
RECOMMENDATION: Veteran author Mary Stolz was curious about a wry, spritely poem about a cat, Pangur Ban, discovered on the border of a 9th-century Irish illuminated manuscript. This book is her attempt to get inside the heart and mind of its anonymous author. Life then was harsh and her book could probably have been that, yet it sings beautifully with life and love, hope and faith, humor and honesty. If you have ever wondered if you will use your talents for God or if they will demand your allegiance for themselves, or if you have been proud of something you have created, you will easily enter into Cormac's joyous struggles of so long ago. E.T., M.T.*

AUTHOR: **Irving Stone**
TITLE: *The Agony and the Ecstasy, a Novel of Michelangelo (1961)*
DESCRIPTION: Michelangelo's passion for sculpture, for his city of Florence, and for God, personifies the turbulent era of the 15th- and 16th-century Italian Renaissance. Though the artist's problems with the several popes he outlived, the wars of the city states, and the daily struggle just to eat and work may seem far removed from today, you may find yourself caught up in his overwhelming desire to create as God had created. If you have ever wondered about the origin of the word "humanism," you will find it here as you see Michelangelo wrestling to unite the best of the Greek view of the body with the true Christian vision of the spirit.
RECOMMENDATION: Stone has the rare ability to bring a whole era to life through a focus on one genius. If you enjoyed *The Agony and the Ecstasy*, you may also enjoy other books by Stone, including *Lust for Life*, his fictional biography of another artist, the tortured Christian of a later era, Vincent Van Gogh. A couple of American women who married Presidents have their own books—Rachel Jackson in *The President's Lady* and Mary Todd Lincoln in *Love is Eternal*. The search by Henry and Sophia

Schliemann for the mythical city of Troy, which developed into the field of archeology, is described in *The Greek Treasure*. L.T.

AUTHOR: **Harriet Beecher Stowe**
TITLE: *Uncle Tom's Cabin (1852)*
DESCRIPTION: Abraham Lincoln told Harriet Beecher Stowe that she "wrote the book that made this great war." Though it may seem sentimental now, over 300,000 Americans bought it during its first year in print. Besides influencing an era, it has contributed unforgettable figures to our cultural memories: the old Uncle Tom; the little Topsy who wasn't born, just "grow'd"; the slave girl Eliza who jumps from ice floe to ice floe in her effort to escape across the Ohio River; and the cruel overseer, Simon Legree.
RECOMMENDATION: If you are interested in this era of history, you will want to compare this classic with the more contemporary but excellent *Jubilee*, by Margaret Walker. M.T.

AUTHOR: **Rosemary Sutcliffe**
TITLE: *The Eagle of the Ninth (1954)*
DESCRIPTION: Marcus, a new Roman cohort commander, is wounded in his first battle with the rebellious British and must recuperate in his uncle's home, where he impulsively buys a British gladiator as his slave. Later, having freed Esca, Marcus and his new friend travel, disguised, into Caledonia (Scotland) to search for the eagle standard of the Ninth Legion with which his father had disappeared years before.
RECOMMENDATION: Rosemary Sutcliffe, who has dozens of books to her credit, has the rare ability to breathe life into "dead" history, and she is at her best in the era of Roman Britain, though the later kings and legends of Britain concern her as well. You'll count the Roman Marcus and the British Esca among your friends and yearn for them to understand the values of the other's way of life. E.T., M.T.*

AUTHOR: **Rosemary Sutcliffe**
TITLE: *Song for a Dark Queen (1978)*
DESCRIPTION: The real person in this book is Queen Boadicea, the matriarch of the Iceni, who in A.D. 60 led a nearly successful revolt against the conquering Romans. You see her through the eyes of the harpist, Cadwan, who observed everything so that he could turn it into songs that praised the queen he loved and the life of the tribe she stood for.

RECOMMENDATION: Rosemary Sutcliffe says that "real people, lost behind their legends, have always fascinated" her; she, in turn, makes them fascinating for you. E.T., M.T.

AUTHOR: **Bodie Thoene**
TITLE: *The Zion Chronicles (1987)*
DESCRIPTION: Includes *The Gates of Zion, A Daughter of Zion, The Return to Zion, A Light in Zion,* and *The Key to Zion,* all published by Bethany House. The months before Israel became a nation in May, 1948 are played out in all their drama and suspense through the lives of a Jewish archaeologist, Moshe Sachar; an emotionally scarred survivor of the Nazi deathcamps, Rachel Lebowitz; an American photojournalist, Ellie Warne; and the American World War II flying ace, David Meyer. Among many others who touch their lives for good or ill are Gerhardt, a former S.S. man, twisted by his hatred of the Jews; Sarai, the sister of one of his Arab henchmen; an old rabbi and other Haganah defending the walls of the Old City of Jerusalem, as well as people whom you will recognize from your history books. There are narrow escapes through labyrinth sewers or over burning rooftops, smuggled weapons and food and partisans, plots and counterplots, agents and double agents, bombings and rescues enough to keep you turning the pages of this wonderful five-volume series. But threaded throughout the intrigue of "the miracle that is Israel" is a strong, sure belief in the redeeming power of Yeshua, the Messiah of Israel, who can heal both individuals and nations.
RECOMMENDATION: This religious vision puts the Zion stories in strong contrast to the more famous *Exodus* by Leon Uris, which equals its drama. However, its characters' main motivation is the powerful but secular desire for freedom. Uris' Ari Ben Canaan says, "The only Messiah that will deliver [us] is a bayonet on the end of a rifle." However, *Exodus* also paints a broader picture of the birth of Israel through flashbacks in various characters' lives, stretching from the steppes of Czarist Russia to the ovens of Auschwitz to the deck of the rescue ship *Exodus* to the kibbutzim carved out of the desert. If *The Zion Chronicles* hooks you on this period of history, as well it might, you may want to give *Exodus* a try. Thoene herself has written a series of "prequels" to the Chronicles called Zion Covenant (*Vienna Prelude, Prague Counterpoint, Munich Signature,* and *Jerusalem Interlude, Danzig Passage,* and *Warsaw Requiem*) in which she follows the fortunes of several minor characters in the Israeli series during the years of World War II. As you might guess from the titles, music plays an important role in them, but they are as suspenseful and faith-infused as the books set in Israel. M.T., L.T.*

AUTHOR: **Margaret Walker**
TITLE: *Jubilee (1966)*
DESCRIPTION: Based on the lives of her great-grandparents, Margaret Walker tells a compelling story of blacks in the south, from slavery days when Vyry was the bastard daughter of a Georgian plantation owner and Randall was a free black blacksmith in the nearby town of Dutton. The story continues through the years of the Civil War and the Ku Klux Klan years of reconstruction that followed.
RECOMMENDATION: Vyry's husband once realized, after a final confrontation with her past, that Vyry was "touched with a spiritual fire and permeated with a spiritual wholeness that had been forged in a crucible of suffering." You too will quickly perceive that whole human greatness that makes her story so remarkable. M.T., L.T.

Two excellent books of historical fiction for young people are out of print and not readily available in public libraries, but we mention them here to you so that perhaps you could go on a treasure hunt in church or school or friends' bookshelves or let the publishers know that you would like to read either of them. **Anne de Vries** was a Dutch author who, better than almost anyone else, captured on paper the essence of World War II as experienced by the De Boers, and especially their teenage son, John. They resisted all that Hitler stood for because they served both their fellow human beings and a higher King who controls all history. Translated into English, it is called *Journey Through the Night* and was published in 1984 by the Canadian publishing house, Paideia Press (Box 1000, Jordan Station, Ontario, Canada, L0R 1SO). M.T., L.T.*

British missionary-author, **Patricia St. John,** much loved for her children's books set in Europe and North Africa, wrote movingly of the destruction of Lebanon in 1973, which still has its repercussions in the continuing Middle East crisis. She gives to us the story of teenage Lamia and her family, middle-class Arab Christians. Redemption in the midst of ashes is her powerful theme, as it is one of de Vries's. In England, Scripture Union titled it *Nothing Else Matters* when it came out in 1982, and in the United States, Moody Press (Chicago, Ill.) gave it the title, *If You Love Me.* E.T., M.T.*

Both books are wonderful for families to read aloud together, even with the youngest of teens. Find them, if you can!

MYSTERY

AUTHOR: **Avi**
TITLE: *The Man Who Was Poe (1989)*
DESCRIPTION: Eleven-year-old Edmund, his twin sister, and Aunty Pru arrive in Providence, Rhode Island, in 1848 after receiving an urgent message from his missing mother. Within weeks his aunt and sister have also disappeared under sinister circumstances. He turns, unwillingly, for help from a stranger who calls himself Auguste Dupin and who sometimes has great insight into Edmund's plight. At other times, however, he is both drunk and indifferent. What Edmund does not know is that "Dupin" is really that fictional character's creator, Edgar Allan Poe, who sees Edmund's real life as a possible plot for a new story. But if he writes it, Sis will have to die.
RECOMMENDATION: You may find yourself fascinated not only by the clever unraveling of Edmund's plot—a mystery in itself—but by this fictional peek into the unstable mind of America's greatest writer of horror stories, Edgar Allan Poe—yet another mystery. E.T.

AUTHOR: **G. K. Chesterton**
TITLE: *Father Brown (1911)*
DESCRIPTION: Father Brown is the most unlikely of detectives, and his methods of analysis are more psychological than the forensics used by Sherlock Holmes. You may therefore find yourself even more fascinated to have the chance to sleuth along with the outwardly bumbling priest who "tries to get [himself] inside the murderer. "Till," as he says, "I really am the murderer. And when I am quite sure that I feel exactly like the murderer myself, of course I know who he is." M.T., L.T.*

AUTHOR: **Tom Clancy**
TITLE: *Red Storm Rising (1986)*
DESCRIPTION: *Red Storm Rising* envelops you in the Soviet Union's critically desperate plot for Middle Eastern oil—a Muslim fanatic has destroyed its major refinery. To ensure that NATO countries will not retaliate for their seizure of that oil, military and diplomatic intrigue is launched on a giant scale. You see events unfold through the eyes of Soviets and Westerners, both key strategists and common soldiers.
RECOMMENDATION: Clancy is the cleanest of the writers of international intrigue; you can read his novels without fear of embarrassingly steamy sex scenes and continuous streams of foul language. L.T.

AUTHOR: **Peter Dickenson**
TITLE: *The Seventh Raven (1981)*
DESCRIPTION: One hundred-one children in dress rehearsal for the annual church opera are taken hostage by three Latin American terrorists who had bungled kidnapping the boy playing the role of the seventh raven—the son of their Mattean ambassador to England.
RECOMMENDATION: Just because this suspense takes place in a church, don't expect that the characters are religious. Instead, you'll discover the relevance of the Elijah-Baal stories—as well as art—to today's unjust political situations. You will also empathize with Doll over her growing awareness of her guilt and her calling in the context of a needy world. Besides being a terrific story, this book gives you lots to think about. Danny, one of the terrorists, says at one point, "I have heard you sing in your opera the song of the King in the Middle [Ahab]. This king in your story is a traitor to the God in your story. So in this world, this real place, which is not a story, you, you, and you, and you are traitors. You are traitors to Man." Are you? M.T.

AUTHOR: **Sir Arthur Conan Doyle**
TITLE: *The Adventures of Sherlock Holmes (1887)*
DESCRIPTION: Sherlock Holmes, who is, according to his companion, Dr. Watson, "the most perfect reasoning and observing machine that the world has ever seen," is therefore one of the world's greatest detectives; in fact, tourists try to find 221 Bacon Street in London, when really the famous lodgings and the famous lodgers are just figments of Sir Arthur Conan Doyle's imagination.
RECOMMENDATION: Put your own reasoning powers to work as you trace with Holmes "the scarlet thread of murder that runs through the colorless skein of life." E.T., M.T.*

AUTHOR: **Virginia Hamilton**
TITLE: *Sweet Whispers, Brother Rush (1982)*
DESCRIPTION: Newbery Honor. The suspense in this story that takes place both on the rough city streets and in rural poverty is not so much the ghost who appears on the first page but in the battle for Dab's life and Tree's security. The mystery, again, is not so much the ghostliness but how the past affects the present.
RECOMMENDATION: Grimly realistic, this story is about a 14-year-old girl essentially abandoned by her parents to bring up her older retarded brother alone. Nonetheless, you may finds strands of love and flashes of hope. E.T., M.T.

AUTHOR: **John Haworth**
TITLE: *Heart of Stone (1984)*
DESCRIPTION: Tim Vaughan is careful not to let Henry Stanwick know too much about himself because he needs the geologist's expertise to be able to hike the impossible stone pinnacles of Madagascar—and to complete his mysterious mission. For his part, Stanwick welcomes the opportunity to take his mind off a faltering romance and an unwanted job offer. But what Stanwick stumbles into is Operation Jezreel, a plot to save the earth—or at least some of the politically enlightened few—from its own imminent collapse.
RECOMMENDATION: Stanwick's adventure, published by Crossway, has enough suspense to keep you turning the pages and a spiritual message overlaying it. M.T., L.T.*

AUTHOR: **Stephen King**
TITLE: *The Shining (1977)*
DESCRIPTION: Teens are among Stephen King's biggest fans and *The Shining* is one of his most popular books (and movies). Jack Torrance, fired from his teaching job for hitting a student, takes his wife, Wendy, and five-year-old son, Danny, to an isolated resort hotel in the Rockies. He will be the winter caretaker and can perhaps get his alcoholism and violent temper under control and his promising writing career back on track. The Overlook, however, has a sleazy history and, once the Torrances are there alone, its past horrors seem to come alive, especially to Danny who has a "shining"—the ability to perceive the future. Where does the evil come from—from a "broken circuit-breaker" in his body chemistry, as Jack thinks—or from a malevolent outside force, such as the haunted hotel itself? You'll find that the question matters very much to you, but as you get caught in the grip of the escalating horror of a likable family self-

destructing, you may temporarily put it aside in a revulsion against such gross violence. The question is vital for Danny who, with the aid of another shiner, Halloran, escapes the Overlook, because innocent though he seems, he carries in his own body the inheritance of his father's violently defective genes.

RECOMMENDATION: Academic critics of Stephen King say that his horror novels can be fit into a tradition of American gothic romances that reaches back to Melville and Edgar Allan Poe, and are a critique of a corrupt and corrupting American society. While that interpretation may be one possibility, King himself says he writes "to terrorize the reader. But if . . . I cannot terrify . . . I will try to horrify; and if I cannot horrify, I'll go for the gross-out. I'm not proud." You have no doubt heard at school every foul word King uses, but their constant repetition becomes part of the degrading atmosphere of the story, which serves to dull you to the full moral horror of the mother's and father's attempting to murder each other while their little boy sees it coming but is unable to prevent it. King says he believes that there is love, but it is nevertheless only a necessary illusion to comfort us on our ultimately lonely path to death." That means that the tranquil end to *The Shining* is also only an illusion. And if it's horror that gives you your kicks, why then, eat, drink, and be merry on it, for tomorrow you will die. Such a philosophy seems to belie all the disdain King has for adults who corrupt innocent children. Ironically, he is one of the most powerful corrupters of them all! L.T.

AUTHOR: **John LeCarré**
TITLE: *The Spy Who Came in from the Cold (1963)*
DESCRIPTION: Alec Leamus has just watched the destruction of his spy network so carefully built up during the years just following the erecting of the Berlin Wall. He returns home to England, supposedly to retire in disgrace, but really to attempt one last time to defeat his East German Communist counterpart. Or is it Leamus who is being manipulated by him?
RECOMMENDATION: LeCarré's most famous spy story is not only an espionage thriller with twists that will keep you reading past your bedtime but it provides a careful and compassionate examination of the central moral dilemmas of spying: Do the ends justify the means? Are a few people worth sacrificing to save many? Do you agree with the experienced but jaded spy, Leamus, that killing is despicable but necessary in a world gone mad? Or with the idealistic but confused Communist, Liz, that though truth is absolute (built into historical processes more important than individuals), individuals are ultimately significant? Or have you formulated a worldview different from either of theirs? M.T., L.T.

AUTHOR: **Alistair MacLean**
TITLE: *The Guns of Navarone (1957)*
DESCRIPTION: Against impossible odds, a hand-picked group of five Allied saboteurs are sent off into the Aegean Sea to make their way to the fortress island of Navarone. They must destroy the German guns that control that strategic crossroad and prevent the British from evacuating 1200 soldiers from Kheros. Among them are two mountain climbing experts, the New Zealander leader, Mallory, and an inwardly fearful British soldier, Stevens. To accomplish their goal, they must scale a sheer precipice never climbed before. A giant Greek, Andreas, who has seen his family and village slaughtered; an American explosives expert, Miller; and Casey Brown, who can fix any engine, make up the rest of the party.
RECOMMENDATION: Besides being a story of compelling action that you won't be able to put down, *The Guns of Navarone* explores the qualities of courage, the notions of what kinds of killing can be justified in a desperate wartime situation, and the common humanity among enemies that makes their lives worth living and sacrificing. Although many of MacLean's later books do not live up to the standard he set in *Navarone*, you do not want to miss this one. M.T., L.T.

AUTHOR: **Margaret Mahy** (See author overview in the Contemporary section.)
TITLE: *The Changeover: A Supernatural Romance (1984)*
DESCRIPTION: Fourteen-year-old Laura must "change over" into a witch so that she can counter-curse the wicked spirit of the dead who is sucking the life out of her young brother, Jacko. She turns for help to Sorry Carlisle, an older boy in her school, the son and grandson of reputed witches. He not only assists in her rebirth as a witch but in awakening for her an awareness of her sexuality. Ordinary, loving families coexist with strange, even demonic ones, in this unusual book set in New Zealand.
RECOMMENDATION: As with the characters in all Mahy's novels, Laura and Sorry and their families are so vividly drawn and so complex that they seem real, hence you may experience a vivid, complex uneasiness at their interaction with the occult world. In some of her other novels, Mahy reveals herself as a person who only believes in the natural world, a place where all we can do is make the best choices we can, so you may legitimately ask, "How does the spirit world of *Changeover* fit that?" Is she saying that reality is anything an author can create? Unlike some of Mahy's other heroines, Laura chooses not to make love with her newfound lover. You will be cheering for her in that as well as in the release of Jacko from Carmony Braque's death mark. M.T., L.T.

AUTHOR: **Margaret Mahy**
TITLE: *The Tricksters (1986)*
DESCRIPTION: Harry, the 17-year-old middle daughter of the five children of Jack and Naomi Hamilton, is anxious for her family's Christmas-midsummer holiday at their New Zealand beach cottage, Carnival Hide. It is famous in local history for the eccentric owner who built and then abandoned it after his son's drowning. The Hamiltons are used to frequent guests, such as Emma and her baby, but when the sinister, conjuring Carnival brothers—are they the villain in Harry's secret romance novel come to life or are they the drowned Teddy resurrected?—join the clan, bizarre tricks sweep away the appearance of family happiness and force all the Hamiltons to confront their own betrayals and guilt.
RECOMMENDATION: As it does for Harry, who falls in love with one of the ghostly Carnival brothers, just when you think you are "going to catch on, the meaning goes away again" in this book full of tricks of appearance, words, and philosophies. Mahy is so skilled a writer that she makes you care about her characters, and so you may feel a full portion of horror at their discoveries and may even become angry, wondering if she is playing word tricks on you all the while you are thinking and feeling hard. M.T., L.T.

AUTHOR: **Walter Dean Myers**
TITLE: *Tales of a Dead King (1983)*
DESCRIPTION: John Robie and Karen Lacey, two American teens chosen to help John's great-uncle, Dr. Leonhardt, with an archaeological dig in Egypt, arrive there to discover that he is missing. In their week-long search for him, they encounter snakes planted in Karen's room, daggers thrown at them in the marketplace, and capture by kidnappers in a deserted village.
RECOMMENDATION: There is action enough for all in this easy-to-read mystery and a gently understated message that "worshiping gold" is not worth the price. E.T.

AUTHOR: **Frank Peretti**
TITLE: *This Present Darkness (1986)*
DESCRIPTION: A typical small town is the unlikely place that the Prince of Darkness has chosen to orchestrate his final assault on Christianity by establishing a world religion, Universal Consciousness. The newly arrived newspaper editor, the pastor of a troubled and divided church, and a brilliant but bitter professor of psychology are some of the key figures in this vast spiritual drama that moves back and forth between the physical and spiritual realms where devils and angels alike plot their strategies. It also moves to a tightly controlled climax and has exciting scenes of

exorcisms, intriguing glimpses of New Age thinking, and vivid pictures of diabolical plots and angelic counterplots.

RECOMMENDATION: This book, published by Crossway, has taken the evangelical world by storm as it highlights themes of commitment and purity that are important in the late 20th century. There are cautions that must be noted, however. First, you should fix in your mind before you read is, that though it is classified here as "suspense" (Peretti has been called the Christian Stephen King!), it could also be classified as "fantasy." It must not be taken literally, any more than Madeleine L'Engle's stories or C. S. Lewis's *Screwtape Letters*, even though it may well convey actual truth, as all stories attempt to do. Second, you must evaluate as you read. Who has power to act in this book—people, or angels and devils, or both? Are people just puppets, reacting as programmed by good and evil forces, or do they exercise a true freedom of will? If you decide primarily for the former view, you may find yourself uneasy at several critical points in the novel. L.T.

AUTHOR: **Ellis Peters**
TITLE: *A Morbid Taste for Bones (1978)*
DESCRIPTION: Ellis Peters has dozens of mysteries to her credit, but probably the best loved are her medieval ones revolving around a Benedictine monastery in Shrewsbury. Her sleuth is Brother Cadfael, a worldly, traveled man retired to the monastery to raise herbs. In this first one, when Brother Columbanus is cured of his madness by a vision of the Welsh St. Winifred, he declares that the saint wants her bones to enhance the prestige of Shrewsbury Abbey. The delegation sent off to retrieve her remains discovers that the Welsh villagers are not anxious to part with them. Even so, they are horrified when their main opponent is found dead. Evidence points to the victim's English suitor, Engelard, but Br. Cadfael is not so sure. He and Sioned, the daughter, contrive both to discover the true murderer and ensure that St. Winifred rests where she belongs.

RECOMMENDATION: With all the puzzles and suspense of a mystery, these Brother Cadfael stories also reveal a shrewd yet sympathetic insight into human nature. Mercy is as apparent as greed and pride. You will find yourself nodding with agreement when Br. Cadfael argues that we must "meet every man as you find him, for we're all made the same under habit or robe or rags. Some made better than others, and some better cared for, but on the same pattern all." M.T., L.T.*

AUTHOR: **Dorothy Sayers**
TITLE: *Strong Poison (1930)*

DESCRIPTION: Sayers wrote 12 mysteries and in *Strong Poison* (critics disagree violently whether *Strong Poison* or *Nine Tailors* is her best), Harriet Vane, a writer of detective stories, has been accused of poisoning her former lover with arsenic. Because her latest book concerns an arsenic poisoning, she is considered an expert on the subject. The case seems airtight to everybody but Lord Peter Wimsey.

RECOMMENDATION: Wimsey, the amateur detective made famous by Sayers, says that "in detective stories virtue is always triumphant. They're the purest literature we have." Do you agree? From time to time you'll be able to see a Lord Peter Wimsey mystery on public television. M.T., L.T.

AUTHOR: **Josephine Tey**
TITLE: *The Daughter of Time (1951)*
DESCRIPTION: Inspector Alan Grant of the Scotland Yard is bored beyond belief as he lies day after day in a hospital with a broken leg. To pass the time, he studies portraits of famous people, using his detective's eye for detail and evidence to discern something of their personalities. King Richard III's portrait intrigues him because history books claim he was one of England's worst villains, killing his young nephews to secure his throne. Yet his face is kindly and sensitive. Could the truth of the 1485 murder be known? Grant is determined to find out.

RECOMMENDATION: Many consider Josephine Tey's *Daughter of Time* to be one of the best mysteries ever written. It is only one of many Elizabeth MacIntosh wrote about Inspector Grant under her Tey pen name or under the name Gordon Daviot. The book takes you right inside the reasoning processes of a master detective, a fascinating place to be. If you've ever wondered how historians, who should be merely detectives themselves, separated by time from their flesh-and-blood evidence, determine what really happened, this lets you into the secret of truth-finding. Do you agree with the old proverb of the title, that "truth is the daughter of time?" M.T., L.T.

AUTHOR: **Phyllis Whitney**
TITLE: *Black Amber (1964)*
DESCRIPTION: *Black Amber* is a typical Phyllis Whitney "suspense thriller romance." In an exotic setting—in this case, Istanbul—a beautiful, plucky young heroine—Tracy Hubbard—confronts sinister forces—both the mysterious circumstances of her sister's suicide and drug smuggling—and, after danger threatens her as well, overcomes them with persistence and intelligence. In the process she finds, of course, true love.

RECOMMENDATION: Mary Stewart and Victoria Holt are the other authors who, along with Whitney, have mastered this gothic (or suspense thriller) romance genre. M.T., L.T.

NONFICTION

AUTHOR: **Joy Adamson**
TITLE: ***Born Free (1960)***
DESCRIPTION: Elsa is a lioness raised from birth by Kenya Game Warden George Adamson and his wife, Joy, but also trained by them to be able to take her place confidently in the wilds, her true home. This story is of their four years together in which Elsa achieved the impossible: both freedom to be a natural wild animal and a friend to humans. You'll learn many fascinating facts about African wildlife while this lioness captivates you as she did the Adamsons. E.T.*

AUTHOR: **Verne Becker, ed.**
TITLE: ***The Campus Life Guide to Surviving High School (1984)***
DESCRIPTION: One of the many *Campus Life* magazine guides now published by Zondervan is this one—not a how-to-study, how-to-balance extra-curriculars kind of guide. This one deals with more basic issues: feelings, loneliness, failure, habits, and family. You'll find this—or other Campus Life guides on friendship, peer pressures, or family life—a real help. E.T., M.T.*

AUTHOR: **Paul Brand and Philip Yancey**
TITLE: ***In His Image (1984)***
DESCRIPTION: A hand surgeon famous for his work with leprosy patients around the world teams up with a professional writer to explore the wonders of the human body. Then they apply the fascinating tidbits and patterns of information metaphorically to the spiritual body of Christ in this richly layered book, a companion volume to their *Fearfully and Wonderfully Made*. Dr. Brand and Yancey want "to throw across" (the literal

Dr. Ben Carson, renowned neurosurgeon and author of the book *Gifted Hands*. Photo by Christine Armstrong and reprinted with permission of Review and Herald Pub. Assoc. For description of this book see page 191.

meaning of the word "symbol") a bridge between the natural visible world of the body to the invisible world of the spirit, because they stand in the tradition of Copernicus, Kepler, Galileo, and Newton, the great scientists of the past who believed the created world revealed God's nature to his people. Dorothy Clark Wilson has written a biography of Dr. Brand's work in India, reconstructing the hands of lepers, *Ten Fingers for God*. Both books are published by Zondervan. L.T.*

AUTHOR: **Ben Carson with Cecil Murphey**
TITLE: *Gifted Hands: The Story of Ben Carson (1990)*
DESCRIPTION: Raised in inner-city Detroit by a mother with a third-grade education, Ben Carson lacked motivation and had a pathological temper. Then his mother decided that her two sons would read books, not watch TV. Today Carson is a world-famous black pediatric neurosurgeon whose story will inspire you to try to beat any odds that may be facing you, as he beat the odds facing him. This book is published by Zondervan. M.T., L.T.*

AUTHOR: **Bruce Catton**
TITLE: *The Civil War (1960)*
DESCRIPTION: The leading historian of the Civil War, Bruce Catton won a Pulitzer Prize citation for this vivid narrative of the years of the war that divided and demoralized the United States. The American Heritage Press edition contains 200 photographs and illustrations. Look for other books by Catton on various aspects of the conflict, including *Mr. Lincoln's Army, A Stillness at Appomattox, A Terrible Swift Sword*, and *Never Call Retreat*. M.T., L.T.*

AUTHOR: **Padraic Colum**
TITLE: *The Golden Fleece, and the Heroes Who Lived Before Achilles (1921)*
DESCRIPTION: Newbery Honor, 1921. Many of the strange and wonderful stories of Greek mythology, including those of Jason and the Golden Fleece, Persephone in the Underworld, Prometheus and the creation of fire, Hercules and his twelve labors, and the battle of wits between Theseus and the Cretan Minotaur, are woven into one splendid tale by this Irish master storyteller. Whether you are already a lover of mythology or whether these timeless tales are new to you, Colum is sure to delight you. A.A.*

Annie Dillard is an author highly praised in literary circles and much appreciated by those in thoughtful religious circles who know her. *Pilgrim* will reward anyone who puts in the effort it takes to read and understand it, especially those who have been disturbed by the problem of natural (not man-made) evil. And if you like *Pilgrim*, you may also enjoy her *American Childhood*, which chronicles her rebellious teenage years. L.T.

AUTHOR: **Annie Dillard**
TITLE: *Pilgrim at Tinker Creek (1974)*
DESCRIPTION: Pulitzer Prize, 1974. Though this journal of a year's natural cycle at Tinker Creek in Virginia is loaded with biblical and literary allusions and scientific minutiae, it really is an attempt by the author to look so closely (and without blinking) at both the horrors and beauties of nature that she can determine if she should praise God for them or reject him. (Unlike the teenager in Gary Paulsen's *The Island*, you understand from Dillard what intense yet exhilarating work this looking is). One image of horror—a giant waterbug sucking the life out of a frog—and one of beauty—a sycamore tree coming alive in a flame of thousands of birds—recurs until she resolves the question whether "all things live by a generous power and dance to a nightly tune; or . . . all things are scattered and hurled, that our every arabesque and grand jéte is a frantic variation on our one free fall." L.T.*

AUTHOR: **Dave Dravecky with Tim Stafford**
TITLE: *Comeback (1990)*
DESCRIPTION: If baseball is a metaphor for the American dream, as Tim Stafford claims, then Dave Dravecky is the ultimate dreamer. His is the story of making it to the top as a major league pitcher against the odds, then being forced to quit because of a cancerous tumor in his pitching arm, and then—against all odds again—returning to pitch in a pennant-race game, only to break his arm yet again while pitching five days later. It will encourage you, or anyone, to come back against whatever odds are facing you. Dravecky's faith in God is the key to both his determination and his joy. M.T., L.T.*

AUTHOR: **Gerald Durrell**
TITLE: *Birds, Beasts and Relatives (1969)*
DESCRIPTION: This is a companion volume to Durrell's hilarious *My Family and Other Animals* about the five years just prior to World War II that his zany family lived on the idyllic island of Corfu. Five outspoken individualists reside with even more individualistic animals, including a donkey, barn owl, five baby hedgehogs, and a spade-footed toad. Odd neighbors and house guests make their appearances as well. All manage

to keep life in an uproar, yet 10-year-old Gerry persists in collecting the wildlife of the island. M.T., L.T.*

AUTHOR: **Freeman Dyson**
TITLE: *Disturbing the Universe (1979)*
DESCRIPTION: A wonderfully literate physicist, who after World War II worked with the physicists famous for inventing the atomic bomb, examines the significant moral dilemmas that science and technology raise for sensitive, compassionate people. He does so by tracing his own scientific life from a young boy genius in England to his richly productive adult career in the United States and even projects us into a future of space colonization. This complex but very readable book is for you if you are passionate about science and literature and willing to think hard about the relationships between them and the great moral dilemmas of our day. L.T.

AUTHOR: **Joni Eareckson**
TITLE: *Joni (1976)*
DESCRIPTION: Joni was an active athlete of 17 when a diving accident made her a quadriplegic for life. She tells in her book about her accident and the months and years that followed as she adjusted to never being able to move again. The well-meaning people told her just to have faith that God would heal her, but she gradually discovered the spiritual significance that her life could have through art and a ministry to others. Joni's story has been made into a movie, and she has written other books about her life and overcoming handicaps in God's power. E.T., M.T.*

AUTHOR: **Loren Eiseley**
TITLE: *All These Strange Hours: The Excavation of a Life (1975)*
DESCRIPTION: The language and imagery in anthropologist Loren Eiseley's autobiographical *All These Strange Hours* sing both true and steel-hard as he describes his days as a drifter, as a thinker, and as a doubter in which his philosophy of "behind nothing/before nothing/worship it the zero" is confirmed. He takes you deep into his mind as a naturalist who has faced the implications of his worldview honestly. It will be a dangerous yet poignantly compelling journey for you if you are a patient and mature reader interested in cultures and science. L.T.

AUTHOR: **Anne Frank**
TITLE: *The Diary of Anne Frank (1947)*

DESCRIPTION: If you haven't read Anne's story in school, then you'll want to meet her on your own. The irrepressible Jewish teenager is hidden in the "secret annex" in Amsterdam with seven others for two years until the Nazis discover them and take her off to Bergen-Belsen. Cherishing the privacy that her diary alone can give her, Anne explores all the emotions common to adolescents everywhere, yet they are especially clarified by her particularly difficult circumstances. Do you agree with the words she wrote just before her capture? ". . .in spite of everything I still believe that people are really good at heart." E.T., M.T.

AUTHOR: **Robin Graham and L. T. Gill**
TITLE: *Dove (1972)*
DESCRIPTION: At the age of 16, Robin Graham quit school and set off to sail across the Pacific Ocean alone in "Dove." Two years later he has accomplished his goal, exploring the lands and peoples along the route, and is determined to continue on around the world. Even the beautiful Patti with whom he had fallen in love on the Fiji Islands could not deter him, nor could dramatic storms nor seductive voices whispering to wreck the boat. Even though he is guided and protected by God, Robin forgets the One who on occasions calms the seas for him. He arrives back in Los Angeles five years after his departure. The Sailor continues his story when, restless, bored, and unfulfilled after his voyage, he and his wife, Patti, seek new adventure in the untamed wilderness of Montana and the God who could fill their spiritual void. L.T.

AUTHOR: **John Howard Griffin**
TITLE: *Black Like Me (1960)*
DESCRIPTION: In 1959 John Howard Griffin, an expert in race relations, decided that he really didn't know the Negro's real problems, and the only way to correct that was to experience them as a Negro. *Black Like Me* is the journal, raw and real, of the six weeks that he was "cast on the junkheap of second-class citizenship" so as to tell "the real story . . . the universal one of men who destroy the souls and bodies of other men (and in the process destroy themselves) for reasons neither really understands." M.T., L.T.

AUTHOR: **John Gunther**
TITLE: *Death Be Not Proud: A Memoir (1949)*
DESCRIPTION: The writer, famous for his travel guides, gives you this memoir of his son, Johnny, who died of a brain tumor when he was 17, but "not so much a memoir . . . in a conventional sense as the story of a long,

courageous struggle between a child and Death." Because Johnny was so exceptionally bright and good and brave and loved, his special qualities infuse this book with a radiant joy. The title is from a wonderful poem by John Donne, quoted in the beginning, as is Johnny's own "Unbeliever's Prayer," at the end. M.T., L.T.

AUTHOR: **Philip Hallie**
TITLE: *Lest Innocent Blood Be Shed (1980)*
DESCRIPTION: What happened in the small French Heugonot village of Le Chambon has been called a miracle of goodness. Though under the surveillance of two pastors, the whole town conspires to save thousands of Jews. This book tells the compelling story of Le Chambon and Pastors Trochme and Theis as well as examines in a more philosophical way how such goodness could happen in a world where evil is rampant. L.T.

AUTHOR: **Virginia Hamilton**
TITLE: *Anthony Burns: The Defeat and Triumph of a Fugitive Slave (1988)*
DESCRIPTION: Hamilton places "an oppressed slave, a common man, . . . at the center of his own struggle" to be free. Anthony Burns was that man, the focus of a riot and court battle in Boston between abolitionists and slave owners after he had escaped and was recaptured. But instead of being just the slave these impersonal forces struggled over in 1854, in this biography Burns becomes a young man keen for freedom in his own right. And, as Hamilton comments, "As long as we know he is free, we too are liberated." E.T.*

AUTHOR: **Virginia Hamilton**
TITLE: *In the Beginning: Creation Stories from Around the World (1988)*
DESCRIPTION: Newbery Honor, 1989. A master storyteller retells 25 creation myths from around the world, including Babylonian, Greek, and the Genesis accounts. Hamilton says that myths are stories about a god or gods . . . superhuman beings . . . and the first people on earth [which are] truth to the people who believe in them and live by them." You may be interested in figuring out for yourself similarities and differences between the stories she includes. Especially look at the character of the creator-god and whether he or she makes mistakes in creation. A.A.

AUTHOR: **Torey Hayden**
TITLE: *One Child (1980)*

DESCRIPTION: Torey Hayden is an educational psychologist who teaches the throwaway children that no one else wants. *One Child* is the true story of 6-year-old Sheila, abandoned by her mother and terribly abused by her uncle, and alcoholic father—she refuses even to talk. Underneath, Hayden discovers a brilliant child with a loving heart who can be healed. Hayden has written books about other children she has worked with as well. M.T., L.T.

AUTHOR: **Jeanne Wakatsuki Houston and James Houston**
TITLE: *Farewell to Manzanar (1973)*
DESCRIPTION: This true story of one ordinary American family's internment for three and a half years during World War II in Manzanar—just because, like the 10,000 others, they happened to be Japanese—brings to life a too-little known shameful episode in American history. Even though they were surrounded by barbed wire, searchlights, and armed guards, they did not stop being American. Cheerleaders, Boy Scouts, sock hops, baton twirling lessons, and high school yearbooks all had their place in the camp. Jeanne's family survived the indignities with their dignity intact, but she shares with you honestly the high price they did pay for that survival. M.T., L.T.

AUTHOR: **Peter Jenkins**
TITLE: *A Walk Across America (1979)*
DESCRIPTION: Peter Jenkins was a young man disillusioned about his country and his future when he started walking across America with his dog, Cooper. Meeting ordinary people of all races, working side by side with them, moving on to the next place, from New York State through the Appalachian Mountains to New Orleans, each rich in history and heritage, restores his faith in himself, his country, and his God. The second book Jenkins wrote, about the rest of his walk to the Pacific Ocean, this time with his new wife, Barbara, is called *The Walk West.* M.T., L.T.*

AUTHOR: **Peter Kreeft**
TITLE: *Between Heaven and Hell (1982)*
DESCRIPTION: The same day that John F. Kennedy was assassinated on November 22, 1963, two other famous men died also—C. S. Lewis and Aldous Huxley. Kreeft imagines the three of them engaging in a dialog that Socrates would have approved of in their life together after death. He sees Kennedy as a modern humanist, Lewis, a Christian theist, and Huxley, an Eastern pantheist. Their dialog hinges, as does that of all history, on the identity of Jesus Christ. Even if you've never had to think as a philosopher

before, you'll find the style of this book intriguing and the ideas stretching. If you like it, there are several other Kreeft books also published by InterVarsity Press, including *Socrates Meets Jesus* and *The Unaborted Socrates.* L.T.*

AUTHOR: **Linda Lawrence**
TITLE: *Rare Beasts, Unique Adventures (1991)*
DESCRIPTION: This book of unusual devotions for college students can be chewed on in small bites or read in larger chunks, but either way should be savored for a long time. It draws on the great devotional literature of all branches and times of the church as well as experiences of today's college students and will especially appeal to you if you are a questioner who wants your faith to be well grounded. It covers matters of the heart, soul, mind, and strength as well as loving your neighbor and yourself. Worth the price of the book (published by Zondervan) is its bibliography called "Books for the Journey" of titles by such spiritual giants as St. Augustine, Dietrich Bonhoeffer, Julian of Norwich, Martin Luther King, Jr., Mother Teresa, and Bishop Tutu. L.T.*

AUTHOR: **Julius Lester**
TITLE: *To Be a Slave (1968)*
DESCRIPTION: Who better to tell what slavery was like than the slaves themselves? Lester has gathered together their stories, from capture in Africa to eventual emancipation during the Civil War, adding his own commentary as a bridge between them. Tom Feelings beautifully illustrated the Scholastic edition. E.T., M.T.*

AUTHOR: **Doris Lund**
TITLE: *Eric (1974)*
DESCRIPTION: Eric was a 17-year-old star soccer player ready to go off to college when he learned that he had leukemia. His mother tells the story of his 4-year feisty fight against that disease and his 4-year love affair with life, learning, and love itself. M.T., L.T.

AUTHOR: **Robert Massie**
TITLE: *Nicholas and Alexandra (1967)*
DESCRIPTION: Over the vast and disintegrating empire of the Russias in the turbulent early 20th century, Nicholas II reigned as Tsar. For a household of a wife, Alexandra, and four lovely daughters, he was a loving husband and father. Then on August 12, 1904, his long-awaited son, Alexis, was born—born with hemophilia—and that "moment . . . the two

disasters"—hemophilia and a disintegrating empire—"were intertwined." Under the hypnotic influence of the Siberian mystic, Rasputin, whom she thought could heal her son, Alexandra refused to allow the Romanov regime to be reformed. And so the stage was set for the Russian Revolution and the murders of all whom she loved. Massie's biography of the last Tsar and Empress is crowded with fascinating details about one of the most fascinating periods of European history. L.T.

AUTHOR: **Gavin Maxwell**
TITLE: *Ring of Bright Water (1960)*
DESCRIPTION: Gavin Maxwell writes about the remote Scottish Hebrides island of "Camusfearna," where he lives, and about its "intense and varied" beauty of landscape and animals—the otters whom he adopted after the death of his dog, the geese and swans, the whales, the stags, the wildcat—with a "transcendent touch of love [that] summons [his] world into being." L.T.

AUTHOR: **Milton Meltzer**
TITLE: *Never to Forget (1976)*
DESCRIPTION: "The heaviest wheel rolls across our foreheads/to bury itself deep somewhere inside our memories," says Mif, a child in the Terezin ghetto (1944). To remember the Holocaust, writes Milton Meltzer, is to "think of what being human means." He helps you do that in this book by gathering together the words of many Jews, from their days in the ghettos of Europe's great cities to the early days of harassments, to Kristallnacht, and finally to the concentration camps. There they went to death or, for some few, clung tenaciously to life, both with great dignity. He allows you to see the Holocaust, not as a matter of appalling statistics but of haunting personal suffering and victories, and to think thereby of what being human means. E.T., M.T.*

AUTHOR: **Milton Meltzer**
TITLE: *The Rescue (1988)*
DESCRIPTION: As a companion volume to *Never to Forget*, Meltzer has told the stories of "righteous Gentiles" throughout Europe who risked what they had to help the Jews. Sometimes a person acted individually, like Frau Schmidt, who left baskets of food for the Jewish woman for whom she had formerly washed clothes. Sometimes they were a network of resistance, like the one Joop and Will belonged to in Holland, or whole communities like Le Chambon (see also *Lest Innocent Blood Be Shed*), or a whole country like Denmark. While inspiring you with hope for the human

race, the book also reminds you that God gives each of us the opportunity to "choose good, choose life" in the face of evil. E.T., M.T.*

AUTHOR: **Nancy Moyer**
TITLE: *Escape from the Killing Fields (1990)*
DESCRIPTION: The Cambodian Holocaust, in which 2 million people were killed by their own ruler, is not as well known as the Jewish Holocaust of World War II. You may only have heard of it through the movie, *The Killing Fields*. This true story published by Zondervan about a young Christian Cambodian woman who had worked for World Vision during the Vietnam War years, will personalize that distant tragedy. May her spirit of Christian love encourage you to make those choices to love your neighbors—even your enemies—as Christ loves them. M.T., L.T.

AUTHOR: **Neil Postman**
TITLE: *Amusing Ourselves to Death (1985)*
DESCRIPTION: TV has affected every part of American society, not only how families relate to each other but also how politicians run for office, how news is conveyed, how teachers teach, and how preachers preach. Neil Postman, a professor of communications, explores just how television is causing the American people to lose its freedoms not due to censorship of ideas or external political pressures but due to trivial and irrelevant images and internal emotional pleasures. We are, he claims, "amusing ourselves to death." Postman writes clearly and provocatively about serious ideas. No one escapes his probe—not the educators who created "The Voyage of Mimi" you may have seen in school, not the makers of "Sesame Street," and certainly not the televangelists. He will surely cause you to think as well as he disturbs the waters of the cultural medium in which you swim. L.T.

AUTHOR: **Tim Stafford**
TITLE: *Worth the Wait (1988)*
DESCRIPTION: Tim Stafford's candid, biblical column in *Campus Life* magazine, "Love, Sex and the Whole Person," has long been a favorite of teens. In this book built from many of his columns, he frankly discusses the practical and theological issue of waiting for sex until marriage. He has also written *Love Story: Questions and Answers about Sex*, which covers such areas as masturbation, singleness, and homosexuality, also published by Zondervan. E.T., M.T.*

AUTHOR: **Corrie ten Boom**
TITLE: *The Hiding Place (1971)*
DESCRIPTION: A Dutch watchmaker and his two "old maid" daughters are the unlikely heroes in the cosmic battle between good and evil as it was focused on Nazi-controlled Holland. Always willing to hide Jews in the name of the Lord Jesus, Corrie, her sister Betsy, and their father were finally betrayed and captured. Corrie and Betsy were taken to Ravensbruck concentration camp where Betsy eventually died a brutal death, but together the sisters brought hope and peace to their sister inmates. Corrie herself discovered "that it is not on our forgiveness any more than on our goodness that the world's healing hinges, but on [God's]. When He tells us to love our enemies, He gives, along with the command, the love itself." A book not to be missed. M.T., L.T.*

AUTHOR: **James Thurber**
TITLE: *The Thurber Carnival (1944)*
DESCRIPTION: Thurber once described his drawings as "having reached completion by some other route than the common one of intent" but his writings as having been actually written since "it is impossible to read any of them from the last line to the first without experiencing a definite sensation of going backward." This collection of his essays, stories, and cartoons is a good, enjoyable introduction to an American humorist. L.T.

AUTHOR: **Bob Wieland as told to Sarah Nichols**
TITLE: *One Step at a Time (1989)*
DESCRIPTION: From his experience as a paramedic in Vietnam, then a legless gym teacher, to being an inspiration to thousands as he walked across America to raise money for the hungry, Bob Wieland is a remarkable man. His athletic prowess and spiritual strength could be a model for anyone—you—as he demonstrates the truth that "nothing is impossible with God." Zondervan has published his story. M.T.

AUTHOR: **Malcolm X as told to Alex Haley**
TITLE: *The Autobiography of Malcolm X (1964)*
DESCRIPTION: Before he was killed by an assassin in 1965, Malcolm X was the best-known leader in the black separatist movement of Elijah Mohammed's Nation of Islam. He worked for blacks to come out from the cesspool of white immorality that controlled ghetto life, find redemption and identity in Islam, and create their own culture. To Alex Haley he told the story of his own life—of sinking to the depths of that cesspool before meeting Allah in prison—and his role of articulating black America's rage.

A New York newspaper reporter who knew him as well as perhaps any white person knew him, says the book is "a testimony to the power of redemption and the force of human personality." L.T.

SCIENCE FICTION

AUTHOR: **Douglas Adams**
TITLE: *Hitchhiker's Guide to the Galaxy (1979)*
DESCRIPTION: Series continues with *The Restaurant at the End of the Universe; Life, the Universe and Everything;* and *So Long and Thanks for All the Fish.* Douglas Adams' quartet of books are not conventional science fiction despite their computers and spaceships. Enormously popular with teens and young adults, they are an off-the-wall, zany trip through time and space with four oddball companions thrown together by the incomprehensible "perversion of physics." Among their discoveries is the fact that Earth is really a computer that was unfortunately destroyed to make way for an interstellar freeway bypass five minutes before its makers (two mice) determined the ultimate question of life's meaning. The answer is 42; the question, reconstructed by the end of the second volume, is "What is 6 x 9?"
RECOMMENDATION: Adams responds to the meaninglessness of 20th century life as he sees it—and projects it—not with serious pronouncements but with a Monty Python kind of humor. Just every once in a while as you read—and laugh—you'll discover that he cannot maintain the mask. For example, the award-winning computer designer of Earth's fjords says, "What does it matter? Science has achieved some wonderful things, of course, but I'd far rather be happy than right any day." "And are you?" "No, that's where it falls down, of course." For insight into the controlling culture of Western teenagers, these books are must reading. M.T., L.T.

AUTHOR: **Isaac Asimov**
TITLE: *The Bicentennial Man and Other Stories (1976)*

DESCRIPTION: Most of the stories in this collection revolve around robots and consider from various intriguing angles—such as communications, triage, autism, genetic engineering—what it means to be human in a technological society where machines can do more than some people. RECOMMENDATION: Isaac Asimov, the prolific writer best known for his science fiction, collected for this anthology some of the stories he wrote in the 1970s. In the introduction that he writes for each story you can see an enormous ego at work! Though the notion of creation does not enter Asimov's stories, the central matters of humanity—free will and determinism, and self-sacrifice, for example—are explored over and over. M.T., L.T.

AUTHOR: **Isaac Asimov**
TITLE: *Foundation (1951)*
DESCRIPTION: First of series, continued by *Foundation Empire* and *Second Foundation*. Isaac Asimov preaches in the first of his famous Foundation series a sophisticated religion of science whose chief characteristic is "that it really works." As the old Galactic Empire is dying, Hari Seldon, a psychohistorian, creates the Foundation, a fringe society of Encyclopedists, cataloging all knowledge so as to foreshorten the inevitable period of barbarism that follows the death of an empire. More importantly, this will allow them to create the Second Empire.
RECOMMENDATION: Old questions of free will and determinism, science and religion, take on clever new twists in the 12,000th year of the Galactic Empire. Asimov is perhaps the best-known science fiction writer of our age, and he does not attempt to disguise his belief system, a rational, humane scientism. L.T.

AUTHOR: **Ray Bradbury**
TITLE: *The Martian Chronicles (1946)*
DESCRIPTION: In a series of short stories that don't relate to each other at first glance except that they follow the various missions to Mars in chronological order, Ray Bradbury paints a picture of an ancient and marvelous civilization that, although it resists in ingenious ways, is destroyed by invaders from earth who are already destroying their own planet.
RECOMMENDATION: Spender is an example of a character who dissents from the goals of the mission, and as such, he provides a telling commentary on what people are really like and how we have allowed science to control us. Calvin Miller, author of the *Singer* poetry trilogy

published by InterVarsity Press, said that when he was a teen, reading Bradbury nurtured his hope. M.T., L.T.*

AUTHOR: **John Christopher**
TITLE: *The Prince in Waiting (1970)*
DESCRIPTION: Series continued in *Beyond the Burning Lands* and *The Sword of the Spirits*. Luke wins a tournament through skill and luck and thereby guarantees that he will be Prince in Waiting of Winchester, a medieval city set in an England of the future, after an ecological holocaust. In so doing, though, he becomes an unwitting tool of the Seers, the priests of the Spiritists, who under cover of their magic, are hoping to restore a civilization based on the now-banned science and technology.
RECOMMENDATION: With Luke, in these three fine books, you will explore the human costs of pride and jealousy as well as the larger theme of when the ends—in this case, the restoration of a beneficent society— justify the means—of deception and treachery. Luke's battle to become the Prince of Winchester parallels the larger battle of the Seers. And always on the edges of both stories are the despised outcasts, the Christians, who show them all another way. E.T.*

AUTHOR: **John Christopher**
TITLE: *The White Mountains (1967)*
DESCRIPTION: Series continued in *The City of Gold and Lead* and *The Pool of Fire*. Will should have been looking forward to his Capping by the Tripods, the ceremony that signaled his transition to adulthood. He was instead approached by a man posing as a crazy vagrant, who confirmed his worst fears about the event. With his despised cousin, Henry, and later a French boy, Beanpole, he runs away from his English town toward Switzerland where a few free men have banded together to fight their domination by the Tripods. In the books that follow, you will find Will and a German boy winning an athletic contest for the "privilege" of serving the Tripods behind a walled city of gold and lead. There they learn that the gruesome masters come from another planet and are planning the extinction of the human race by altering the environment. Finally the freedom fighters bravely attack the three cities but find themselves divided as to how to use and preserve their hard-won freedom.
RECOMMENDATION: Will is a very human hero, flawed by a quick temper and a tendency to take the easy, undisciplined way. Nevertheless, he and his friends take a daring stand for what it means to be human because they have "the vital spark of defiance" against evil repression. You will find yourself cheering them on through all their dangers. E.T.*

AUTHOR: **Arthur C. Clarke**
TITLE: *2001: A Space Odyssey (1968)*
DESCRIPTION: The computer, Hal, has been created "innocent; but, all too soon, a snake enters his electronic Eden." Therefore, he betrays his two human fellow astronauts, Poole and Bowman. Bowman nevertheless continues on *Discovery* to one of the rings of Saturn, there to determine if the evolution of the whole human race had been programmed by an extraterrestrial, TAM-1. Hal may have been created, but soon Bowman is re-created—to be master of his old world.
RECOMMENDATION: Clarke is a prolific writer of science fiction, and this is his most famous, really based on the movie of the same name. Even without all the special effects of the screen version, you will sense the arrogance of science without God, as you are compelled to keep turning the pages of this story. L.T.

AUTHOR: **Sylvia Louise Engdahl**
TITLE: *Enchantress from the Stars (1970)*
DESCRIPTION: Elana, a student at the Federation's Anthropological Center, her fiancé Evrek, and her father are diverted to the planet Andrecia, where colonists from the Imperial Forces threaten to destroy the Youngling (less evolved) "civilization." To rid Andrecia of the Imperial Forces, they carefully manipulate a sensitive, courageous Youngling, Georyn, who, in the manner of a medieval knight, had set off to conquer what he thought was a Dragon. However, Elana's task is complicated by her own impetuous actions, her growing awareness of Georyn's full humanity, and the clash of three worldviews—magical, scientific, and her own "more advanced" amalgamation of the two. Something, or someone, will have to be sacrificed to save Andrecia.
RECOMMENDATION: This fine story works well on several levels—the surface's exciting plot itself (which may remind you of Star Trek stories), the anthropological exploration of how cultures evolve and how belief in either magic or science can be both helpful and limiting, and—at the deepest level—the theme of the necessity of hope, love, and self-sacrifice to the significance of human existence. Whom do you think sees most truly in this story—the naive Youngling, Georyn; the disillusioned Imperial Agent, Jarel; or the rash but loving anthropologist, Elana? E.T., M.T.

AUTHOR: **Frank Herbert**
TITLE: *Dune (1965)*
DESCRIPTION: First of a six-volume series. Frank Herbert was one of the first of the great modern science-fiction writers to create an alien world that

captures the imagination of millions of readers. *Dune*, is about the forbidding desert planet, Arrakis, where the mind-altering and life-lengthening spice needed by the rest of the universe is harvested. The House of Atreides is headed by Duke Leto, with his 15-year-old son, Paul, and his concubine, Lady Jessica. She is trained in the sisterhood, Bene Gesserit, to total mental and physical mastery not only of her own life but of the whole human race's through genetic breeding. They must not only work out their own precarious destiny but also prevent the evil House of Harkonnen from totally exploiting the planet. After the Duke's death and their escape into the harsh, waterless communities of the Freemen in the interior, it is Paul and his mother who fulfill—or is it manipulate?—the prophesies of a Messiah rescuer.

RECOMMENDATION: If you're intrigued by questions of power and purpose, knowledge and destiny, you'll be glad to explore them with Herbert. And you may find it ironic that in a person-created world of great complexity, where his characters' every gesture can "move a gigantic lever across the known universe," Herbert has one of his most appealing characters realize just before his death that, "his father and all the other scientists were wrong . . . the most persistent principles of the universe were accident and error." L.T.

AUTHOR: **H. M. Hoover**
TITLE: *Another Heaven, Another Earth (1981)*
DESCRIPTION: Gareth is struggling to keep the diminishing numbers of her Xilan community alive and well. On a foray out to gather herbs, she meets four humans exploring her planet for possible colonization, who are now anxious to study her and the "lost colony." Instead, they infect each other with illnesses and so become a picture of the conflicting values of a humane but dying agricultural civilization and a surviving but impersonal technological society.

RECOMMENDATION: Do you feel that Hoover thinks that it is possible to build a bridge between technology and humane values? Is Hoover suggesting that these are our two choices at this point in the evolution of the earth, or should we look for yet another option? M.T.

AUTHOR: **H.M. Hoover**
TITLE: *The Bell Tree (1982)*
DESCRIPTION: Jenny goes on a vacation-expedition from her planet to another with her father. There she meets Eli, their lonely but thoughtful guide, and encounters a surrealistic landscape full of giant angry animals, trees that ring like bells, and an ancient yet hostile treasure.

RECOMMENDATION: Perhaps all science fiction settings are "surrealistic," but this one, particularly, raises the question of how Jenny or Eli—or you the reader—can determine what is real. Or is Jenny (or you) supposed to conclude that it is too dangerous to understand what is real, just as she discovers that it isn't wise to understand an alien mind? M.T.

AUTHOR: **Monica Hughes**
TITLE: *Beyond the Dark River (1981)*
DESCRIPTION: On the Canadian prairies 45 years after the nuclear holocaust, a small Hutterite community and an isolated Indian tribe live separately in fear of the City that was destroyed as Sodom and Gomorrah were. When Benjamin ventures out in search of a healer who can help the mysteriously ailing children of his Bruderhof, he finds Daughter-of-She-Who-Came-After. The Indian girl-healer is astonished by the customs of the religious community, but she is also attracted by both the boy and the adventure he offers. They go into the forbidden City to find a cure at the old University library but find instead much more than that.
RECOMMENDATION: Hughes seems to be saying that modern technologies lead to death, and, though they have profound problems, simple communities of faith, whether biblical or animistic, can provide alternative ways to bring life. As the Israelites of old, Benjamin and Daughter-of-She-Who-Came-After—and the readers who come to admire them both—are asked to choose between life and death. E.T., M.T.*

AUTHOR: **Monica Hughes**
TITLE: *The Keeper of the Isis Light (1981)*
DESCRIPTION: Olwen is the sole human survivor on the planet Isis where her parents had been the lightkeepers. On her 16th birthday her robot, Guardian, gives her a present that makes her joy in the beauty of Isis complete. But also, that day her life changes forever with the arrival of the spaceship *Pegasus*. She and Mark, one of the young settlers, fall in love despite the mask she must wear to protect herself from alien germs. However, on a mountain climbing expedition, Mark sees Olwen maskless and in horror falls over a cliff, creating a crisis of identity for the settlers, for Guardian, and for the young couple themselves.
RECOMMENDATION: On an alien planet, questions of what it means to be fully human seem to be more urgent. Monica Hughes would have you consider with Olwen and Mark the counterbalanced needs for both companionship and the freedom to be true to yourself. M.T.

AUTHOR: **Ursula LeGuin**
TITLE: *The Left Hand of Darkness (1969)*
DESCRIPTION: You may not know that Ursula LeGuin, who is famous for her children's fantasy series, is also an author of adult science fiction. In this award-winning book, she wonders, "What if . . . ?" What if men and women were androgynous (both male and female) so that sexuality did not determine our cultural patterns (women having babies, for example, and being primary care-givers), a very "hot" question today indeed! She sets her androgynous society on an ice-age planet on the edge of the galaxy in the Ekumenical Year, 1490. Genly Ai is the lone Envoy from the confederation of civilized planets with the job of persuading the Karhides to join them. The only person who seems to trust him is the Prime Minister, Estraven. Or does he? Therein lies the story. Perhaps more than anything else, it is about the possibility of friendship between different peoples.
RECOMMENDATION: LeGuin defines science fiction as a thought experiment ("What if . . . ?") that does not predict the future but describes the present. It is a metaphor, she says in her introduction to *The Left Hand of Darkness*, based on the contemporary realities of science, technology, and a mindset that says there is no absolute truth. Read the introduction, as interesting as the story itself, if you'd like to explore how novelists are lying to tell the truth. L.T.

AUTHOR: **C. S. Lewis**
TITLE: *Out of the Silent Planet (1952)*
DESCRIPTION: Series continues with *Perelandra* and *That Hideous Strength*. Out on a walking tour, a professor, Ransom, is kidnapped by two evolutionary scientists, who take him to Malacandra as an offering to a strange species, the sorns. If they are successful, they can continue their plans to take the gold and prepare to defy death by planting a civilized colony there. Ransom escapes only to fall in with some hrossa who are astonished that he is from the silent planet that has been abandoned by their ruler, Malaldil. For his part, he is astonished to find that the hrossa's instincts "so closely resembled the unattained ideals" of man. The struggle between Ransom and Weston continues in the subsequent volumes.
RECOMMENDATION: Like most science fiction writers, C. S. Lewis (of Narnia fame) is holding up a mirror on contemporary society as much as he is projecting a possible future. You will recognize echoes of a theistic worldview as well as barbed satire of a science that tries to be independent of God. M.T., L.T.*

AUTHOR: **Nevil Shute**
TITLE: *On the Beach (1957)*
DESCRIPTION: After the Third World War, an Australian naval officer and his wife and baby, an American submarine officer, and a young Australian woman must make their lives count for something, knowing that the radiation sickness is slowly creeping to their remote corner of the world. Shute quotes from a famous T. S. Eliot poem, "This is the way the world ends / Not with a bang but a whimper" as he explores just how that momentous event might be for rather ordinary people.
RECOMMENDATION: Some critics feel that the characters are so ordinary that they are flat, making it difficult to identify with or learn anything from them. What do you think? Perhaps a bang would be better than a whimper? L.T.

AUTHOR: **William Sleater**
TITLE: *Interstellar Pig (1984)*
DESCRIPTION: Barney is bored on a vacation at the beach until a strange and beautiful threesome move into the cottage next door. These bizarre people are intent on discovering the secrets of Barney's cottage, which had once been owned by a sea captain and his lunatic brother who cried out that he'd murdered the Devil. They entice Barney into a board game of intergalactic control, the object of which is to capture the pink Piggy. Slowly Barney realizes that they are the strange interstellar creatures come to life and they want the Piggy to gain control of their destiny—and his.
RECOMMENDATION: One of the things you will have to puzzle out as you read this book is which Piggy-message can be relied on: the ship murderer's "It's how you respond to your fate that determines your destiny" or the yearbook nonsense that Barney inadvertently programs into it. Or doesn't it matter in Sleater's scheme of things? M.T.

AUTHOR: **Jules Verne**
TITLE: *Twenty Thousand Leagues Under the Sea (1870)*
DESCRIPTION: Early in the 20th century someone commented that "the advance of the peoples is merely living the novels of Jules Verne." So it would seem with his imaginative projection of submarine life and warfare. The mysterious Captain Nemo, who has some sort of grudge against society, commands the submarine *Nautilus* on which Pierre Aronnax, professor from the Museum of Paris, and Ned Land, expert harpoonist, find themselves captive.

RECOMMENDATION: Besides predicting scientific advances, Verne began a new kind of writing. He is considered by many to be the father of science fiction. E.T.*

AUTHOR: **H. G. Wells**
TITLE: *The Island of Doctor Moreau (1896)*
DESCRIPTION: H. G. Wells, along with Jules Verne, is the second contender for the title: father of science fiction. His *Island of Doctor Moreau* is one of his most intriguing plots, especially in this day of genetic engineering. When Wells wrote about the experiments that the self-styled "god," Doctor Moreau, performed on his remote island to create manlike creatures from the beasts, he was exploring the dark side of the evolutionary theory he otherwise welcomed, because it seemed to free man from God. The question for him became, Can man create any better than God did?
RECOMMENDATION: You may be interested in comparing *Island* to Daniel DeFoe's *Robinson Crusoe*, where a man is also isolated on a remote island but responds to his circumstances, particularly concerning his faith, quite differently. L.T.

AUTHOR: **H. G. Wells**
TITLE: *The War of the Worlds (1898)*
DESCRIPTION: *The War of the Worlds* is not reread today so much for its literary value but for its historical value. Not only did it do much to form our popular conceptions of Martians, but when it was read aloud on the radio early in this century, listeners panicked, thinking that Martians had really landed. M.T.

TRIED AND TRUE

AUTHOR: **Chinua Achebe**
TITLE: ***Things Fall Apart (1959)***
DESCRIPTION: Okonkwo, though he is the son of a weak man, has carved out a leadership role for himself in his tribe through hard work and determination. However, "things fall apart" for him—and, indeed, for all of precolonial West Africa—with the arrival of the white missionaries. Or did they fall apart for this proud man because his pride and fear of weakness led him to violate some of the tribe's most sacred traditions? The Nigerian Achebe takes you to the heart of another culture in this sympathetic yet unflinching examination of Okonkwo's village life. L.T.

AUTHOR: **James Baldwin**
TITLE: ***Go Tell It on the Mountain (1953)***
DESCRIPTION: *Go Tell it on the Mountain,* without wincing at all from the raw realities of Harlem life, tells the story of the salvation experience of a young, illegitimate black boy. John hates his hypocritical stepfather, the preacher Gabriel, who really only loves his "true" sons, the dead Royal, son of his mistress, and the weak Roy, son of John's mother. In all the vivid language and ceremony of the black church, you experience John's transformation by God's love on the mountain top, just as you experience the bondage (often explicitly sexual) that had held John as it held Gabriel, and the women in his life. For the most mature reader. L.T.

AUTHOR: **Charlotte Brontë**
TITLE: ***Jane Eyre (1847)***
DESCRIPTION: Long a favorite of may teenagers, *Jane Eyre* has the ingredients of a thrilling romance: a high-spirited orphan heroine deter-

"Pip Leaves the Village"—illustration by F. W. Pailthorpe for Charles Dickens' *Great Expectations.* For description of this book and other books by Charles Dickens, see pages 215– 16.

mined to make her own way by training to be a governess; a wealthy, aloof master of an English country estate; mysteriously set fires, seances, and strange appearances by a madwoman; and a happily-ever-after resolution to the plot. M.T., L.T.*

AUTHOR: **Emily Brontë**
TITLE: *Wuthering Heights (1847)*
DESCRIPTION: *Wuthering Heights* is well named, for it definitely rises to stormy heights (wuthering means "stormy"). The cold sweep of the northern moors is an apt setting for the stormy intertwining of the Earnshaws and the Lintons and the brooding stranger, Heathcliffe, taken in by Mr. Earnshaw when Heathcliffe was only 14. Earnshaw's favoritism to the boy over his own two children, Hindley and Catherine, sets the stage for the jealousies that blow up into mismatched romances and revenge. These work themselves out into three generations who live at Wuthering Heights. All the passions of Emily Brontë's book run deeper and more violently than in her sister's *Jane Eyre*. M.T., L.T.*

AUTHOR: **Pearl Buck**
TITLE: *The Good Earth (1931)*
DESCRIPTION: Chinese peasants are tied to the natural cycle of the earth, which supplies their every need. So it is with Wang Lung, an ambitious peasant, who works hard and shrewdly takes advantage of the misfortune that natural disasters bring to others. He survives them but pays the price of living too far above the land as he attains wealth. His wife, O-lan, his children—the favored sons, the despised feeble-minded daughter—and the concubine of his wealthy days: All are sympathetically drawn so that you can walk in the shoes of people who live a very alien way of life and thought from your own. L.T.

AUTHOR: **John Bunyan**
TITLE: *Pilgrim's Progress (1676)*
DESCRIPTION: While unjustly imprisoned in a British jail, Bunyan wrote this allegory of the journey from this world to the next of a pilgrim named Christian. Seeking the Celestial City from his home in the City of Destruction, Christian faces the Slough of Despond, receives bad advice, loses his burden in the House of the Interpreter, climbs the Hill of Difficulty, fights with the monster Apollyon, passes through the Valley of the Shadow of Death, is tempted in Vanity Fair, is troubled in Doubting Castle, and must cross the Dark River before he can reach his destination. There are many editions available, but one your whole family might especially enjoy is

the 1985 Eerdman's edition, called *Dangerous Journey*, illustrated by Alan Parry, who animated the story for British television. A.A.*

AUTHOR: **Albert Camus**
TITLE: *The Plague (1947)*
DESCRIPTION: *The Plague* is one of Camus' more readily understandable books. If you are willing to put in the effort to think deeply, Camus will take you on a rewarding journey exploring the existentialists' dilemma; in his own words, "Can one be a saint without God?" When bubonic plague hits the North African port city of Oran, all the residents quarantined there are forced to react to the disaster according to their own principles. The book focuses on what meaning those who seek to help their fellow sufferers can wrest out of life. Camus has won the Nobel prize for literature. L.T.

AUTHOR: **Willa Cather**
TITLE: *Death Comes for the Archbishop (1926)*
DESCRIPTION: Jean Marie Latour, French missionary to the Ohio regions in the 1840s, is made Vicar Apostolic of New Mexico. With Father Joseph Vaillant, his boyhood friend, he makes his way across the vast continent to the newly annexed region where lax Mexican priests and superstitious Navaho are not happy to see him. Nevertheless, they persist and over the years build up a diocese to the point where it could even support its own cathedral. Not a fast-paced book but as calm and determined as the soul of Latour, it unfolds the rewarding story of the lives and devotions of these two priests as well as the land and people that so captivated them until death comes for the Archbishop—Latour himself—many years later. L.T.*

AUTHOR: **Willa Cather**
TITLE: *My Antonia (1918)*
DESCRIPTION: Jim Burden, an eastern orphan who grew up on the vast prairies of Nebraska at his grandparents' farm but who left to study at Harvard, tells the story of an immigrant girl, Antonia Shimerda. Antonia helps her beloved father carve out a living from the prairie, learns English from Jim, joins the hired girls in the town of Black Hawk in their daily work and evening fun, decides what moral values she will live by, and eventually returns (unlike Jim) to the soil that has nurtured her. Typically American, Antonia's story is both lyrical and deceptively simple and has been enjoyed for generations. L.T.

AUTHOR: **Joseph Conrad**
TITLE: *Lord Jim (1900)*

DESCRIPTION: Jim, a wanderer and an outcast, works various seaport jobs until he finally arrives on the East Indian Ocean island of Patustan. What he is running from is his self-hatred for abandoning a sinking ship full of Muslim pilgrims after the captain and mates, drunkenly and cowardly, left him in charge. He had thus betrayed his own deepest morality and could never escape a haunting sense of failure. On Patustan, however, he is trusted by the natives and finally earns an opportunity to redeem himself. L.T.

AUTHOR: **James Fenimore Cooper**
TITLE: *The Last of the Mohicans (1826)*
DESCRIPTION: The exciting plot of this tale of pursuit and captivity and rescue and siege during the French and Indian Wars has kept readers on the edges of their seats for over 150 years. Two British sisters are being escorted to the fort where their father is commander, when they are intercepted by some Indians aiding the French. Besides its vivid actions, *The Last of the Mohicans* is rich in description of Indian lore. M.T., L.T.*

AUTHOR: **Stephen Crane**
TITLE: *The Red Badge of Courage (1894)*
DESCRIPTION: Some consider *The Red Badge of Courage* America's greatest Civil War novel. It certainly changed the way Americans wrote about war as it "ript away the gilt and glitter that had so long curtained [its] horror, and with a stern realism pictured for us the bloody grime of it all." The nameless youth of the brief story, however, emerges as a common man's hero who survives the blood of battle, not reduced to an animal but having grown to be a man who understands and loves his world. L.T.

AUTHOR: **Charles Dickens**
TITLE: *Great Expectations (1860)*
DESCRIPTION: Though *Great Expectations* does not have the comic relief of the typical Dickens character sketches, it has an absorbing enough plot to overcome its rather gloomy feeling. Pip is an orphan whose great expectations for life are intertwined with those of a vindictive, jilted old maid, Miss Havisham, and a mysterious, grateful, escaped prisoner, Abel Magwitch. Discovering the identity of the benefactor who enables him to gain a London education, his life's love, and the proper attitude with which to live satisfactorily—these make up Pip's story. M.T., L.T.

AUTHOR: **Charles Dickens**
TITLE: *A Tale of Two Cities (1859)*

DESCRIPTION: Many teens who first read Dickens when *A Tale of Two Cities* is assigned in school, should find it a satisfying story. It is full of true-to-life yet larger-than-life characters who act out their heroism and their deceit, their private sorrows and public political passions, against the huge panorama of the French Revolution of the late 18th century. The true love between Lucie Manette and the fine French aristocrat, Charles Darnay, who is made to pay for the crimes his family has committed against the common French people, and the sacrifice that the weak, alcoholic Sydney Carton has opportunity to make, join to form the structure of the book. If you only read one book by Dickens in your lifetime, perhaps this should be the one. M.T., L.T.*

AUTHOR: **Lloyd C. Douglas**
TITLE: *Magnificent Obsession (1929)*
DESCRIPTION: Why is it that evil is so much more attractive in books than good? Many people believe it is almost impossible for authors to make good attractive. However, Douglas's *Magnificent Obsession* is an exception to that "rule": It is the chronicle of playboy Robert Merrick, whose life is saved at the expense of an eminent brain surgeon, Dr. Wayne Hudson. Challenged to make his own life worthwhile by taking Dr. Hudson's place, including accepting Hudson's belief in the Higher Power, Merrick enters medical school and eventually perfects techniques that save the life of Hudson's attractive young widow. L.T.

AUTHOR: **Daphne DuMaurier**
TITLE: *Rebecca (1938)*
DESCRIPTION: A dead woman, Rebecca, dominates the action and the thoughts of the characters of Daphne DuMaurier's classic romantic suspense novel. The narrator is the insecure and timid second wife of Maxim de Winter, owner of the magnificent Manderley estate. Rebecca was his adored first wife, or so it seems to the narrator as she feels the full force of the staff's resentment. Slowly the truth about Rebecca's character and death come to light and with them come both tragedy for the estate and resolution for the newly married couple. *Rebecca* is considered the supreme example of this favorite genre. M.T., L.T.

AUTHOR: **Shusaku Endo**
TITLE: *The Samurai (1980)*
DESCRIPTION: In 1613 Hasekura, a lowly samurai from a desolate corner of Japan in the service of a powerful feudal lord, accompanies Velasco, an ambitious Franciscan priest who longs to be named Bishop of Japan, on a

treacherous sea voyage to Mexico. From there they go to Europe, seeking to guarantee trading privileges in return for more missionaries—Franciscans, not the rival Jesuits. Hasekura is persuaded that he must outwardly embrace the emaciated Lord on the crucifix who so offends his sensibilities, in order for the mission to succeed. But when he returns to Japan four years later, he discovers that Japan no longer wants corrupting outside influences, economic, political, or religious, and that Christians are being martyred. Hasekura was a real samurai who really made this journey, but Endo, considered one of Japan's finest novelists, has documented far more than a physical journey in this remarkable historical novel. Hasekura's spiritual journey to faith is portrayed with both its terrible costs and its high rewards. Joining Velasco's and Hasekura's journeys will surely enrich your own. For the reader ready to venture into new territory. L.T.

AUTHOR: **Edna Ferber**
TITLE: *Giant (1952)*
DESCRIPTION: In Texas, where everything is giant-sized—ranches, wealth, social and political hobnobbing, the gap between the haves and the have-nots—Leslie Benedict, her rancher husband, Bick, and two independent-minded children, Jordan and Luz, make the appropriate gestures to size. But is their lifestyle the very cause of everything that is coming home to haunt them? L.T.

AUTHOR: **Edna Ferber**
TITLE: *So Big (1924)*
DESCRIPTION: Pulitzer Prize, 1925. Selina lives a hand-to-mouth but nevertheless whimsical life with her gambler father who has conveyed to her a sense of the joy in experiencing life. It is this intense sense that life is magic that Selina attempts to retain after she educates herself and finds a job—teaching in a Dutch farming community in Illinois. More than that, she wants her son, Dirk, to inherit that same zest. To her disappointment, he compromises with the material, corporate-ladder-climbing world and must ultimately decide where his values lie and whether he will only be "so big." L.T.

AUTHOR: **C. S. Forester**
TITLE: *The African Queen (1940)*
DESCRIPTION: In 1914 the Germans commandeered everything on the German Central African mission station where Rose Sayer had lived for ten years under the thumb of her now-dying missionary brother. She escapes with the British cockney miner, Charlie Allnutt, who irregularly

delivered their supplies. Determined to damage Germany by destroying its ship blocking the only British entrance into German territory, Rose, with the befuddled Allnutt in tow, makes for the lake in his well-stocked *African Queen*. Never mind that she has never managed anything before in her life, never mind that the Ulanger River had never been navigated, and never mind that events strange and sinful enough to shock any missionary's soul would face them. A wonderfully tender story, though its amorality may bother you. Rose is not, by anyone's standards, a typical missionary. L.T.

AUTHOR: **C. S. Forester**
TITLE: *Captain Horatio Hornblower (1937)*
DESCRIPTION: Exciting sea battles, both won and lost, make up most of Captain Horatio Hornblower's fascinating story, first as commander of a frigate giving secret British aid to a Spanish American dictator who wants to be free from Spain's rule, and then of a larger frigate now allied to Spain against France. Taken captive at the Battle of Gibraltar, a disguised Hornblower later escapes from the French, returning to England as a hero and to a reward for having remained faithful to his sickly wife. L.T.

AUTHOR: **Paul Gallico**
TITLE: *The Snow Goose (1940)*
DESCRIPTION: This is a moving short story about a deformed artist who lives alone in a bird sanctuary, a girl from the nearby village, and the injured Canadian snow goose who brings them together. Meant to be read aloud. A.A.*

AUTHOR: **Rumer Godden**
TITLE: *In This House of Brede (1969)*
DESCRIPTION: Philipa Talbot is a successful career woman in her forties when she decides to enter the Benedictine monastery for nuns called Abbey of Brede. There she can practice the unceasing cycle of prayer, praise, and work "without sloth or haste." Her former boss, the Permanent Secretary for the British government, predicts she will last six months, but the story takes us through Philipa's first seventeen years, moving through crises of faith to a final sacrifice. Or is it fulfillment? The story is as much about the Benedictine Order as it is about Philipa. L.T.

AUTHOR: **Rumer Godden**
TITLE: *Kingfishers Catch Fire (1953)*
DESCRIPTION: Sophie Barrington Ward, a genteelly poor young widow— against the advice of everyone, British and Indian—decides to remain

alone in the primitive region of Kashmir with only her two children. Despite her good intentions to make her way among the peasants there, the dire warnings seem to be coming true. Finally even her daughter, Teresa, is in grave danger. Does Sophie have a duty to those who injured Teresa? The whole village is involved in the repercussions of the beating, as you will be. And you, too, will have "richer eyes" for having seen the kingfishers of Kashmir as only Godden can bring them to life. L.T.

AUTHOR: **Rumer Godden**
TITLE: *The River (1946)*
DESCRIPTION: Harriet, the second of four children of a British manufacturing family living in India, experiences across one winter a death, a birth, guilt, and love. As a result, there are "cracks in [the] wholeness of her unconsciousness" where she is reaching to understand the meaning of the flow of life. You will most likely see your own tentative understanding of the enormity of life and your own small yet significant place in it through this beautifully written book. M.T., L.T.

AUTHOR: **William Golding**
TITLE: *The Lord of the Flies (1954)*
DESCRIPTION: Did you know that "lord of the flies" is the English equivalent of Beelzebub, or the Devil? It seems particularly appropriate for a fable or parable about the modern condition of the human race. But Golding's devil is not an external force—very modern, very psychological, it resides in the deepest part of our hearts. Golding sets his story on a remote island where a group of British schoolboys have crash-landed. In this "paradise" they have the chance to create a civilization from scratch, but their venture becomes a struggle between order and reason (Ralph) and anarchy and wildness in human hearts (Jack). This exploration of what most Christians call total depravity seems heightened because children, in contrast to adults, are supposed to be "innocent." Do you see yourself and your classmates in the behavior of these boys? Does Golding present any way out of this brutal situation he has created? (This book is often assigned in school even before you may feel yourself ready to handle it.) M.T., L.T.

AUTHOR: **Elizabeth Goudge**
TITLE: *The Dean's Watch (1960)*
DESCRIPTION: The old humble artisan-watch repairman, Isaac Peabody, chances to meet the ugly, formidable Dean of the city's cathedral, Adam Ayscough, who is childless and only tolerated by his beautiful but cold wife.

The meeting brought them not only the pleasure of an unexpected friendship, but for the Dean the affection of his parishioners; and for Isaac faith in the God he has always doubted. This is a touching and profoundly beautiful book with clock symbolism worked naturally throughout. Other books by Goudge include *The Child From the Sea*, *The Castle on the Hill*, and *The Heart of the Family*. L.T.*

AUTHOR: **Graham Greene**
TITLE: *The Power and the Glory (1940)*
DESCRIPTION: Set in the poverty-stricken villages of Mexico, *The Power and the Glory* is about the tensions between the revolutionary police lieutenant and the last priest in the district, whom he is hunting down. This "whiskey priest" has failed in so many ways—particularly his drunkenness, his fathering a child—but stubbornly persists in his duties despite the persecution. Although the novel is gripping by virtue of its suspenseful plot, it is also compelling in its psychological probe of the motives and actions of a sinful saint. It was the novel that gave modern master, Graham Greene, the most satisfaction to write as he explored a paradox: "the idealistic police officer who stifled life from the best possible motives, [and] the drunken priest who continues to pass life on." For the mature reader. L.T.

AUTHOR: **Ernest Hemingway**
TITLE: *Farewell to Arms (1929)*
DESCRIPTION: *Farewell to Arms* is Hemingway's novel about the Italian front of World War I. Frederic Henry is an American ambulance driver for the Italian army who meets a British nurse, Catherine Barkley. They fall in love and, after he is wounded, she nurses him and they consider themselves married. Just after he learns that "Cat" is pregnant, Henry must go back to the front but gets caught in a disorderly, harried retreat. The book might just be like dozens of other war novels except for those few passages where Henry, who doesn't like to think, does so anyway, reflecting on the meaning of it all. What do you think of his idea that "if people bring so much courage to this world, the world has to kill them to break them, so of course it kills them"? L.T.

AUTHOR: **James Hilton**
TITLE: *Lost Horizon (1933)*
DESCRIPTION: If you've always thought of Shangri-la as a lush, peaceful Paradise Island, you will be surprised to learn that it is an imaginary lamasery in Tibet. Hugh Conway, a competent but undistinguished counsel

at a remote British outpost, is being evacuated after putting down an uprising in 1931, when the plane carrying him, another consul, an American embezzler, and a missionary woman, is diverted and then crashes in a high Tibetan valley. As the pilot dies, he calls out the name "Shangri-la," and so the survivors set out for it. They eventually learn that it is a Buddhist monastery (lamasery) headed by a 250-year-old former Catholic priest who wants to create a community able to reintroduce civilization after the coming World War. No one has ever been allowed to leave—the promise of long life beckons them anyhow—but when a chance comes, should Conway take it? L.T.

AUTHOR: **William Hudson**
TITLE: *Green Mansions (1904)*
DESCRIPTION: An old man, Abel, tells the story of his youthful adventuring in the South American jungles, where he patiently coaxes friendship from a strange, birdlike girl, Rima, hiding away from the Indians. A legend says that she is the daughter of the spirit Didi, but Abel knows her to be an intensely lonely girl who longs to communicate in the fluttering, birdlike language she had learned from her long-dead mother. They set out to find that mother, but disaster strikes them both. Is Hudson saying in this legend that has become a classic, that nature herself is like Rima, longing to tell us of herself but unable to do so completely? L.T.

AUTHOR: **Victor Hugo**
TITLE: *Les Miserables (1862)*
DESCRIPTION: Revived in a highly popular stage version, this book is a very long but enthralling picture of life in post-revolutionary France. Jean Valjean is imprisoned for 19 years for stealing a loaf of bread to feed his starving sister. Afterward, befriended by a bishop who gives Valjean the recovered silver he has stolen, the ex-convict disguises himself as a priest and opens a factory. In his new role as benefactor, he must evade the ever-vigilant policeman, Javert, and also help the blackmailed beauty, Fantine, and her daughter, Cosette. Powerful not only in its depictions of the miserable social conditions of the Parisian slums, *Les Miserables* is also considered one of the best stories of all times. L.T.*

AUTHOR: **Kathryn Hulme**
TITLE: *The Nun's Story (1956)*
DESCRIPTION: Unable to marry the man she loves, Gabrielle becomes a nun and discovers more of the world than she could ever have dreamed as she nurses in an insane asylum on a mission station in the Congo, where

uprisings of the "natives" ever threaten, and in the Belgian underground during World War II. As Sister Luke she struggles to keep her vows of poverty, chastity, and obedience to God. L.T.

AUTHOR: **James Joyce**
TITLE: *Portrait of the Artist As a Young Man (1916)*
DESCRIPTION: If you've ever wondered about whether your particular place in the cosmos is significant to anyone, you may well be hooked by the beginning of James Joyce's *Portrait of the Artist,* an autobiography (disguised as a novel) of the schoolboy, Stephen Dedalus. In a series of five sections, each ending in an "Epiphany," or crisis experience of enlightenment, the book traces Stephen's growth toward manhood—and away from God. He experiences both conflict with his family and challenges to his political loyalty to Ireland. He experiences his first sexual encounter and resulting religious guilt, a loss of faith and friendship, and always a desire for the beauty of art that compels him above all else to find his identity outside all the social and personal forces that shape his world. For the mature reader. L.T.

AUTHOR: **Rudyard Kipling**
TITLE: *Kim (1901)*
DESCRIPTION: *Kim* is the story of a half-caste Indian-Irish orphan boy who grows up totally Indian in the back streets of Lahore. He attaches himself to a wandering holy man in search of the river that will wash away his sins and immediately becomes involved in the intrigue of the secret service and counter-intelligence. Kim has to submit to the Roman Catholic schooling his father insists on, but the focus of his curiosity and intelligence is on the life of a secret agent. His adventures have captivated readers for nearly a century. L.T.

AUTHOR: **Charles and Mary Lamb**
TITLE: *Tales from Shakespeare (1807)*
DESCRIPTION: The brother-and-sister team of Charles and Mary Lamb retold twenty of Shakespeare's plays as the exciting stories they are, hoping that young people would learn to love the most famous of all British authors. Across almost two centuries, countless people have met the master through these faithfully told tales. You may be glad to be numbered among them. A.A.

AUTHOR: **Harper Lee**
TITLE: *To Kill a Mockingbird (1960)*

DESCRIPTION: Scout and Jem Finch are growing up in Alabama during the Depression, children of the local attorney, Atticus. All sorts of odd folk, genteel and not so, make life fascinating for these intelligent, curious children. But things turn ugly when their father defends a black man, Tom Robinson, who is accused of assaulting a white woman. They learn to do what Atticus advises—stand in the shoes of someone else and walk around for a while. This is one story, turning a gentle but persistent light on the soul of America, the souls of all peoples, that you would be a lesser person for having missed. M.T., L.T.*

AUTHOR: **C. S. Lewis**
TITLE: *Till We Have Faces (1956)*
DESCRIPTION: In what is probably his least known fiction, C. S. Lewis of Narnia and science fiction fame retells the ancient but most compelling Cupid and Psyche myth from the perspective of Psyche's older, ugly, and adoring sister. Psyche is the youngest daughter of a weakening king, so beautiful and so good that the jealous priest of the local deity demands she be sacrificed to The Brute to appease the gods. If you read this story carefully, especially if you are familiar with mythology, you will be greatly rewarded, not only with a great story but with discovering parallels or reverberations of the Christian gospel. But even if these are not readily apparent, the story also exposes two ancient ways of life, Greek and pagan, and the universal human heart. L.T.*

AUTHOR: **George Orwell**
TITLE: *Animal Farm (1946)*
DESCRIPTION: This story has been called an allegory, a fable, and a parable, so don't be surprised to discover people-like qualities in the animals of *Animal Farm*. The pigs and other animals take over control of Manor Farm from its incompetent, drunken owner, determined to create a utopian society of equality, respect, and adequate provisions. However, before Napoleon Pig declares himself lord of Manor Farm again, the animals come to know all too well that "all animals are equal but some animals are more equal than others." George Orwell's allegory-fable-parable has given us much to think about since World War II. M.T., L.T.

AUTHOR: **George Orwell**
TITLE: *1984 (1949)*
DESCRIPTION: Did you know that the phrase "Big Brother is watching you" comes from Orwell's satire, *1984*? Written in 1949 to "predict" what kind of a totalitarian society could develop by 1984, Orwell created the

story of Winston Smith who lives in the drab world of Oceania where "Big Brother" spies on every citizen's every action by way of two-way television monitors. Winston, a writer in the Ministry of Truth who revises the government's predictions to fit what actually happened, nevertheless thinks it is safe to rebel . . . a little, anyway, with the encouragement of a bookstore owner, Mrs. Charrington, and the love of beautiful Julia. But is it? Do you see parallels to our own post-1984 world? M.T., L.T.

AUTHOR: **Boris Pasternak**
TITLE: *Dr. Zhivago (1958)*
DESCRIPTION: If you are ambitious and if you are interested in the events of the Russian Revolution, then you may truly enjoy reading *Dr. Zhivago*. It is the story of Yurii, a poet-physician who gets caught up in the student riots prior to the 1917 revolution. He marries Tonia, a childhood companion; is injured while serving as a doctor on the front during World War I; is nursed back to health by the great love of his life, Lara; and is pressed into service by the various factions during the post-war turmoil both in Moscow and in the Urals to which he has fled. Through all the events of his life so torn apart by revolutionary madness, Yurii Zhivago maintains a mystical innocence that he conveys not only in his relationships with people but in his poems, published at the end of the novel. There the great theme of Christ's crucifixion and resurrection is revealed as the standard by which he judges the great sweep of history through which he has lived. L.T.

AUTHOR: **Alan Paton**
TITLE: *Cry, the Beloved Country (1948)*
DESCRIPTION: Alan Paton's heart-rending, poetic novel was the first to dramatize the conflict between the races in South Africa and has never been equaled in its impact around the world. It is the story of two fathers who have lost sons because of apartheid. Rev. Stephen Kumalo has a son, Absalom, who has been snared by the vice in black townships. Arthur, the son of Mr. Jarvis, a white man who has attempted to help the blacks, is accidently shot by Absalom. Kumalo and Jarvis cry not only for their sons but also for their beloved country. What makes their story so memorable is how Paton reveals through them his deep conviction that only love can overcome the hate-spawning fear that grips South Africa, a love that can redemptively spring from such sorrow as these two fathers share. This book will echo in your memory for a long, long time. M.T., L.T.*

AUTHOR: **Mary Renault**
TITLE: *The King Must Die (1958)*
DESCRIPTION: Mary Renault has no peer when it comes to bringing the ancient Greek world, both mythical and historical, to life for modern readers. *The King Must Die* is her vivid recreation of the legend of Theseus, the son of Poseidon, heir to Athens' King Aigeus, and self-offered sacrifice to the Minotaur of Crete's King Minos. Courage and wits, loyalty and treachery, love and passion, dark, blood-filled religion and airy reason all play their roles in this vivid story. If you love mythology or history, you should love *The King*. If you don't have those prerequisites, it may just crack the door open to a whole new world for you. M.T., L.T.

AUTHOR: **Mary Renault**
TITLE: *The Last of the Wine (1956)*
DESCRIPTION: Through the life of the narrator, Alexian of Athens, you can enter the great and tragic days of the Peloponnesian War. You see all their nobility—for along with Alexian the student, you meet Socrates, Plato, and other scholars. You see all their baseness—for with Alexis the soldier, athlete, and citizen, you are privy to the conniving, the lust for wealth and power, the sieges, the slavery, and the acceptable homosexual relationships (delicately handled by Renault). The Greek ideals of harmony, proportion, and order prevail as long as Socrates is free to be a gadfly to Athens. He is the novel's true hero, as is the Greece about which Renault writes so well. L.T.

AUTHOR: **Nevil Shute**
TITLE: *A Town Like Alice (1950)*
DESCRIPTION: A young British secretary and an Australian soldier are both made prisoners of war by the Japanese in Malaysia, meeting only briefly during their 6-year ordeal. She is marched 1200 miles around the jungles, and he is crucified for stealing food for her, but both become stronger individuals than they had been. After the war they seek each other out, test whether their feelings for each other are truly love, and find mutual commitment to the undeveloped outback of Australia. Shute said that the true story of courageous women prisoners in Sumatra was more appealing to him as basis for a novel than anything he could concoct out of his imagination. You will probably agree with him. L.T.

AUTHOR: **Betty Smith**
TITLE: *A Tree Grows in Brooklyn (1943)*

DESCRIPTION: Francie Nolan is the book-loving daughter of a good-hearted but drink-weakened father and a hard-working janitress mother. She and her brother and parents struggle against poverty and hardship to maintain a family life and gain an education in their Brooklyn tenement community at the turn of the century. Francie herself determines to read all the books in the library in alphabetical order. How she achieves her goals in such an unpromising environment, how a tree grows in Brooklyn, is her story. M.T., L.T.

AUTHOR: **Aleksandr Solzhenitsyn**
TITLE: *One Day in the Life of Ivan Denisovich (1963)*
DESCRIPTION: Ivan Denisovich Shokhov was an ordinary Russian carpenter, a man like millions of others put into Stalin's forced labor camps in the name of socialism. This remarkable book takes him through one day, from reveille to lights out, one day of the 3,653 like it in his sentence, thereby revealing the "spiritual squalor, corruption, frustration and terror" of the place, but also his "passionate outcry for dignity and justice." Even the Soviet official who wrote a preface when it made its revolutionary appearance in 1962 said that "this novel, which is so unusual for its honesty and harrowing truth, . . . strengthens and ennobles us." L.T.

AUTHOR: **John Steinbeck**
TITLE: *The Pearl (1945)*
DESCRIPTION: You will be moved by this short novel about an Indian fisherman, Kino, whose baby son is bitten by a scorpion. Kino hunts for the Pearl of the World so that he can afford to pay the evil town doctor to treat his son. The ancient harmonious music, which Steinbeck built into the rhythms of the language and which accompany all that Kino, Juana, and the baby do, are disturbed by the Pearl that promises so much wealth. L.T.

AUTHOR: **James Thurber**
TITLE: *The Thirteen Clocks (1950)*
DESCRIPTION: Look for a new edition of this slim volume—both a fairy tale and a satire on the genre of fairy tales, about a duke frozen in time because he is such a cold creature, and the princess whom he has imprisoned, and, of course, the prince charming who rescues her. E.T.*

AUTHOR: **Mark Twain**
TITLE: *Huckleberry Finn (1885)*
DESCRIPTION: This book is often assigned in English classes, but that is no reason not to want to read it! Huck, say some people, is Everyboy. His

clever mind, which sees through the trickery and stupidity of others; his high but idiosyncratic ethical standards; his moral dilemmas over the slavery of his companion, the runaway Jim (causing some to feel that the book should be banned because of its racism); his refusal to be "civilized" (by a corrupt civilization?); and his adventures on the raft floating down the Mississippi make this book an essentially American experience not to be missed. E.T., M.T.*

AUTHOR: **Mark Twain**
TITLE: *Tom Sawyer (1876)*
DESCRIPTION: How Tom Sawyer got out of whitewashing the fence, how he fell in love with the imperious Becky Thatcher, how he and Huck Finn witnessed a murder by Injun Joe, how they arrived at their own funerals, and how justice was eventually served and the boys rewarded—these are all part of the American mystique about growing up in the simpler days near the Mississippi River and should be a part of everyone's growing up today. E.T., M.T.*

AUTHOR: **Jessamyn West**
TITLE: *Friendly Persuasion (1943)*
DESCRIPTION: This gentle story is about a Quaker family. Jess, the husband, in the nursery stock business, and his wife, Eliza, the minister, live in the bounty of southern Indiana before the Civil War. Music is forbidden to the Quakers, but early on, Jess buys an organ to satisfy a longing in his soul. The outrageous organ, pacifism, suspicion of modernity, and other Quaker convictions all are important in this chronicle of three generations. L.T.

AUTHOR: **Thorton Wilder**
TITLE: *The Bridge of San Luis Rey (1927)*
DESCRIPTION: "On Friday noon, July the twentieth, 1714, the finest bridge in all Peru broke and precipitated five travelers into the gulf below." So begins this short, thoughtful novel about those five people whose lives intertwined and through whose stories Brother Juniper hoped that he could justify the ways of God to the people he worked with. He made his attempt because he believed that "either we live by accident and die by accident, or we live by plan and die by plan." L.T.*

GLOSSARY

Aestheticism—artistic beauty and taste as a basic standard; ethical and other standards are secondary.

Allegory—a story (parable, myth, or fable) that veils its deeper meaning by letting readers discover it for themselves.

Allusion—a passing or casual mention of something.

Anarchy—a society without laws or governmental control; confusion; chaos.

Animism—a belief that gives all natural objects souls or spirits.

Convivial—fond of feasting, drinking, merry company; friendly, agreeable.

Daimon—(1) a god or (2) a demon; deity, fate, fortune.

Deism—a belief that God created the world and then abandoned it.

Dualism—a theory that mind and body are the two basic realities.

Eclectic—not following one system, but taking bits and pieces from different sources.

Elemental—simple, basic.

Elitism—consciousness or pride in belonging to a select group.

Erotica—literature or art dealing with sex.

Existentialism—a belief that people make themselves who they are. It is not a full-fledged worldview. Atheistic existentialism says God does not exist; theistic existentialism has God in the equation.

Fatalistic—believing that all events are subject to fate or chance.

Genre—kind; sort; style.

Humanism—a philosophy in which human beings—their rights and interests—are the sole value.

Ideology—a defined and closed system that typifies what people believe, which allows no questions.

Illusion—something that deceives by producing a false impression.

Lyrical—having a musical quality.

Metaphor—a word or phrase that suggests a likeness; as in, "A mighty fortress is our God." God is not literally a fortress; he is like a fortress.

Mores—the moral views or folkways of a group.

New Age—began with a belief that a new species will evolve. A worldview that borrows bits and pieces from other non-Christian worldviews, influenced by Eastern thought and mysticism.

Nihilism—nothingness or nonexistence; a denial of real existence.

Pantheism—identifies the universe with God—so that god is in everything that exists.

Paradoxical—something that seems self-contradictory, often two ideas that seem in opposition to each other.

Phenomenon—(1) an observable fact, occurence or circumstance; (2) something that impresses one as being extraordinary.

Scientism—a belief in science as the final word on everything.

Surrealistic—a style of art or literature that stresses the subconscious or non-rational.

Theism—a belief in one God as creator and ruler of the universe.

Theme of a story—the idea, the general truth about life or a people brought out in a story or other literary work.

Vicarious—felt or enjoyed through the experience of another person.

INDEX